The Complete PC Repair and Troubleshooting Lab Guide

Donald Casper
MCT, MCSE, MCNI
Eastern Idaho Technical College

Cheryl Schmidt, Consulting Editor

Scott/Jones Inc.
P.O. Box 696
El Granada, California 94018
Voice: 650-726-2436
Facsimile: 650-726-4693
e-mail: marketing@scottjonespub.com
Web page: www.scottjonespub.com

ISBN 1-57676-117-7

The Complete PC Repair and Troubleshooting Lab Guide

Donald Casper
Eastern Idaho Technical College

Copyright 2003 Scott/Jones, Inc.

All rights reserved. No part of this book may be reproduced or transmitted in any form without written permission of the publisher.

ZYX   432

ISBN: 1-57676-117-7

The publisher wishes to acknowledge the memory and influence of James F. Leisy. Thanks, Jim. We miss you.

Page Design & Composition: Stephen Adams, Adams Design
Copyediting & Proofreading: Sheila Butler
Cover Design: Martie Bateson Sautter
Production Management: Audrey Anderson
Book Manufacturing: Versa Press, Inc.

Scott/Jones Publishing Company
Editorial Group: Richard Jones, Mike Needham, Denise Simon, Leata Holloway, Joe Burns, and Patricia Miyaki
Production Management: Audrey Anderson
Marketing and Sales: Victoria Judy, Page Mead, Hazel Dunlap, Hester Winn and Donna Cross
Business Operations: Michelle Robelet, Cathy Glenn, Natasha Hoffmeyer and Bill Overfelt

A Word About Trademarks
All product names identified in this book are trademarks or registered trademarks of their respective companies. We have used the names in an editorial fashion only, and to the benefit of the trademark owner, with no intention of infringing the trademark.

Additional Titles of Interest from Scott/Jones

Computing with Java™: Programs, Objects, Graphics,
   Second Edition and Second Alternate Edition
From Objects to Components with the Java™ Platform
Advanced Java™ Internet Applications, Second Edition
   by Art Gittleman

Developing Web Applications with Active Server Pages
   by Thom Luce

Starting Out with Visual Basic
Standard Version of Starting Out with C++, Third Edition
Brief Version of Starting Out with C++, Third Edition
Starting Out with C++, Third Alternate Edition
   by Tony Gaddis

C by Discovery, Third Edition
   by L.S. and Dusty Foster

Assembly Language for the IBM PC Family, Third Edition
   by William Jones

The Visual Basic 6 Coursebook, Fourth Edition
QuickStart to JavaScript
QuickStart to DOS for Windows 9X
   by Forest Lin

Advanced Visual Basic.Net, Third Edition
   by Kip Irvine

HTML for Web Developers
Server-Side Programming for Web Developers
   by John Avila

The Complete A+ Guide to PC Repair
The Complete Computer Repair Textbook, Third Edition
   by Cheryl Schmidt

Windows 2000 Professional Step-By-Step
Windows XP Professional Step-By-Step
   by Leslie Hardin and Deborah Tice

The Windows 2000 Professional Textbook
Prelude to Programming: Concepts and Design
The Windows XP Textbook
   by Stewart Venit

The Windows 2000 Server Lab Manual
   by Gerard Morris

Contents

Introduction **vii**
Features **vii**
Why Certification? **vii**
A+ Core Hardware Service Technician Examination Objectives **viii**
A+ Operating System Technologies Examination Objectives **ix**
Lab Setup **x**
Your Work Area **xi**
Lab Procedures **xii**

Chapter 1 Introduction to Computer Repair 1
  Lab 1.1 Understanding Computer Terminology **2**
  Lab 1.2 External Ports Identification **7**
  Lab 1.3 Identify Internal Cables and Connectors **9**
  Lab 1.4 Installing Windows 98 **13**
  Lab 1.5 Installing Windows NT Workstation **18**
  Lab 1.6 Installing a Service Pack on Windows NT Workstation **24**
  Lab 1.7 Installing Windows 2000 Professional **26**

Chapter 2 On the Motherboard 31
  Lab 2.1 System Board Identification **32**
  Lab 2.2 Microprocessor/Slot/Socket Identification **36**
  Lab 2.3 Replacing a Microprocessor **39**
  Lab 2.4 Expansion Bus Identification **42**
  Lab 2.5 System BIOS Identification **45**
  Lab 2.6 Replacing the System BIOS **47**
  Lab 2.7 Installing a System BIOS Flash Upgrade **50**
  Lab 2.8 Chipset Identification **52**

Chapter 3 System Configuration 55
  Lab 3.1 Basic CMOS Configuration **56**
  Lab 3.2 Disabling Devices within CMOS **59**
  Lab 3.3 Assigning System Resources within CMOS **62**
  Lab 3.4 Viewing System Information in Windows 98 **64**
  Lab 3.5 Using Windows 98 Device Manager **67**
  Lab 3.6 Viewing System Information in Windows NT Workstation **71**
  Lab 3.7 Managing Devices in Windows NT Workstation **74**

Contents

Lab 3.8 Viewing System Information in Windows 2000 Professional **78**
Lab 3.9 Using Windows 2000 Professional Device Manager **81**

Chapter 4 Disassembly and Assembly 85
Lab 4.1 Computer Disassembly and Assembly **86**
Lab 4.2 System Module Identification **90**

Chapter 5 Basic Electronics and Power 93
Lab 5.1 Volts, Amps, Ohms, and Watts **94**
Lab 5.2 Power Supply Identification **95**
Lab 5.3 Power Supply Removal and Installation **97**
Lab 5.4 Calculating Power Supply Requirements for Your Workstation **100**
Lab 5.5 Measuring Input Line Voltages **102**
Lab 5.6 Measuring/Troubleshooting Internal System Voltages **108**
Lab 5.7 Installing a Surge Suppressor **114**
Lab 5.8 Installing a UPS **116**
Lab 5.9 PC Shock Hazards **120**

Chapter 6 Logical Troubleshooting 123
Lab 6.1 Troubleshooting Fundamentals **124**
Lab 6.2 Practical Troubleshooting **128**
Lab 6.3 CMOS Beep Codes and Error Codes **129**
Lab 6.4 Diagnostic Utilities **131**
Lab 6.5 P.O.S.T. Cards (Power On Self-Test Cards) **134**
Lab 6.6 Basic Maintenance Procedures **136**
Lab 6.7 Creating a Preventive Maintenance Plan **139**
Lab 6.8 Backing Up Data in Windows 98 and Windows 2000 **141**
Lab 6.9 Installing Virus Protection **146**
Lab 6.10 Creating an ERD in Windows NT Workstation **149**
Lab 6.11 Creating an ERD in Windows 2000 Professional **151**
Lab 6.12 Using Regedit to Backup the Windows 98 Registry **153**
Lab 6.13 Restoring Your Data from a Backup in Windows 98 and 2000 Pro **155**
Lab 6.14 Using an ERD to Recover Windows NT Workstation **159**
Lab 6.15 Using Recovery Console to Recover Windows 2000 **161**
Lab 6.16 Using an ERD to Recover Windows 2000 Pro **163**
Lab 6.17 Using Regedit to Restore the Windows 98 Registry **165**

Chapter 7 Memory 169
Lab 7.1 Memory Module Identification **170**
Lab 7.2 Installing/Upgrading System RAM **173**

Chapter 8   Floppy Drives   **177**

- Lab 8.1   Installing a Second Floppy Drive   **178**
- Lab 8.2   Formatting a Floppy Disk Using Windows 98, NT Workstation, and 2000 Professional   **180**
- Lab 8.3   Creating a Bootable Floppy   **184**

Chapter 9   Hard Drives   **187**

- Lab 9.1   Installing an EIDE Hard Drive   **188**
- Lab 9.2   Installing a SCSI Hard Drive   **190**
- Lab 9.3   Creating and Formatting Disk Partitions   **193**
- Lab 9.4   Using Windows 98, NT, and 2000 Disk Utilities   **199**

Chapter 10   Multimedia Devices   **203**

- Lab 10.1   Installing an EIDE CD-ROM   **204**
- Lab 10.2   Installing a SCSI CD-ROM Drive   **207**
- Lab 10.3   Installing a Sound Card in Windows 98, NT, and 2000   **209**

Chapter 11   Serial Devices, Mice, and Keyboards   **213**

- Lab 11.1   Installing an Internal Modem in Windows 98, NT, and 2000   **214**
- Lab 11.2   Installing an External Modem in Windows 98, NT, and 2000   **218**
- Lab 11.3   Installing a Serial Mouse   **222**
- Lab 11.4   Installing a PS2 Mouse   **224**

Chapter 12   Video   **227**

- Lab 12.1   Installing a Video Adapter in Windows 98, NT Workstation, and 2000   **228**
- Lab 12.2   Updating a Video Driver in Windows 98, NT Workstation, and 2000   **231**
- Lab 12.3   Installing a Second Video Adapter and Monitor in Windows 2000   **236**

Chapter 13   Printers   **239**

- Lab 13.1   Installing a Printer in Windows 98   **240**
- Lab 13.2   Installing a Printer in Windows NT Workstation   **243**
- Lab 13.3   Installing a Printer in Windows 2000 Professional   **246**
- Lab 13.4   Laser Printer Fundamentals   **249**
- Lab 13.5   Ink Jet Printer Fundamentals   **252**
- Lab 13.6   Troubleshooting Printers   **255**

Appendix A Using DOS in a Windows Environment 259
- Lab A.1 Opening a DOS Window in Windows 98, NT, and 2000 **260**
- Lab A.2 Finding Help for Using DOS Commands **264**
- Lab A.3 Starting an Application from the DOS Command Line **267**
- Lab A.4 Managing the File System from the DOS Command Line **268**

Appendix B Using Windows 98 273
- Lab B.1 Basic Windows 98 Operation **274**
- Lab B.2 Managing the File System in Windows 98 **279**
- Lab B.3 Installing an Application in Windows 98 **282**
- Lab B.4 Starting an Application in Windows 98 **284**

Appendix C Using Windows NT Workstation 287
- Lab C.1 Basic Windows NT Operation **288**
- Lab C.2 Managing the File System in Windows NT **293**
- Lab C.3 Installing an Application in Windows NT **296**
- Lab C.4 Starting an Application in Windows NT **297**

Appendix D Using Windows 2000 Professional 299
- Lab D.1 Basic Windows 2000 Operation **300**
- Lab D.2 Right-click Managing the File System in Windows 2000 **306**
- Lab D.3 Installing an Application in Windows 2000 **310**
- Lab D.4 Starting an Application in Windows 2000 **311**

Appendix E Using Windows XP 313
- Lab E.1 Installing Windows XP Professional **314**
- Lab E.2 Basic Windows XP Operation **319**
- Lab E.3 Managing the File System in Windows XP **325**
- Lab E.4 Installing an Application in Windows XP **328**
- Lab E.5 Starting an Application in Windows XP **329**

Appendix F CMOS Beep and Error Codes 331

Appendix G Standard IRQ, I/O, and DMA Assignments 335

Appendix H PC Power Connector Diagrams 337

The Complete PC Repair and Troubleshooting Lab Guide

Introduction

Whether you are highly experienced in PC repair and troubleshooting or are just beginning to explore computers and computer repair, *The Complete PC Repair and Troubleshooting Lab Guide* is the book you need! The guide is designed to prepare you for the CompTIA (Computer Technology Industry Association) A+ certification tests, or it can be used to sharpen your existing PC troubleshooting and repair skills.

Features

The guide features over 100 labs that map directly to the CompTIA A+ Certification objectives. Each lab begins with an introduction, an explanation of the CompTIA A+ Objectives the lab maps to, and a complete required materials list. This is followed by step-by-step instructions written in easy-to-understand, yet technically correct, language. Lab and Safety notes are provided to define key terms, acronyms, and safety procedures. Review questions are provided with some labs to reinforce the skills practiced within the lab.

In addition, there are several appendices that provide a wealth of PC repair and troubleshooting reference material.

Why Certification?

In today's competitive technology employment market, the prospective employee needs an edge in order to stand out from the crowd. Industry certifications help provide that edge! Obtaining certification increases your ability to obtain employment by proving your skill set to a potential employer. Technicians with certifications tend to receive higher salary levels and quicker promotions. For more information about A+ certification and the CompTIA Organization, visit www.comptia.org.

viii   The Complete PC Repair and Troubleshooting Lab Guide

A+ Core Hardware Service Technician Examination Objectives

Objective 1.0 Installation, Configuration, and Upgrading	Labs
1.1 Identify basic terms, concepts, and functions of system modules, including how each module should work during normal operation and during the boot process.	1.1, 4.2, 5.1, 5.
1.2 Identify basic procedures for adding and removing field replaceable modules for both desktop and portable systems	2.3, 4.1, 5.3, 5.4, 8.1, 9.1, 9.2, 10.1, 10.2, 10.3, 11.1, 11.2, 11.3, 11.4, 12.1, 12.3,
1.3 Identify available IRQs, DMAs, and I/O addresses and procedures for device installation and configuration	3.4, 3.5, 3.6, 3.7, 3.8, 3.9, 11.1, 11.2, 11.4
1.4 Identify common peripheral ports, associated cabling, and their connectors	1.2, 1.3, 11.3
1.5 Identify proper procedures for installing and configuring IDE/EIDE devices	1.4, 4.1, 8.1, 9.1, 10.1
1.6 Identify proper procedures for installing and configuring SCSI devices	1.4, 4.1, 9.2, 10.2
1.7 Identify proper procedures for installing and configuring peripheral devices	3.5, 3.7, 3.9, 5.4, 10.1, 10.2, 10.3, 11.1, 11.2, 11.4
1.8 Identify hardware methods of upgrading system performance, procedures for replacing basic subsystem components, unique components, and when to use them	2.2, 2.3, 2.4, 2.6, 5.3, 5.4, 7.1, 7.2, 10.1, 10.2, 10.3, 12.1, 12.2, 12.3
Objective 2.0 Diagnosing and Troubleshooting	Labs
2.1 Identify common symptoms and problems associated with each module and how to troubleshoot and isolate the problems	5.5, 5.6, 6.1, 6.2
2.2 Identify basic troubleshooting procedures and how to elicit problem symptoms from customers	5.5, 5.6, 6.1, 6.2, 6.3, 6.4, 6.5
Objective 3.0 Preventive Maintenance	Labs
3.1 Identify the purpose of various types of preventive maintenance products and procedures and when to use them	5.7, 5.8, 6.6, 6.7, 6.8, 6.13
3.2 Identify issues, procedures, and devices for protection within the computing environment, including people, hardware, and the surrounding workspace	5.7, 5.8, 5.9, 6.6, 6.7, 6.9, 6.10, 6.11, 6.12, 6.14, 6.15, 6.16, 6.17
Objective 4.0 Motherboards, Processors, And Memory	Labs
4.1 Distinguish between the popular CPU chips in terms of their basic characteristics	2.2
4.2 Identify the categories of RAM (Random Access Memory) terminology, their locations, and physical characteristics	7.1, 7.2

A+ Core Hardware Service Technician Examination Objectives (continued)

4.3 Identify the most popular type of motherboards, their components, and their architecture (bus structures and power supplies)	2.1, 2.2, 2.4, 2.8
4.4 Identify the purpose of CMOS (Complimentary Metal-Oxide Semiconductor), what it contains, and how to change its basic parameters	2.5, 2.6, 2.7, 3.1, 3.2, 3.3, 6.3
Objective 5.0 Printers	**Labs**
5.1 Identify basic concepts, printer operations, and printer components	13.1, 13.2, 13.3, 13.4, 13.5
5.2 Identify care and service techniques and common problems with primary printer types	13.4, 13.5, 13.6
Objective 6.0 Basic Networking	**Labs**
6.1 Identify basic networking concepts, including how a network works and the ramifications of repairs on the network	

A+ Operating System Technologies Examination Objectives

Objective 1.0 Operating System Fundamentals	**Labs**
1.1 Identify the Operating System's functions, structure, and major system files to navigate the operating system, and how to get needed technical information	1.1, 3.4, 3.6, 3.8, 8.2, 8.3, 9.3, 9.4, A.1, A.2, A.3, B.1, B.2, B.3, C.1, C.2, C.3, D.1, D.2, D.3, E.1, E.2, E.3, E.4
1.2 Identify basic concepts and procedures for creating, viewing, and managing files, directories, and disks. This includes procedures for changing file attributes and the ramifications of those changes (For example, Security Issues)	6.8, 6.13, 8.2, 8.3, 9.3, 9.4, A.1, A.2, A.3, A.4, B.1, B.2, B.3, B.4, C.1, C.2, C.3, C.4, D.1, D.2, D.3, D.4, E.1, E.2, E.3, E.4, E.5
Objective 2.0 Installation, Configuration, and Upgrading	**Labs**
2.1 Identify the procedures for installing Windows 9X and Windows 2000, and bringing the software to a basic operational level	1.4, 1.5, 1.7, E.1
2.2 Identify steps to perform an operating system upgrade	1.5, 12.1, 12.2
2.3 Identify the basic system boot sequences and boot methods, including the steps to create an emergency boot disk with utilities installed for Windows 9X, Windows NT, and Windows 2000	6.10, 6.11, 6.12, 6.14, 6.15, 6.16, 6.17

A+ Operating System Technologies Examination Objectives (continued)

2.4 Identify procedures for loading/adding and configuring application device drivers, and the necessary software for certain devices	10.1, 10.2, 10.3, 11.1, 11.2, 11.3, 11.4, 12.1, 12.2, 12.3, 13.1, 13.2, 13.3, B.3, C.3, D.3, E.4
Objective 3.0 Diagnosing and Troubleshooting	**Labs**
3.1 Recognize and interpret the meaning of common error codes and startup messages from the boot sequence, and identify steps to correct the problems	6.2, 6.3
3.2 Recognize common problems and determine how to resolve them	3.5, 3.7, 3.9, 6.15, 6.16
Objective 4.0 Networks	
4.1 Identify the networking capabilities of Windows, including procedures for connecting to the network	
4.2 Identify concepts and capabilities relating to the Internet, and basic procedures for setting up a system for Internet access	12.2, B.3, C.3, D.3, E.4

Lab Setup

In order to complete the labs in this manual, each student should have access to a workstation that meets the following minimum specifications:

- Pentium 133 MHZ
- 64 MB RAM
- 2 GB Hard Drive
- CD-ROM Drive
- Floppy drive
- NIC (Network Interface Card)
- Mouse or other pointing device
- VGA Video adapter and monitor

During the Chapter 1 labs, each student will install Windows 98, Windows NT Workstation, and Windows 2000 Professional on their workstations in a multi-boot configuration. This configuration will allow the student to complete all except the networking and Windows XP labs. For the networking labs, two or more students may work together to accomplish the labs. To complete the optional Windows XP labs, your workstation must meet the following specifications:

- Intel Pentium (or compatible) 233 MHz (300 MHz recommended)
- 64 MB RAM (128 MB RAM recommended)
- 2 GB hard disk with 650 MB free space
- VGA video adapter and monitor
- Mouse or other pointing device
- CD-ROM or DVD-ROM drive
- Network Adapter (for network installations)

In addition to the minimum workstation configuration, you should have the following components available:
- Windows 98 SE installation CD
- Windows NT Workstation installation CD
- Windows 2000 Professional installation CD
- (optional) Windows XP installation CD
- Installable Windows application
- Parallel printer/printer cable/driver disk
- Internal and External modem
- Sound Card/Speakers
- Surge Protector or UPS (Uninterruptible Power Supply)
- Category 5 UTP (Unshielded Twisted Pair) network cable
- RJ45 connectors
- Ethernet UTP network hub
- Several blank 3.5" floppy disks

Your Work Area

The following tools and equipment should be available at each student's work area:
- Static grounding mat
- Static grounding wrist strap
- Screwdriver set
- TORX driver set
- Needle nose pliers
- Multi-meter (Volt/Ohm meter)
- Anti-static bags
- Cat. 5 network cable strippers/crimpers

Optional
- Hemostats
- Side cutters
- Soldering iron/solder
- Flashlight

Lab Safety

Ensure that you follow all lab safety rules, both those that pertain to the individual labs and those in place for the classroom. Be especially aware of shock hazards, sharp edges, etc.

ESD Prevention

A computer's circuitry is very delicate and is easily damaged by external forces. ESD, or Electrostatic Discharge, has a very high potential for causing damage to the electrical components on the computer's system board and expansion cards. As little as 20–30 volts of ESD can cause permanent damage. The ESD shocks we are familiar with usually range between 1,000 and 3,000 volts. We can easily shock and damage electrical components without even being aware we did so.

Whenever you are working inside a computer's case, at a minimum you should wear a properly grounded wrist strap. This will channel any damaging ESD to a ground and protect the computer's circuitry. If possible, your work area should also be equipped with a grounding mat.

Lab Procedures

Each lab begins with an introduction, followed by an explanation of the skills practiced within the lab and the CompTIA objectives the lab maps to.

Before beginning each lab, ensure that all materials on the required materials list are available. Also, thoroughly read any special notes or instructions that accompany the lab.

Follow each lab step and procedure in order. The labs will build upon each other, and if you skip steps, you may discover that subsequent labs will not work properly.

If you see *italicized* words in the lab procedure, this means that you must supply some input for the procedure to work properly. Your Instructor will be able to help you supply the proper input.

Continue with each lab until you see **End of Exercise**. At this point, have your Instructor review your work and initial the Instructor Check line.

At the completion of each lab, review the Lab Notes section before moving to the next lab.

CHAPTER 1

Introduction to Computer Repair

1.1 Understanding Computer Terminology 2

1.2 External Ports Identification 7

1.3 Identify Internal Cables and Connectors 9

1.4 Installing Windows 98 13

1.5 Installing Windows NT Workstation 18

1.6 Installing a Service Pack on Windows NT Workstation 24

1.7 Installing Windows 2000 Professional 26

2 Introduction to Computer Repair

Lab 1.1 Understanding Computer Terminology

Introduction

It is important for the computer technician to understand computer terminology, including commonly used acronyms. In this lab you will review commonly used computer terminology and acronyms.

Maps to the following CompTIA A+ Objectives

A+ Core Hardware Service Technician Objectives
- Objective 1.1

A+ Operating System Technologies Objectives
- Objective 1.1

Required Materials
- Lab manual
- Lab textbook

Lab Procedure

Study the following list of computer terms and their associated acronyms, then write a short description of the term.

☐ Random Access Memory, RAM

___

___

☐ Read Only Memory, ROM

___

___

☐ Enhanced Integrated Drive Electronics, EIDE

___

___

☐ Small Computer Systems Interface, SCSI

___

___

Lab 1.1 Understanding Computer Terminology

- Hard Disk Drive, HDD

_____

_____

- Floppy Disk Drive, FDD

_____

_____

- Compact Disk–Read Only Memory, CD-ROM

_____

_____

- Serial Port, COM port

_____

_____

- Parallel Port, LPT port

_____

_____

- Universal Serial Bus, USB

_____

_____

- Basic Input Output System, BIOS

_____

_____

- Complimentary Metal–Oxide Semiconductor, CMOS

_____

_____

4 Introduction to Computer Repair

- Compact Disk-Recordable, CD-R

- Compact Disk-Rewritable, CD-RW

- Cache on a Stick, COAST

- Single Inline Memory Module, SIMM

- Dual Inline Memory Module, DIMM

- Cathode Ray Tube, CRT

- Liquid Crystal Display, LCD

- Direct Memory Access, DMA

Lab 1.1 Understanding Computer Terminology

☐ Input Output Port, I/O Port

_____

_____

☐ Interrupt Request, IRQ

_____

_____

☐ Industry Standard Architecture, ISA

_____

_____

☐ Peripheral Component Interconnect, PCI

_____

_____

☐ Accelerated Graphics Port, AGP

_____

_____

☐ Master Boot Record, MBR

_____

_____

☐ File Allocation Table, FAT

_____

_____

☐ Personal Computer Memory Card Industry Association, PCMCIA

_____

_____

6 Introduction to Computer Repair

☐ Plug and Play, PnP

_____

_____

End of Exercise

✓ Instructor Check _____

> ### 💡 Lab Notes
>
> The computer terms presented in this lab are a sampling of the terms in common use today. For a more complete understanding of computer terminology, study the glossary in the back of your textbook.

Student Notes

_____

_____

_____

_____

_____

_____

_____

_____

_____

_____

Lab 1.2   External Ports Identification

Introduction

It is important for the PC Technician to be able to visually identify computer components including peripherals, modules, and ports. In this exercise you will identify the external ports on an AT-style computer.

Maps to the following CompTIA A+ Objectives

A+ Core Hardware Service Technician Objectives
- Objective 1.4

Required Materials
- Lab manual

Lab Procedure

Study the following graphic and then enter the corresponding letter next to each of the following port descriptions:

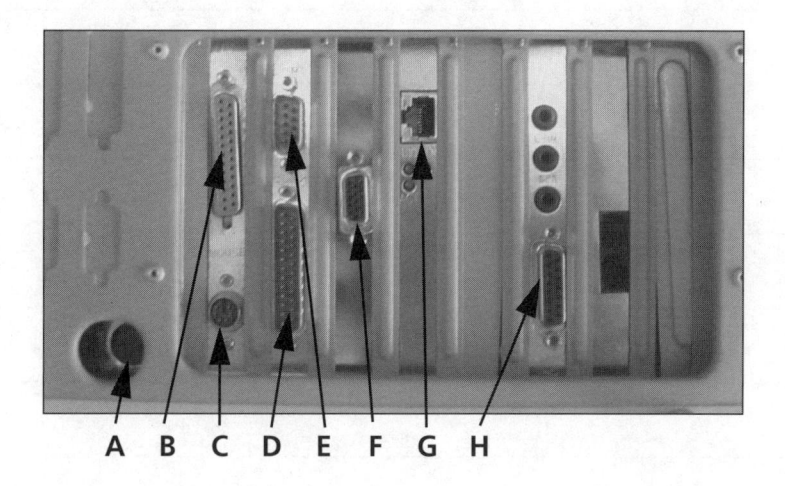

___   Parallel Port: 25-pin female port used for printer and scanner connections

___   DB-15 Game Port: 15-pin female port used for game controller and midi input connections.

___   5-pin DIN: female port used for ATX-style keyboard connections.

___   PS-2 Mouse Port: used for PS-2 mouse connections.

___   COM1: 9-pin male port used for serial connections.

___   RJ-11 port: 4-pin data port used for analog telephone connections.

___   SVGA port: 15-pin, 3-row, female port used for video display connections.

___   COM 2: 25-pin male port used for serial connections.

End of Exercise

✓ Instructor Check _____

> ### 💡 Lab Notes
>
> There are several other types of external ports that are not represented by the above graphic. Among these are Ethernet Ports, USB Ports, external SCSI ports, and the PS2-style keyboard port.
>
> **Key Terms**
>
> **SVGA:** Super Video Graphics Adapter
>
> **COM:** Communications Port
>
> **DIN connector:** Round connector with a locator slot that restricts orientation
>
> **DB connector:** D-Shell connector allows connecting only one way

Student Notes

_____

_____

_____

_____

_____

_____

_____

_____

_____

_____

Lab 1.3 Identify Internal Cables and Connectors

Introduction
In this lab you will identify common internal cables and connectors.

Maps to the following CompTIA A+ Objectives

A+ Core Hardware Service Technician Objectives
- Objective 1.4

Required Materials
- Lab workstation

Lab Procedure
1. Using proper Electrostatic Discharge (**ESD**) precautions, remove the workstation case. (Figure 1.3.1)

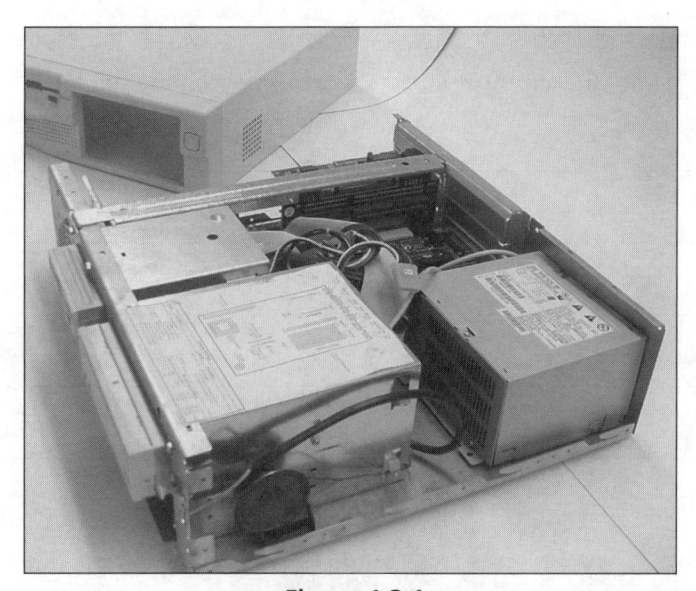

Figure 1.3.1

10 Introduction to Computer Repair

2. Remove the flat ribbon cable from your hard disk drive. (Figure 1.3.2)

Figure 1.3.2

☐ How many pins does the hard disk drive cable have?

_____

☐ What is the significance of the colored stripe on the ribbon cable?

_____

_____

_____

_____

_____

3. Remove the flat ribbon cable from the floppy disk drive. (Figure 1.3.3)

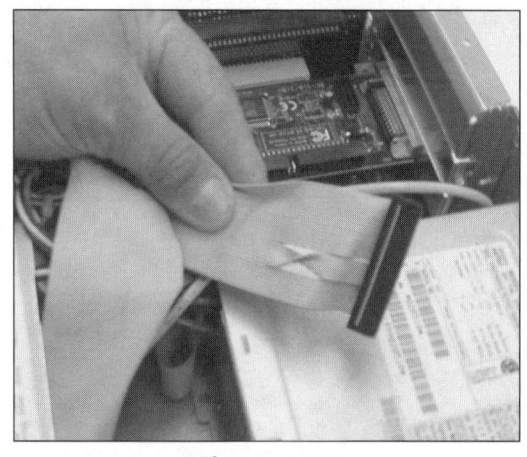

Figure 1.3.3

Lab 1.3   Identify Internal Cables and Connectors   11

☐ How many pins does the floppy drive cable have?

_____

_____

☐ What is the significance of the "twist" in the floppy ribbon cable?

_____

_____

_____

_____

_____

☐ How many floppy disk drives can be attached to the ribbon cable?

_____

4. Remove the power (MOLEX) connectors from the hard disk and floppy drives. (Figure 1.3.4)

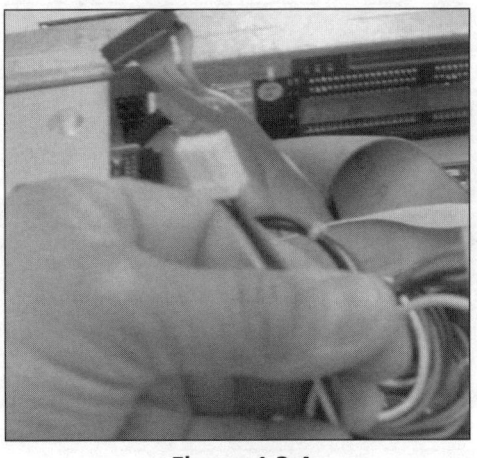

Figure 1.3.4

☐ What voltages are present at the hard disk and floppy drive power connectors?

_____

_____

5. Replace all cables and connectors you removed in the above exercise. Before replacing the workstation's cover, start the system and ensure that it boots properly. If the system operates properly, shut down, then reinstall the cover.

End of Exercise

✓ Instructor Check _____

💡 Lab Notes

Safety Note: Whenever you open your computer's case, ensure that you are using proper ESD (Electrostatic Discharge) precautions, i.e., static wrist strap, grounding mat, etc.

Student Notes

Lab 1.4 Installing Windows 98

Introduction

This is a two-part lab. In Part One you will prepare a hard disk for an installation of Windows 98 by deleting all existing disk partitions, creating a FAT 16 partition and formatting the partition. In Part Two you will do a clean install of Windows 98 on the new partition.

Maps to the following CompTIA A+ Objectives

A+ Core Hardware Service Technician Objectives
- Objectives 1.5 and 1.6

A+ Operating System Technologies Objectives
- Objective 2.1

Required Materials
- Workstation meeting the minimum classroom requirements
- Windows 98 installation CD-ROM
- Windows 98 setup boot disk
- Blank 3.5" floppy disk

Part One: Preparing the hard disk for Windows 98 installation

1. Insert the **Windows 98 setup boot disk** into the floppy drive and start your workstation.

   > **Note:** If your workstation is not configured to boot from the floppy drive, enter CMOS setup and configure your boot order setting.

2. When prompted, select **Start Computer with CD-ROM Support**, then press **Enter**.
3. At the "**A**" prompt, type **FDISK** and press **Enter**. The FDISK utility will start. (Figure 1.4.1)

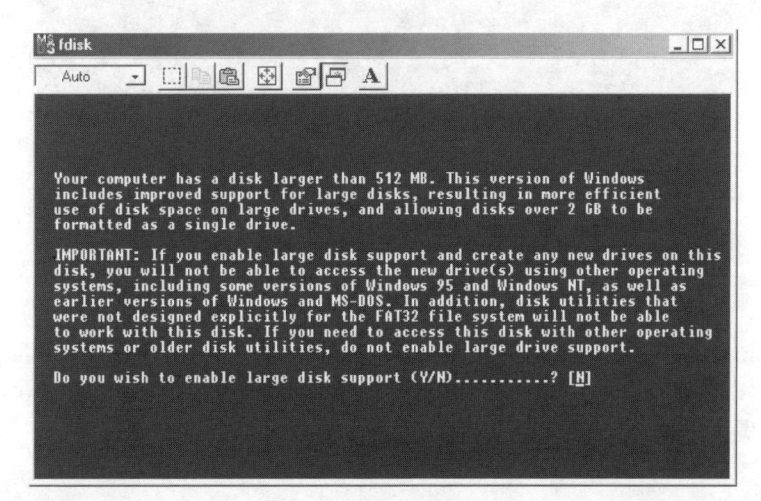

Figure 1.4.1

14 Introduction to Computer Repair

4. When prompted to enable **Large Disk Support**, select the "**N**" key, then press **Enter**.

> **Note:** If you enable Large Disk Support, FDISK will create FAT 32 partitions rather than FAT 16 partitions, and the subsequent operating system installations will not work!

☐ What are some advantages of using FAT 32 instead of FAT 16?

_____

_____

_____

_____

_____

5. From the **FDISK Options screen**, select **option 4** and press **Enter**. The partition information screen will be displayed showing all currently configured partitions. Make note of the partitions and then press the **ESC** key.

6. From the **FDISK Options screen**, choose **option 3** and press **Enter**. From the **Delete DOS Partition or Logical DOS Drive** screen, delete all of the partitions noted in step 5 above. When all partitions are deleted, press the **ESC** key to return to the **FDISK Options** screen.

7. From the **FDISK Options screen**, select **option 1** and press the **Enter** key. Select **Option 1**, **Create Primary DOS Partition**, and press **Enter**. (Figure 1.4.2)

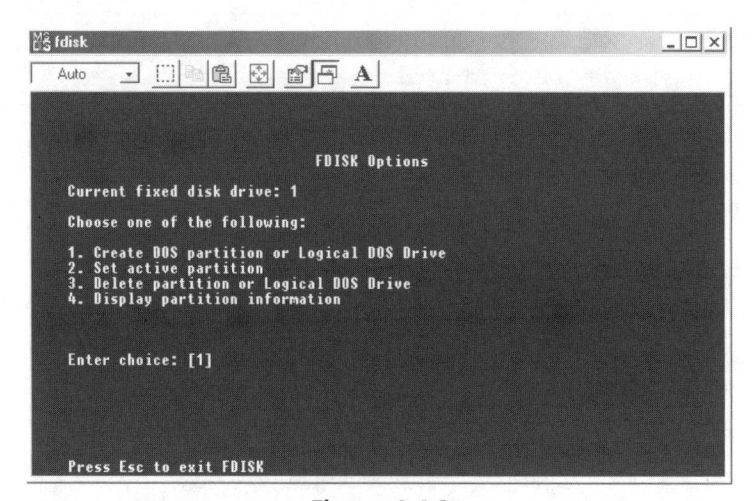

Figure 1.4.2

8. When prompted to use the maximum available size for the partition and make it active, select the "**N**" key and press **Enter**. Type **500** for the partition size and press **Enter**. Press the **ESC** key to return to the **FDISK Options** screen.

9. From the **FDISK Options screen**, select **option 2** and press the **Enter** key. Enter the number of the partition you just created (Should be #1) and press **Enter**. Press the **ESC** key to return to the **FDISK Options screen**.

   ☐ In step 9 you made the partition the ACTIVE partition. What is the significance of making a partition ACTIVE?

   _____

   _____

   _____

   _____

   _____

10. Press the **ESC** key twice to exit the **FDISK** utility and reboot the PC with the Windows 98 startup disk in the floppy drive. When prompted select **Start Computer with CD-ROM Support** and press **Enter**. Note the **drive letter** assigned to your CD-ROM drive.

11. At the "**A**" prompt, type **FORMAT C:** and press **Enter**. Confirm the format operation by pressing the "**Y**" key. When the format operation is finished, type **WIN98_DRIVE** as the volume label and press **Enter**.

Part Two: Installing Windows 98

1. Insert the Windows 98 Installation CD-ROM into the CD drive. Using the drive letter noted in step 10 above, navigate to the CD-ROM drive, type **SETUP**, and press **Enter**. Windows 98 **setup** will start.

2. Press **Enter** to allow setup to check your system. When the results of the check are displayed press the "**X**" key. Windows will copy files needed for setup. When the **Windows 98 Setup screen** appears, select **CONTINUE**.

3. Choose **C:\WINDOWS** as the installation directory, then select **Next**.

4. From the **Setup Options screen** choose **TYPICAL**, then select **Next**.

5. From the **Windows Components screen** choose **Install the Most Common Components**, then select **Next**.

6. At the **Identification screen**, type **WIN98_XX**, (with *XX* being a number assigned by the Instructor) as the computer name, and **WORKGROUP** as the workgroup name. Type **A+ Training Computer** as the computer description then select **Next**.

7. At the **Establishing Your Location screen** choose your **Country or Region** from the list then select **Next**.

8. At the **Startup Disk screen** select **Next**. When prompted, insert a floppy disk into the drive "**A**" and click **OK**. Setup will copy the files necessary to create a Windows 98 Startup disk. When setup completes the startup disk creation click **OK** then select **Next**. Setup will begin installing Windows 98 on your computer.

9. When prompted, remove all floppy disks from the drives and select **RESTART**. Windows will restart.

Introduction to Computer Repair

10. When prompted enter **your name**, your **Company name** (if applicable), then select **Next**.
11. At the **License Agreement screen** choose **I Accept The Agreement**, then select **Next**.
12. Enter your **product key** (supplied with the installation CD-ROM), then select **Next**. Select **Finish**. Setup will begin setting up your hardware and Plug and Play devices.
13. At the **Date/Time Properties screen**, choose the correct **date, time, and time zone**, select **APPLY**, then click **OK**.
14. When setup finishes configuring your system the computer will automatically restart. When the computer restarts, enter a **user name and password** then click **OK**. Confirm the password and click **OK**.
15. If prompted, allow Windows to search for drivers for any detected hardware.
16. Windows will finalize your system settings and open the **Welcome To Windows 98 screen**. Close the Welcome To Windows 98 screen to begin using Windows 98.

End of Exercise

✓ Instructor Check _____

Lab Notes

It is imperative you follow the above instructions exactly! You will be installing three different operating systems on your computer, and these instructions must be followed for the installations to be successful!

Key Terms

Windows 98 SE: Windows 98 Second Edition

FDISK: The Windows 98 built-in partitioning utility

FORMAT: Before a hard disk can be used for data storage, it must be partitioned and formatted. Formatting prepares the partition for the specific type of file system you will be using.

Student Notes

Student Notes

18 Introduction to Computer Repair

Lab 1.5 Installing Windows NT Workstation

Introduction

Windows NT Workstation is a 32-bit Operating System designed to be used in a workstation role. In this lab you will install Windows NT Workstation on your class workstation.

Maps to the following Comp TIA A+ Objectives

A+ Operating System Technologies Objectives
- Objective 2.1
- Objective 2.2

Required Materials
- Workstation meeting the minimum classroom requirements with Windows 98 installed
- Windows NT Workstation installation CD-ROM
- Blank 3.5" floppy disk

Lab Procedure

> **Note:** Windows NT Workstation setup can be started on one of four ways
> 1. Windows NT setup Boot disks
> 2. Bootable CD-ROM drive
> 3. Across the Network
> 4. From within an existing Windows installation (autorun)
>
> For this exercise you will begin setup from within Windows 98.

1. With your workstation started and running Windows 98, insert the Windows NT Workstation installation CD-ROM into the CD drive. The disk will autorun. (Figure 1.5.1)

   > **Note:** If the autorun feature is turned off, open My Computer and double-click the CD-ROM.

Lab 1.5   Installing Windows NT Workstation   19

Figure 1.5.1

2. Choose **Windows NT setup**. You will be prompted for the location of the Windows NT files. Verify that the proper file location is displayed, then press **Enter**. Setup will enter the **FILE COPY phase** of setup. (Figure 1.5.2)

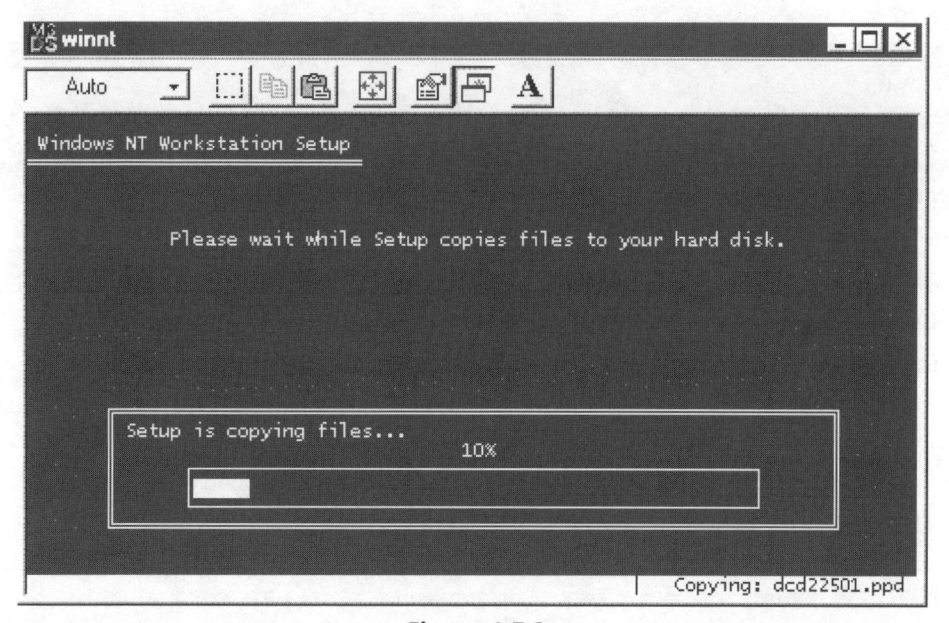

Figure 1.5.2

3. When the file copy phase of setup completes, press **Enter** to return to windows, then **Shut down** and **Restart** the computer. When setup resumes, it will enter the **TEXT phase** of setup.
4. At the **Welcome to Setup** screen, press **Enter** to setup Windows NT.
5. Verify that setup has recognized your mass storage devices (controllers), and press **Enter**.
6. **Page Down** through the Windows NT Licensing Agreement and press the "**F8**" key to agree to the license.
7. Verify that the listed **hardware and software components** match your computer and press **Enter**.
8. Use the **up and down arrow keys** to select **UNPARTITIONED** space on your hard drive and press the "**C**" key to create a partition.
9. Enter **500MB** as the size for the new partition, then press **Enter**.
10. Using the **up and down arrow keys**, select the **newly created partition**, then press **Enter**.
11. Choose **Format The Partition Using The NTFS File System**, then press **Enter**. Setup will format the partition.

> **Note:** The initial format will be FAT 16. Setup will convert the partition to NTFS during a later portion of setup.

12. Verify that **\WINNT** is listed as the installation directory, then press **Enter**.
13. Press **Enter** to allow setup to examine your hard disks. When setup completes the examination, it will begin copying files to your hard disk. When the file copy completes, press **Enter** to **restart** your computer.

> **Note:** When Windows NT restarts, setup will start the conversion of the partition to the NTFS file system. When the conversion is complete, setup will automatically restart the computer a second time.

14. After your computer restarts, setup will enter the **GUI phase** of setup. When prompted, press **Enter** to allow setup to gather information about your computer.
15. From the **Setup Options** screen, choose **TYPICAL**, then select **Next**.
16. From the **Name And Organization** screen, type your **name and organization information**, then select **Next**.
17. Enter your **CD Key** information (provided with the installation CD), then select **Next**.
18. Type **WINNT_XX** (**XX** being a number provided by your Instructor) for your computer name, then select **Next**.
19. At the **Administrator Account** screen, **type and confirm a password** for the Administrator account, then select **Next**.

> **Note:** Passwords are case sensitive. For convenience, use **password** (all lower case) as your password.

Lab 1.5 Installing Windows NT Workstation

20. Choose **Yes, Create an Emergency Repair Disk**, then select **Next**.
21. Choose **Install The Most Common Components**, then select **Next**.
22. Select **Next** to install **Windows NT Networking**.
23. Choose **This Computer Will Participate on a Network**, select **Wired to the Network**, then select **Next**.
24. Choose **Start Search** to have setup search for your network adapter. If setup is unable to find your network adapter, choose **Select From List** and either **select your adapter from the list** or **provide the appropriate driver**. When your network adapter appears in the **Network Adapters** window, select **Next**.
25. Verify that the **TCP/IP protocol** is checked and select **Next**. Select **Next** to install the selected components.
26. When prompted to use **DHCP** select **NO**.
27. From the TCP/IP Properties screen choose **Specify an IP Address**, enter **10.0.0.X** (**X** being a number assigned by the Instructor) in the **IP Address field**, and **255.0.0.0** in the **subnet mask field**. Click **OK** to accept the IP address settings.
28. Select **Next** to start the network.
29. Verify that **WINNT_XX** appears in the computer name field, select **Make This Computer A Member of WORKGROUP**, ensure the WORKGROUP name is WORKGROUP, then select **Next**.
30. Select **Finish** to finish setup.
31. At the **Date/Time Properties** screen, select the proper **date**, **time**, **and time zone**, then select **Close**.
32. At the **Display Properties** screen, choose the **TEST** button. Click **OK** to test your display settings. The test screen will be displayed for five seconds. If the test screen was displayed properly, click **OK** three times to accept the settings.

> **Note:** If the test screen was NOT displayed properly, adjust the settings and re-test.

33. Windows NT setup will begin a final file copy process, and will then set security on the system files.
34. After setup saves your configuration you will be prompted to create an **Emergency Repair Disk**. Insert a blank disk into the floppy drive and click **OK**.
35. When the Emergency Repair Disk creation process completes, remove the floppy disk and select **Restart Computer**.
36. When the computer restarts, you will be given the option to choose your Operating System. Choose **Windows NT Workstation Version 4.00** then press **Enter**.

22 Introduction to Computer Repair

37. When prompted, press **CTRL + ALT + Delete** to log on. Enter **Administrator** as the **user name**, the **password** you entered in step 19 above, then click **OK**. Close the **Welcome To Windows NT** screen to begin using Windows NT Workstation. (Figure 1.5.3)

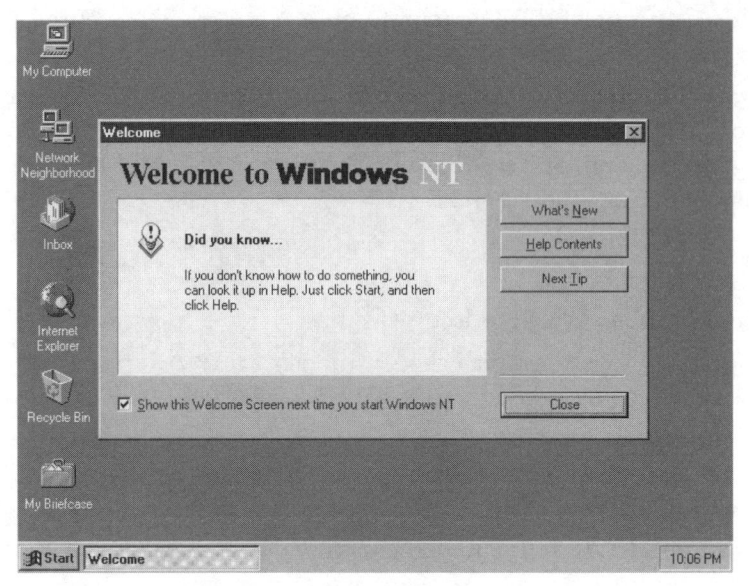

Figure 1.5.3

End of Exercise

✓ Instructor Check _____

💡 Lab Notes

Key Terms

NTFS: Windows NT allows you to use either the standard Windows FAT 16 file system or the NTFS file system. NTFS provides several file system enhancements, including more efficient allocation of disk storage and file-level security both locally and across the network.

File Copy phase, Text Phase, GUI Phase of setup: The installation process for Windows NT enters these three distinct phases during the installation process.

Student Notes

_____

_____

_____

Student Notes

Lab 1.6 Installing a Service Pack on Windows NT Workstation

Introduction

In this lab you will download and install the latest service pack for Windows NT Workstation.

Maps to the following CompTIA A+ Objectives

A+ Operating System Technologies Objectives
- Objective 2.2

Required Materials
- Workstation with Windows NT installed and configured
- Internet access

Lab Procedure

1. To download a service pack for Windows NT Workstation, go to: http://www.microsoft.com. Search for and download the latest Windows NT Workstation service pack executable to your local hard drive. (Figure 1.6.1)

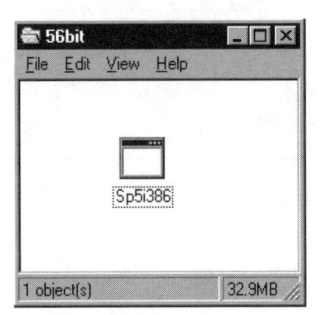

Figure 1.6.1

2. Double-click the service pack executable or, from the **Start Menu,** choose **Run**, type the path and file name of the service pack executable, and click **OK**.
3. Setup will extract the service pack files. (Figure 1.6.2)

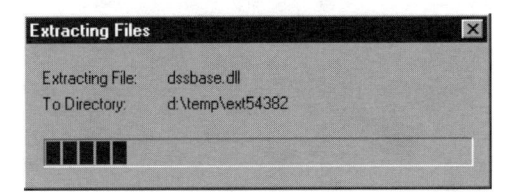

Figure 1.6.2

4. When setup is finished extracting the service pack files, the Windows NT Service Pack startup window will open. Choose **Accept the License Agreement**, and **Back up files for uninstall**, then select **Install**.
5. Service pack setup will back up your existing files and install the new service pack.

Lab 1.6 Installing a Service Pack on Windows NT Workstation

6. When Windows NT Service Pack setup completes, select **Restart** to start your computer with the new service pack files. (Figure 1.6.3)

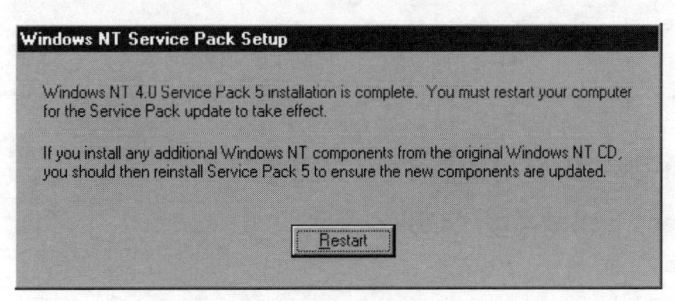

Figure 1.6.3

End of Exercise

✓ Instructor Check _____

> ### 💡 Lab Notes
>
> Service packs are provided to upgrade an Operating System's performance and fix known "bugs." In order for Windows NT to be fully compatible with Windows 2000, service pack 4 or greater must be installed.

Student Notes

_____
_____
_____
_____
_____
_____
_____
_____

Lab 1.7 Installing Windows 2000 Professional

Introduction

In this lab you will install and configure Windows 2000 Professional on your workstation.

Maps to the following CompTIA A+ Objectives

A+ Operating System Technologies Objectives
- Objective 2.1

Required Materials

- Lab workstation with Windows 98, Windows NT Workstation, and Windows NT Service Pack 4 or greater installed
- Windows 2000 Installation CD-ROM

Lab Procedure

> **Note:** Windows NT Workstation setup can be started on one of four ways
> 1. Windows NT setup Boot disks
> 2. Bootable CD-ROM drive
> 3. Across the Network
> 4. From within an existing Windows installation (autorun)
>
> For this exercise you will begin setup from within Windows 98 or Windows NT.

1. Start your workstation and ensure that Windows 98 or Windows NT Workstation loads properly.
2. Insert the **Windows 2000 Professional** installation disk into the CD-ROM drive. The disk will autorun.

> **Note:** If the autorun feature is turned off, open My Computer and double-click the CD-ROM.

Lab 1.7 Installing Windows 2000 Professional 27

3. Choose **Install Windows 2000**. The **Windows 2000 Setup** screen will open. (Figure 1.7.1)

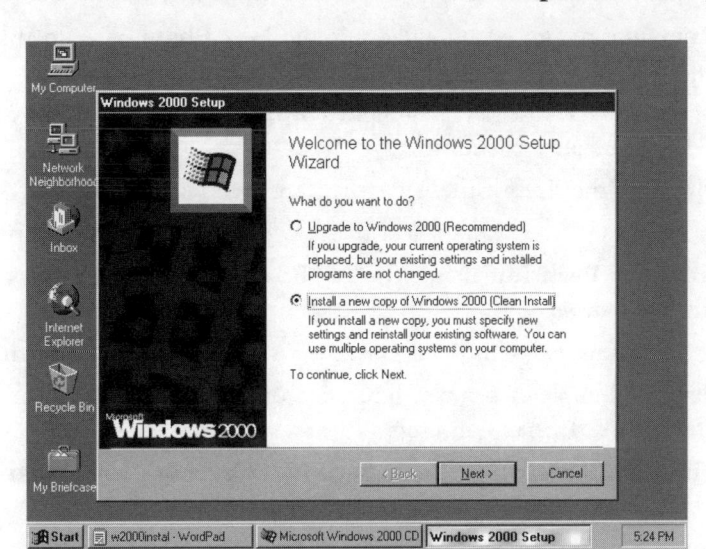

Figure 1.7.1

4. Choose **Install a new copy of Windows 2000**. Then select **Next**. The **File Copy phase** of setup will start.
5. At the **License Agreement** screen, select **I Accept the Agreement**, then click **Next**.
6. At the **Product Key** screen, type in your product key number (provided with installation CD), then select **Next**. (Figure 1.7.2)

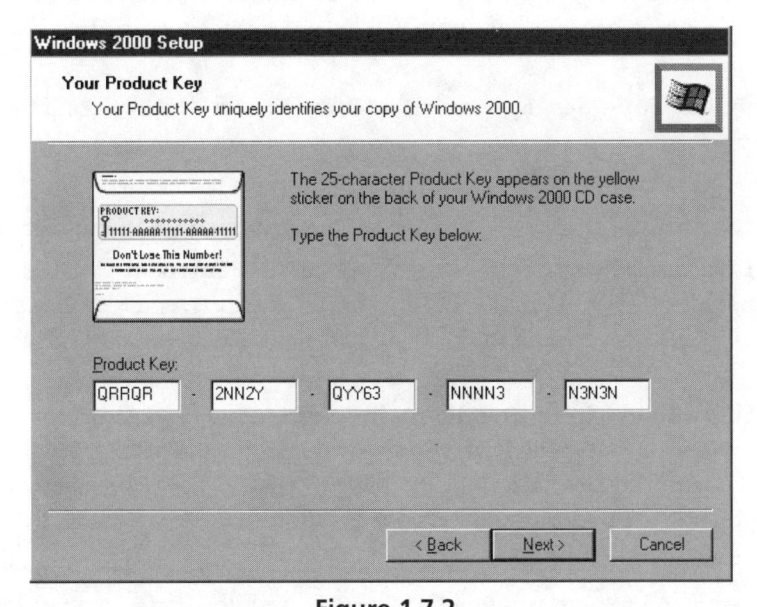

Figure 1.7.2

7. At the **Select Special Options** screen, you can customize language, installation, and accessibility options.
8. At the **Upgrading to the Windows 2000 NTFS File System** screen, choose **No Do Not Upgrade My Drive**, then select **Next**.

9. Setup will copy files needed for setup, then restart your computer.
10. When your computer restarts, setup will begin the **Text Phase** of setup. When prompted, press **Enter** to continue setting up Windows 2000 Professional.
11. Using the up and down arrow keys, highlight **Unpartitioned Space** on your hard drive, and press the "**C**" key to create a partition.
12. Type in **1000 MB** as the size for the new partition, then press **Enter**.
13. Using the up and down arrow keys, select the new partition, then press **Enter**.
14. Choose **Format the Partition using the NTFS file system**, then press **Enter**. Setup will begin formatting the drive.
15. When the format is finished, setup will examine your hard drive then begin copying files.
16. When the file copy completes, setup will reboot your computer. When the computer reboots, setup will enter the **GUI phase** of setup.
17. When the **Windows 2000 Professional Setup Wizard** starts, click **Next**. Setup will begin detecting and installing devices on your computer.
18. At the **Regional Settings** screen, you can customize Windows 2000 for different regions and languages. Select **Next** to accept the default settings.
19. At the **Personalize your Settings** screen, type your name and the name of your organization, then select **Next**.
20. At the **Computer Name** and **Administrator Password** screen, type **WIN2000XX** (where **XX** is the number assigned by your instructor). For the computer name, enter and confirm a password for the Administrator Account, then select **Next**.

> **Note:** For convenience, use **password** (all lower case) for your password).

21. At the **Date and Time Settings** screen, enter the correct date, time, and time zone, then select **Next**.
22. Setup will begin detecting and installing networking components.
23. At the **Networking Settings** screen, choose **Custom Settings**, then select **Next**.
24. At the **Networking Components** screen, highlight the **Internet Protocol** (TCP/IP), then select **Properties**. Choose **Use the Following IP Address**, enter 10.0.0.*X* (*X* being a number supplied by your Instructor) in the IP address field, 255.0.0.0 in the Subnet Mask field, click **OK**, and then select **Next**.
25. At the **Workgroup or Computer Domain** screen, choose **No, this computer is not on a network**, or **is on a network without a domain**, ensure **Workgroup** appears in the **Workgroup or Computer Domain** field, then select **Next**. Setup will begin installing Windows 2000 components and performing final configuration tasks.
26. When the Windows 2000 Professional setup completes, select **Finish** to restart your computer.
27. When the computer restarts, you will be presented with the option to start multiple operating systems. Choose Microsoft Windows 2000 Professional and press **Enter**.
28. When the **Windows 2000 Professional Network ID Wizard** starts, select **Next**. Choose **Users must enter a user name and password to use this computer**, then select **Next**. Click **Finish** to close the wizard.

Lab 1.7 Installing Windows 2000 Professional 29

29. At the **Log on to Windows** screen, enter **Administrator** as the user, type your **password**, and then click **OK**.
30. Close the **Getting Started with Windows 2000** screen to start using Windows 2000 Professional. (Figure 1.7.4)

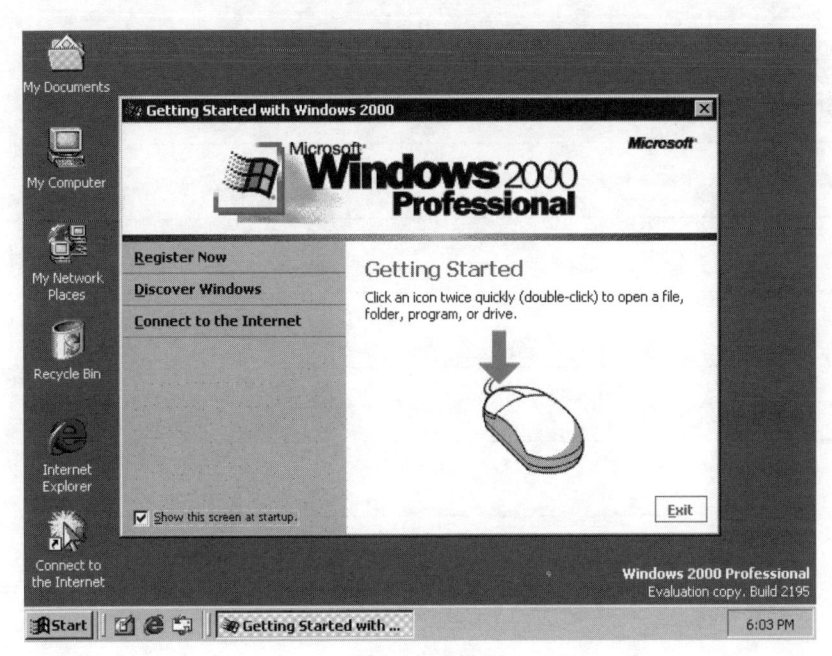

Figure 1.7.3

End of Exercise

✓ Instructor Check _____

💡 Lab Notes

In this exercise, you installed Windows 2000 Professional using the NTFS file system. Both Windows NT and Windows 2000 Professional will be able to access all partitions on your workstation. Windows 98 will only be able to access the FAT 16 partition (C-Drive). If you create any files that you wish to have available for all three Operating Systems, save them on the C-Drive.

Student Notes

Student Notes

CHAPTER 2
On the Motherboard

2.1 System Board Identification 32

2.2 Microprocessor/Slot/Socket Identification 36

2.3 Replacing a Microprocessor 39

2.4 Expansion Bus Identification 42

2.5 System BIOS Identification 45

2.6 Replacing the System BIOS 47

2.7 Installing a System BIOS Flash Upgrade 50

2.8 Chipset Identification 52

32 On the Motherboard

Lab 2.1 System Board Identification

Introduction

It is important for the PC technician to be able to identify popular system board configurations. In this lab you will identify the three most popular motherboard styles.

Maps to the following CompTIA A+ Objectives

A+ Core Hardware Service Technician Objectives
- Objective 4.3

Required Materials
- Lab Manual

Lab Procedure

1. Study the following system board pictures and descriptions, then label the following figures according to the type, AT, ATX, or Planar.
   - **AT System Boards:** AT System Boards can be identified by a lack of on-board integrated components such as video adapters, sound cards, and network adapters. These components are normally installed as add-on expansion cards. The AT-style keyboard connector is a 6-pin DIN connector. (Figure 2.1.1)

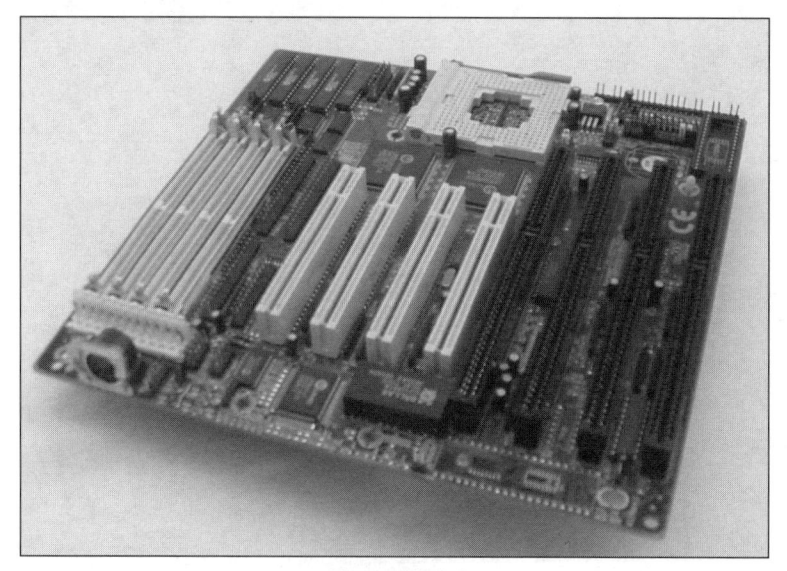

Figure 2.1.1

Lab 2.1 System Board Identification 33

- **ATX System Boards:** ATX System Boards can be identified by the presence of integrated components such as video adapters, sound cards, USB ports, and network adapters. The keyboard and mouse connectors are of the PS2 (5-pin mini-din) type. (Figure 2.1.2)

Figure 2.1.2

- **Planar System Boards:** Planar-style System Boards can be identified by the absence of expansion bus slots on the board. There is usually a single expansion slot in which a specialized expansion board is inserted. Expansion cards such as video adapters, sound cards, and network adapters are inserted into the expansion board. (Figure 2.1.3)

Figure 2.1.3

34 On the Motherboard

2. Using proper ESD precautions, remove the case from your workstation, then answer the following questions.

   ☐ What type of system board is installed in your workstation?

   _____

   _____

   ☐ If you have an ATX system board, identify the ports and list them below:

   _____

   _____

   _____

   _____

   _____

   ☐ In the figures above, circle the keyboard port on the AT system board.
   ☐ In the figure above, how many expansion slots are available on the Planar board?

   _____

   _____

End of Exercise

✓ Instructor Check _____

Student Notes

_____

_____

_____

_____

_____

Student Notes

36 On the Motherboard

Lab 2.2 Microprocessor/Slot/Socket Identification

Introduction

Due to the constant improvements in microprocessor designs, there are many different types of microprocessors, slots, and sockets. It is important for the PC technician to be able to identify proper microprocessor and socket combinations.

Maps to the following CompTIA A+ Objectives

A+ Core Hardware Service Technician Objectives
- Objectives 1.8, 4.1, and 4.3

Required Materials
- Lab manual
- Lab workstation

Lab Procedure

1. Using proper ESD precautions, remove your workstation cover.
2. Study the following microprocessor slot and socket definitions and then answer the following questions:
   - **Socket 4**: Socket 4 is a 273-pin PGA socket that supports the Classic Pentium 60/66.
   - **Socket 5**: Socket 5 is a 320-pin PGA socket that supports the Classic Pentium 75/90/100/120.
   - **Socket 7**: Socket 7 is a 321-pin SPGA socket that supports Pentium MMX, AMD K5, AMD K6, Cyrix M II, and Cyrix Media GX.
   - **Super Socket 7**: Super Socket 7 is a 321-pin SPGA socket that supports AMD K6-2, and AMD K7.
   - **Socket 8**: Socket 8 is a 387-pin SPGA socket that supports Pentium Pro.
   - **Socket 370**: Socket 370 supports Celeron processors.
   - **Slot 1**: Slot 1 is a 242-pin slot that supports Pentium II and Pentium III.
   - **Slot A**: Slot A supports AMD Athlon Processors.
   - **Socket 423**: Socket 423 supports Pentium IV processors.
   - What type of processor and slot combination is in your workstation?

Lab 2.2 Microprocessor/Slot/Socket Identification

- What type of processors will your system board support?

  _____
  _____
  _____
  _____
  _____

- Refer to your system board documentation. What are the system bus speed and clock multiplier settings?

  _____
  _____

- Multiply the system bus speed by the clock multiplier. Is the result the same as your processor's rated speed?

  _____
  _____

3. When finished, replace your workstation's cover.

End of Exercise

✓ Instructor Check _____

Student Notes

_____
_____
_____
_____
_____
_____

Student Notes

Lab 2.3 Replacing a Microprocessor

Introduction

Microprocessors are Field-Replaceable Units. As a PC technician, you will need to know how to remove and replace microprocessors.

Maps to the following CompTIA A+ Objectives

A+ Core Hardware Service Technician Objectives
- Objectives 1.2 and 1.8

Required Materials
- Lab workstation

Lab Procedure

1. Using proper ESD precautions, remove the workstation cover.
2. Locate and remove the microprocessor cooling fan and/or heat sink. (Figure 2.3.1)

Figure 2.3.1

40 On the Motherboard

3. Remove the microprocessor from its slot or socket by releasing the microprocessor retaining mechanism. (Figure 2.3.2)

Figure 2.3.2

4. Ensure that the system bus speed and clock multiplier are set properly for the new microprocessor.

   Note: Refer to the system board documentation for information on setting the bus speed and multiplier.

5. Insert the new microprocessor into the slot or socket, and secure the retaining mechanism.
6. Replace the microprocessor cooling fan, then start the workstation and verify that it boots properly.

End of Exercise

✓ Instructor Check _____

Student Notes

Student Notes

42 On the Motherboard

Lab 2.4 Expansion Bus Identification

Introduction

Due to the constant improvements in computer designs, there are many different types of expansion buses. It is important for the PC technician to be able to identify the various bus types and the expansion cards that go in them.

Maps to the following CompTIA A+ Objectives

A+ Core Hardware Service Technician Objectives
- Objectives 1.8 and 4.3

Required Materials
- Lab manual
- Lab workstation

Lab Procedure

1. The following four bus types are the most common types found in modern computers:
   - **AGP:** Accelerated Graphics Port, used for high-speed video
   - **PCI:** Peripheral Component Interconnect, used for high-speed input/output devices
   - **ISA:** Industry Standard Architecture, older 16-bit slot used by older (legacy) devices
   - **VL-Bus:** VESA-Local Bus, older 32-bit local bus
2. Study the figures on the following page. Label the expansion slot as to Bus type, and draw a line to the corresponding expansion card.

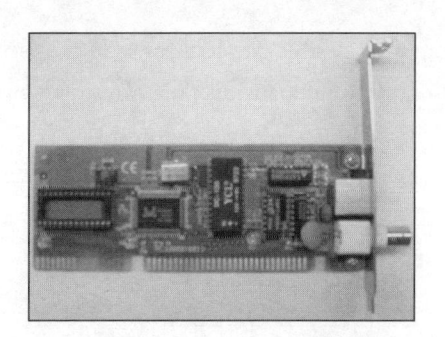

Lab 2.4 Expansion Bus Identification 43

☐ Bus Type

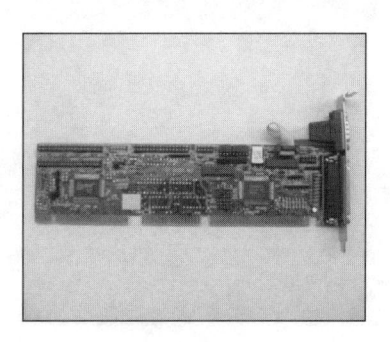

_____

☐ Bus Type

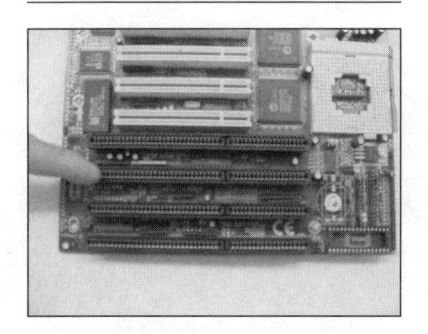

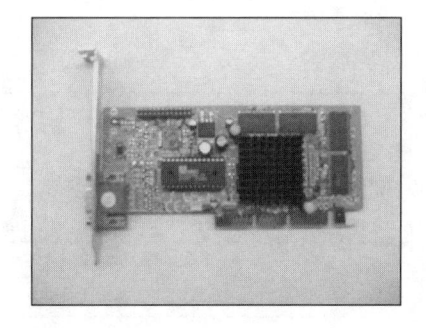

_____

☐ Bus Type

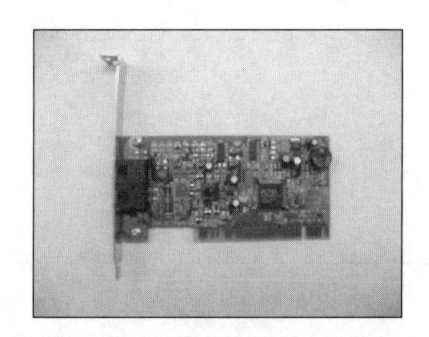

_____

☐ Bus Type

_____

44   On the Motherboard

3. Using proper ESD procedures, remove the workstation cover.
   □ Identify the expansion slots on your workstation and list them below.

___

___

___

___

___

End of Exercise

✓ Instructor Check _____

Student Notes

Lab 2.5 System BIOS Identification

Introduction
System BIOS provides basic input/output information during system startup and operation.

Maps to the following CompTIA A+ Objectives

A+ Core Hardware Service Technician Objectives
- Objectives 4.4

Required Materials
- Lab manual
- Lab workstation

Lab Procedure
1. Using proper ESD precautions, remove the workstation cover.
2. Locate the system BIOS on your system board. (Figure 2.5.1)

Figure 2.5.1

46 On the Motherboard

☐ What is the manufacturer name and model number of your system BIOS?

_____

_____

End of Exercise

✓ Instructor Check _____

> 💡 **Lab Notes**
>
> **Note:** Common BIOS manufacturers include: Award, AMI, Phoenix, MR BIOS, Quadtel. In addition, some computer manufacturers have their own proprietary BIOS.

Student Notes

_____

_____

_____

_____

_____

_____

_____

_____

_____

_____

Lab 2.6 Replacing the System BIOS

Introduction
In this lab you will remove and replace the System BIOS.

Maps to the following CompTIA A+ Objectives

A+ Core Hardware Service Technician Objectives
- Objectives 1.8 and 4.4

Required Materials
- Lab workstation

Lab Procedure
1. Using proper ESD precautions, remove your workstation's cover.
2. Locate the system BIOS, and grip the BIOS with a chip-puller tool. (Figure 2.6.1)

Figure 2.6.1

48   On the Motherboard

3. With even upward pressure, remove the BIOS from its socket. (Figure 2.6.2)

Figure 2.6.2

4. Insert the new BIOS into the socket and, with even downward pressure, fully insert the BIOS into the socket.
5. Start the workstation and ensure that it boots properly.

End of Exercise

✓ Instructor Check _____

> ### 💡 Lab Notes
>
> 1. Some system BIOS are soldered in and not replaceable. Check the system board documentation to see if your specific BIOS is replaceable.
> 2. In some cases it will become necessary to replace the system BIOS in order to add functionality to your workstation. This increased functionality may include support for new computer components, or enhanced support for existing components.
> 3. Some POST diagnostic cards require the technician to replace the existing system BIOS with a specialized diagnostic BIOS. This allows more thorough diagnostics on the system components.

Student Notes

Lab 2.7 Installing a System BIOS Flash Upgrade

Introduction

Most BIOS manufacturers design their components to be "flashable." This allows the BIOS to be upgraded without removal and replacement. In this exercise you will download and install the latest BIOS flash update for your system BIOS.

Maps to the following CompTIA A+ Objectives

A+ Core Hardware Service Technician Objectives
- Objective 4.4

Required Materials
- Lab workstation
- Internet access

Lab Procedure

1. From a workstation with Internet access, access the Web site for your system BIOS manufacturer. Use the system BIOS information you gathered in Exercise 2.5.
2. Browse to and download the latest BIOS update for your system BIOS.
   - What is the file name for the BIOS flash upgrade you downloaded?

   _____

   _____

3. Once the flash upgrade is downloaded, follow the BIOS manufacturer's instructions to install the BIOS upgrade on your workstation.

End of Exercise

✓ Instructor Check _____

> **Lab Notes**
>
> Use the following URLs to access BIOS manufacturer's Web sites:
> - Phoenix BIOS: http://www.phoenix.com
> - Award BIOS: http://www.phoenix/com
> - AMI Bios: http://www.ami.com
> - Mr. BIOS: http://www.mrbios.com
> - Generic BIOS Support: http://www.bioscentral.com
>
> For all other proprietary BIOS manufacturers (Compaq, Dell, etc.), browse to the respective computer manufacturer's Web site.

Student Notes

52 On the Motherboard

Lab 2.8 Chipset Identification

Introduction

In this lab you will identify your workstation's chipset.

Maps to the following CompTIA A+ Objectives

A+ Core Hardware Service Technician Objectives
- Objective 4.3

Required Materials
- Lab workstation

Lab Procedure

1. Using proper ESD precautions, remove the workstation cover.
2. Locate the system board chipset. (Figure 2.8.1)

Figure 2.8.1

- What is the make and model of your system board chipset?

_____

_____

3. Replace the workstation cover, and start the workstation.

End of Exercise

✓ Instructor Check _____

Student Notes

Student Notes

CHAPTER 3

System Configuration

3.1 Basic CMOS Configuration   56

3.2 Disabling Devices within CMOS   59

3.3 Assigning System Resources within CMOS   62

3.4 Viewing System Information in Windows 98   64

3.5 Using Windows 98 Device Manager   67

3.6 Viewing System Information in Windows NT Workstation   71

3.7 Managing Devices in Windows NT Workstation   74

3.8 Viewing System Information in Windows 2000 Professional   78

3.9 Using Windows 2000 Professional Device Manager   81

Lab 3.1 Basic CMOS Configuration

Introduction

In this lab you will explore the available CMOS configuration settings.

Maps to the following CompTIA A+ Objectives

A+ Core Hardware Service Technician Objectives
- Objective 4.4

Required Materials
- Lab workstation

Lab Procedure

1. Power on your PC. During the initial startup, you should receive a prompt explaining how to enter setup.

   > **Note:** If no prompt is displayed, refer to the motherboard manufacturer's manual for directions on how to enter setup.

   - What is the method for entering your workstation's CMOS setup?

   _____

   _____

   _____

   _____

   _____

2. Enter your PC's CMOS setup utility. From the opening screen, several categories of setup options are available to you.

   - List the available options below:

   _____

   _____

   _____

   _____

   _____

Lab 3.1   Basic CMOS Configuration   57

3. Familiarize yourself with the available setup categories and options, then answer the following questions:
   - Where do you find the setup options for your EIDE controller?

   _____

   _____

   - Where do you set the Date and Time for your PC?

   _____

   _____

   - Where do you configure the Boot Sequence for your PC?

   _____

   _____

   - What would happen if you were to disable the Primary and Secondary IDE Controllers?

   _____

   _____

   _____

   _____

   - Is your onboard FDD (floppy disk drive) controller enabled or disabled?

   _____

   _____

   - If you made any configuration settings you wanted saved, how would you save your settings and exit the setup utility?

   _____

   _____

   _____

   _____

58 System Configuration

4. Exit the setup utility without saving, and allow your PC to boot normally.

End of Exercise

✓ Instructor Check _____

> ### 💡 Lab Notes
>
> *Key Terms*
>
> **CMOS:** Complimentary Metal Oxide Semiconductor, the component that holds the system configuration information, allowing the system to start
>
> **CMOS Setup:** The utility that allows a user to enter system configuration information
>
> **Boot Sequence:** The sequence in which the System BIOS will search disk drives looking for the system bootfiles

Student Notes

_____
_____
_____
_____
_____
_____
_____
_____
_____
_____

Lab 3.2 Disabling Devices within CMOS

Introduction
In this lab you will use the CMOS configuration utility to disable system devices.

Maps to the following CompTIA A+ Objectives

A+ Core Hardware Service Technician Objectives
- Objective 4.4

Required Materials
- Lab workstation

Lab Procedure
1. Start your workstation and enter the CMOS configuration utility.
2. Open the setup category where the integrated peripherals options are set.
   - List the available integrated peripherals options below:

   _____
   _____
   _____
   _____
   _____

3. Select the onboard serial (COM) Port 1 option.
   - What settings options are available for serial (COM) Port 1?

   _____
   _____
   _____
   _____
   _____

System Configuration

4. Select the option to disable serial (COM) Port 1.
   - What will be the result of disabling serial (COM) Port 1?

   _____
   _____
   _____
   _____

5. Select the option to disable the onboard parallel (LPT) Port 1.
   - What will be the result of disabling parallel (LPT) Port 1?

   _____
   _____
   _____
   _____

6. Exit the CMOS configuration utility without saving your settings.

End of Exercise

✓ Instructor Check _____

> ### 💡 Lab Notes
>
> *Key Terms*
>
> **Serial/COM port:** An external computer port used for serial data communications (commonly used for MODEM and Mouse connections)
>
> **Parallel/LPT Port:** An external computer port used for parallel data communications (commonly used for printer connections)
>
> **Integrated Peripherals:** Devices that are integrated onto the system board

Student Notes

Lab 3.3 Assigning System Resources within CMOS

Introduction

In this lab you will use the CMOS setup utility to assign system resources to system devices.

Maps to the following CompTIA A+ Objectives

A+ Core Hardware Service Technician Objectives
- Objective 4.4

Required Materials
- Lab workstation

Lab Procedure

1. Start your workstation and enter the CMOS configuration utility.
2. Open the setup category where integrated peripherals options are set.
3. Select the configuration options for the onboard parallel (LPT) port.
   - What is your current setting for the parallel (LPT) port?

   _____

   _____

   - What setup options are available for the parallel (LPT) port?

   _____

   _____

   _____

   _____

   _____

4. Select a different I/O and IRQ setting for the parallel (LPT) port.
   - What will be the effect of this setting change?

   _____

   _____

   _____

   _____

   _____

5. Exit the CMOS configuration utility without saving your settings.

End of Exercise

✓ Instructor Check _____

> ### Lab Notes
>
> *Key Terms*
>
> **I/O:** Input/output. Commonly used to refer to a port where input and output data is transferred
>
> **IRQ:** Interrupt Request. A mechanism whereby a peripheral can request attention from the microprocessor

Student Notes

Lab 3.4 Viewing System Information in Windows 98

Introduction

In this lab you will use the System Information utility in Windows 98 to view system information.

Maps to the following CompTIA A+ Objectives

A+ Core Hardware Service Technician Objectives
- Objective 1.3

A+ Operating System Technologies Objectives
- Objective 1.1

Required Materials
- Workstation with Windows 98 installed and configured

Lab Procedure

1. From the **Start Menu**, choose **Programs**, **Accessories**, **System Tools**, and then select **System Information**. The Microsoft System Information utility will open. (Figure 3.4.1)

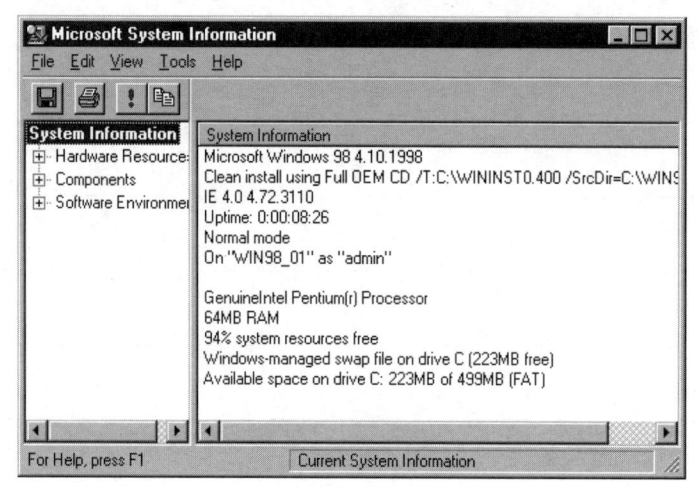

Figure 3.4.1

Lab 3.4 Viewing System Information in Windows 98 65

2. Double-click the hardware resources category, then select IRQs. The system IRQ usage information will be displayed. (Figure 3.4.2)

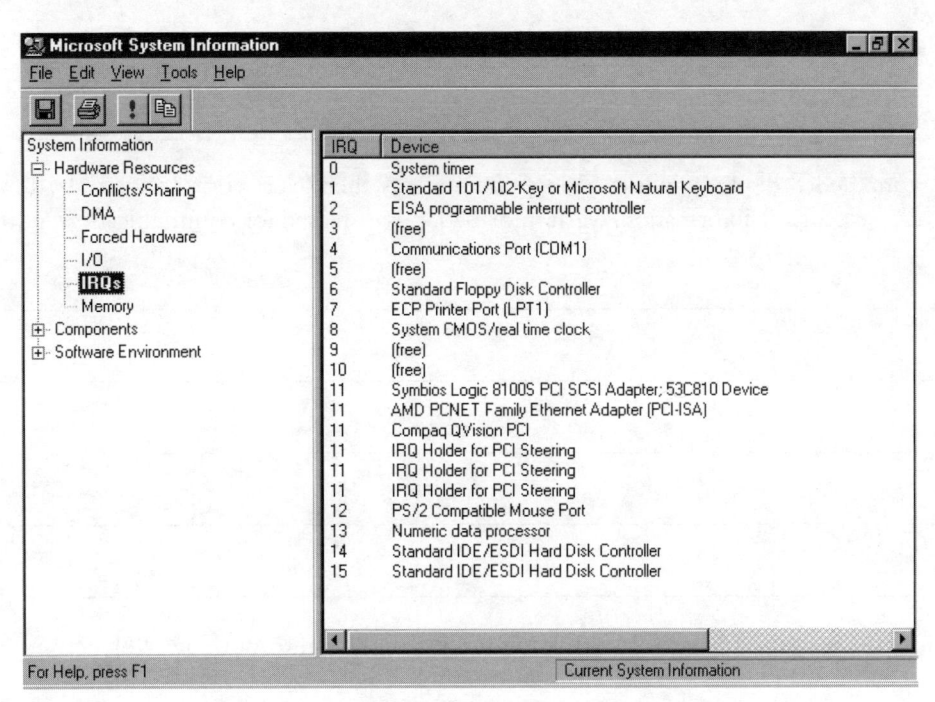

```
Microsoft System Information
File Edit View Tools Help

System Information                IRQ   Device
├─ Hardware Resources             0     System timer
│  ├─ Conflicts/Sharing           1     Standard 101/102-Key or Microsoft Natural Keyboard
│  ├─ DMA                         2     EISA programmable interrupt controller
│  ├─ Forced Hardware             3     (free)
│  ├─ I/O                         4     Communications Port (COM1)
│  ├─ IRQs                        5     (free)
│  └─ Memory                      6     Standard Floppy Disk Controller
├─ Components                     7     ECP Printer Port (LPT1)
└─ Software Environment           8     System CMOS/real time clock
                                  9     (free)
                                  10    (free)
                                  11    Symbios Logic 8100S PCI SCSI Adapter; 53C810 Device
                                  11    AMD PCNET Family Ethernet Adapter (PCI-ISA)
                                  11    Compaq QVision PCI
                                  11    IRQ Holder for PCI Steering
                                  11    IRQ Holder for PCI Steering
                                  11    IRQ Holder for PCI Steering
                                  12    PS/2 Compatible Mouse Port
                                  13    Numeric data processor
                                  14    Standard IDE/ESDI Hard Disk Controller
                                  15    Standard IDE/ESDI Hard Disk Controller

For Help, press F1                              Current System Information
```

Figure 3.4.2

3. Explore the remaining categories of system information that are available, then answer the following questions:

   ▫ What hardware resources can be viewed with the system information utility?

   _____

   _____

   _____

   _____

   ▫ Open the I/O hardware resource category. What I/O address ranges are being used by your video adapter?

   _____

   _____

System Configuration

- Open the memory hardware resource category. What memory address ranges are being used by your video adapter?

  _____

  _____

- From the left display window, choose components, then select ports. In the right display window, select basic information. What information is displayed for communications port COM 1?

  _____

  _____

  _____

  _____

  _____

4. Close the Microsoft System Information utility and return to Windows 98.

End of Exercise

✓ Instructor Check _____

Student Notes

_____

_____

_____

_____

_____

_____

_____

Lab 3.5   Using Windows 98 Device Manager

Introduction

In this lab you will use Windows 98 Device Manager to manage devices.

Maps to the following CompTIA A+ Objectives

A+ Core Hardware Service Technician Objectives
- Objectives 1.3 and 1.7

A+ Operating System Technologies Objectives
- Objective 3.2

Required Materials
- Workstation with Windows 98 installed and configured

Lab Procedure

1. From the **Start Menu**, choose **Settings**, then select **Control Panel**.
2. From control panel double-click **System**, then select **Device Manager**. (Figure 3.5.1)

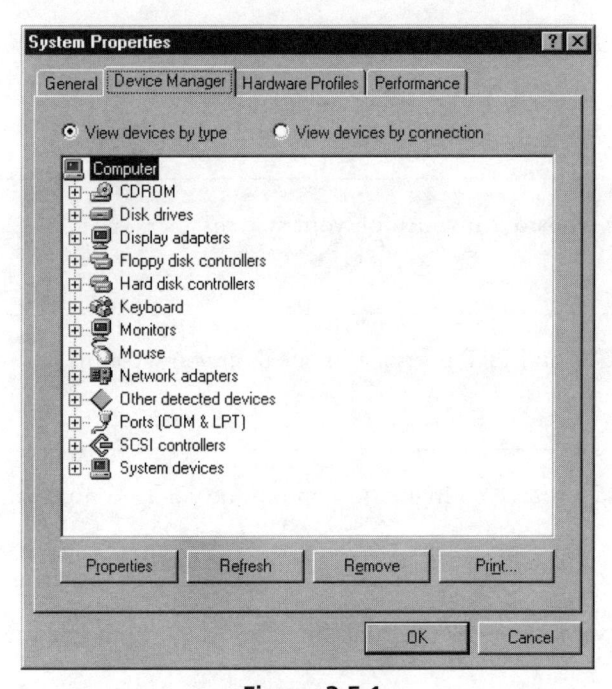

Figure 3.5.1

3. From the systems properties window, double-click disk drives. The system's installed disk drives will be displayed.

68　System Configuration

4. To view the properties of a disk drive, highlight one of the drives and select properties. (Figure 3.5.2)

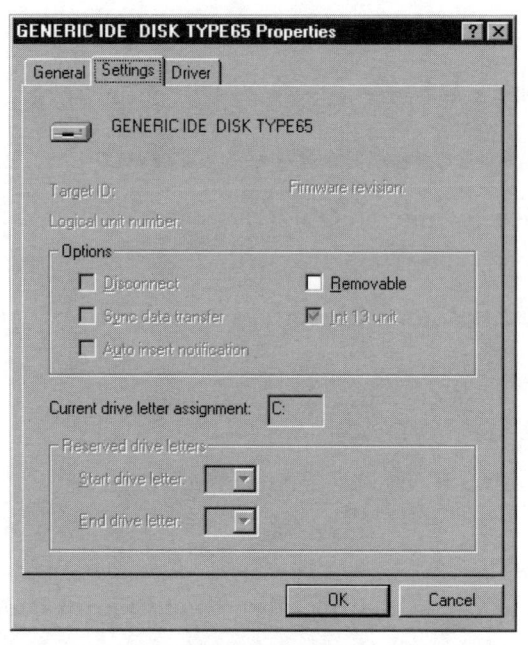

Figure 3.5.2

5. Explore the remaining device manager categories then answer the following questions:
   ▫ What is the file version number for your standard floppy disk controller driver?

   _____

   ▫ What type of keyboard is installed on your system?

   _____

   ▫ How many COM and LPT ports are installed on your system?

   _____

   ▫ Can drivers and resource configuration options be changed from within Device Manager?

   _____

6. From within **Device Manager**, expand the ports category, choose the LPT 1 port, then select **Properties**.

Lab 3.5 Using Windows 98 Device Manager 69

7. From the **General** properties page select **Disable in this hardware profile**, then click **OK**. (Figure 3.5.3)

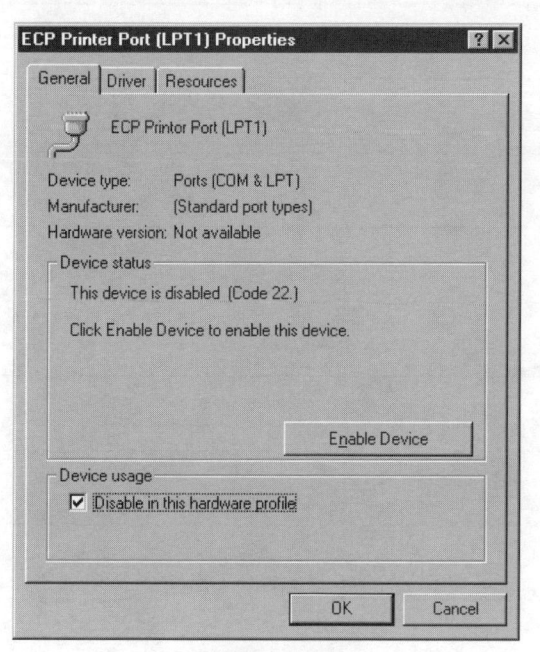

Figure 3.5.3

☐ What will be the result of this configuration setting?

_____

_____

_____

_____

_____

8. From the properties of the LPT 1 port, enable the port then click **OK**. Close the **Device Manager** utility.

End of Exercise

✓ Instructor Check _____

Student Notes

Lab 3.6 Viewing System Information in Windows NT Workstation

Introduction

In this lab you will use Windows NT Diagnostics to view system information.

Maps to the following CompTIA A+ Objectives

A+ Core Hardware Service Technician Objectives
- Objective 1.3

A+ Operating System Technologies Objectives
- Objective 1.1

Required Materials
- Workstation with Windows NT workstation installed and configured

Lab Procedure

1. From the **Start Menu** choose programs, administrative tools, and then select **Windows NT Diagnostics**. (Figure 3.6.1)

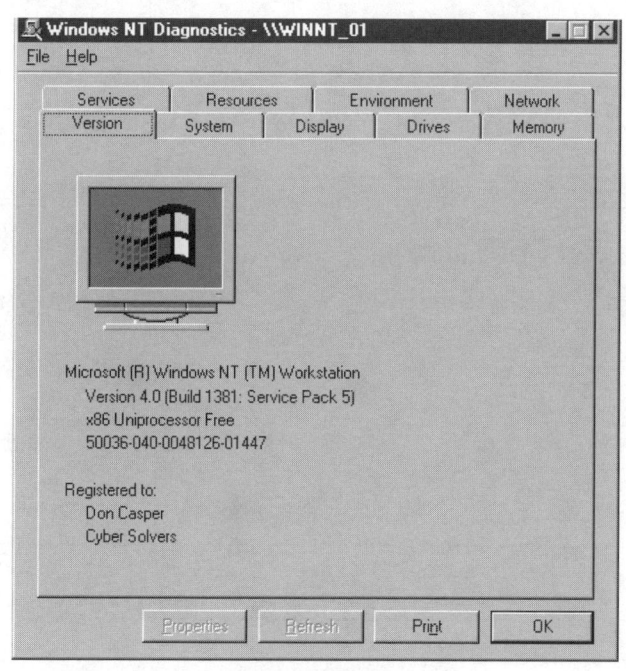

Figure 3.6.1

2. In the **Windows NT Diagnostics** utility you can view system information about resources, drives, memory, network, services, and other system settings. Explore the available system information tabs, and answer the following questions:

72 System Configuration

☐ What are the resolution settings for your video adapter?

_____

_____

☐ What I/O address range is assigned to your video adapter?

_____

☐ How many CD-ROM drives are listed as installed on your computer, and what drive letters are assigned to them?

_____

_____

☐ What is the state of the spooler service on your computer?

_____

☐ What is the value of the processor_identifier system variable?

_____

☐ What is the **BIOS DATE** for your system BIOS?

_____

3. Close the Windows NT Diagnostic utility and return to Windows NT Workstation.

End of Exercise

✓ Instructor Check _____

Student Notes

_____

_____

_____

_____

Student Notes

74 System Configuration

Lab 3.7 Managing Devices in Windows NT Workstation

Introduction

In this lab you will use the built-in utilities in Windows NT Workstation to manage devices.

Maps to the following CompTIA A+ Objectives

A+ Core Hardware Service Technician Objectives
- Objectives 1.3 and 1.7

A+ Operating System Technologies Objectives
- Objective 3.2

Required Materials
- Workstation with Windows NT Workstation installed and configured

Lab Procedure

1. From the **Start Menu** choose **Settings**, then select **Control Panel**. The Windows NT Control Panel utility will open. (Figure 3.7.1)

Figure 3.7.1

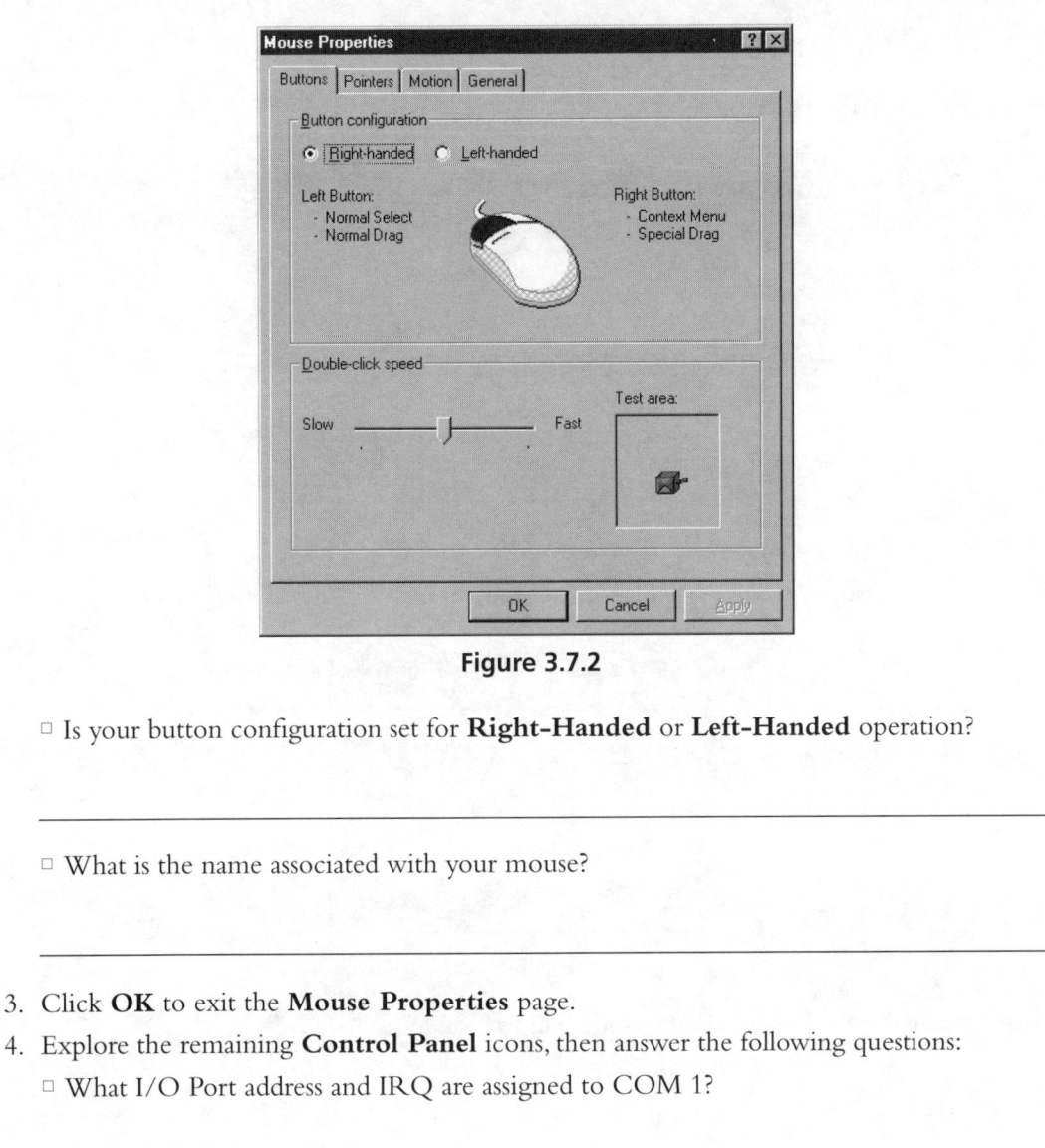

Lab 3.7 Managing Devices in Windows NT Workstation 75

2. Double-click the mouse icon. The **Mouse Properties** page will be displayed. (Figure 3.7.2)

Figure 3.7.2

- Is your button configuration set for **Right-Handed** or **Left-Handed** operation?

___

- What is the name associated with your mouse?

___

3. Click **OK** to exit the **Mouse Properties** page.
4. Explore the remaining **Control Panel** icons, then answer the following questions:
   - What I/O Port address and IRQ are assigned to COM 1?

___

___

- Can you change the I/O address and IRQ assignments for COM 1?

___

- What tape devices are installed on your system?

___

___

76 System Configuration

☐ What is the device status of your network adapter?

___

5. Double-click the **Devices** icon. Choose the floppy device, then select startup. (Figure 3.7.3)

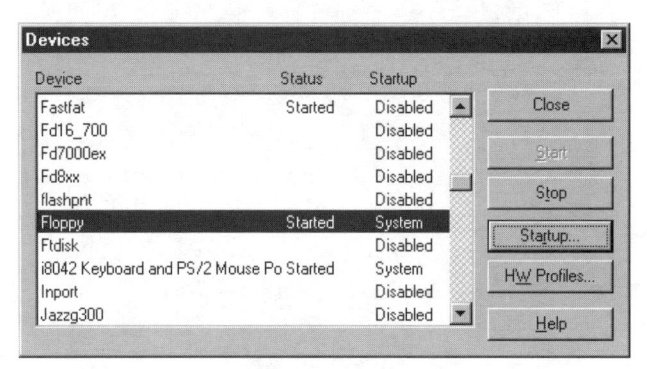

Figure 3.7.3

6. From the startup type window, select **Disabled**, then click **OK**. (Figure 3.7.4)

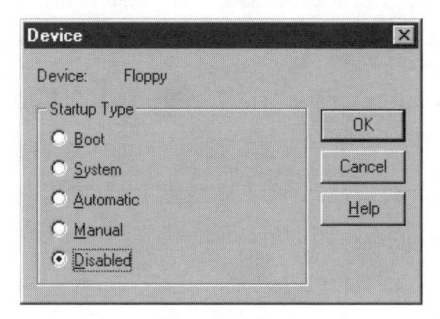

Figure 3.7.4

☐ What will be the effect of this configuration change?

___
___
___
___
___

7. Change the **Floppy device Startup Type** back to **Automatic**, close the **Control Panel** utility, and return to Windows NT Workstation.

End of Exercise

✓ Instructor Check _____

Student Notes

Lab 3.8 Viewing System Information in Windows 2000 Professional

Introduction

In this lab you will use the System Information utility in Windows 2000 to view system information.

Maps to the following CompTIA A+ Objectives

A+ Core Hardware Service Technician Objectives
- Objective 1.3

A+ Operating System Technologies Objectives
- Objective 1.1

Required Materials
- Workstation with Windows 2000 Professional installed and configured

Lab Procedure

1. From the **Start Menu**, choose **Programs**, **Accessories**, **System Tools**, and then select **System Information**. (Figure 3.8.1)

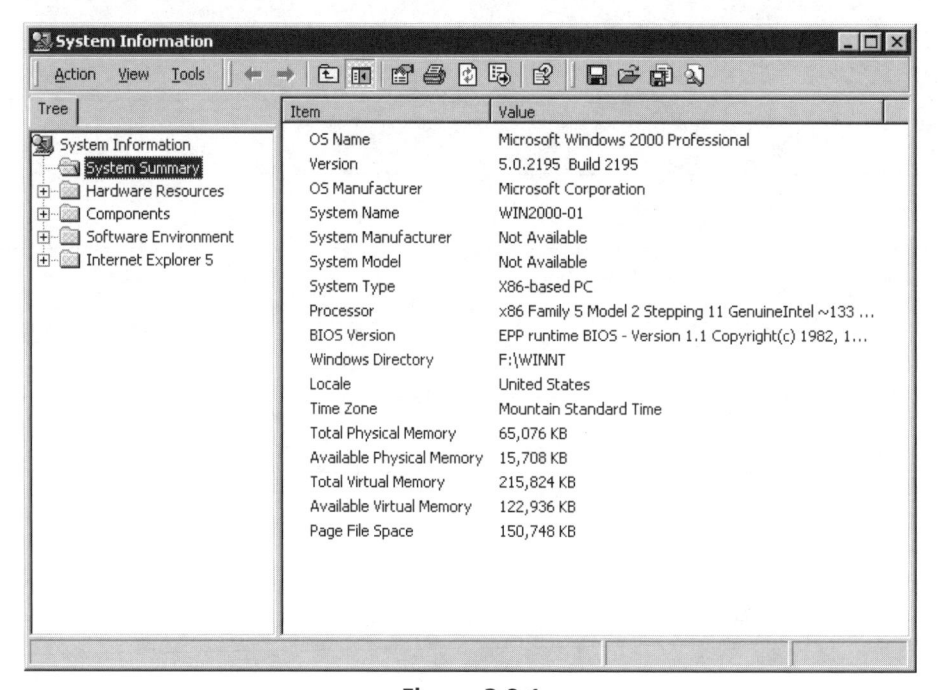

Figure 3.8.1

Lab 3.8 Viewing System Information in Windows 2000 Professional 79

2. In the system information utility window, double-click the hardware resources category. (Figure 3.8.2)

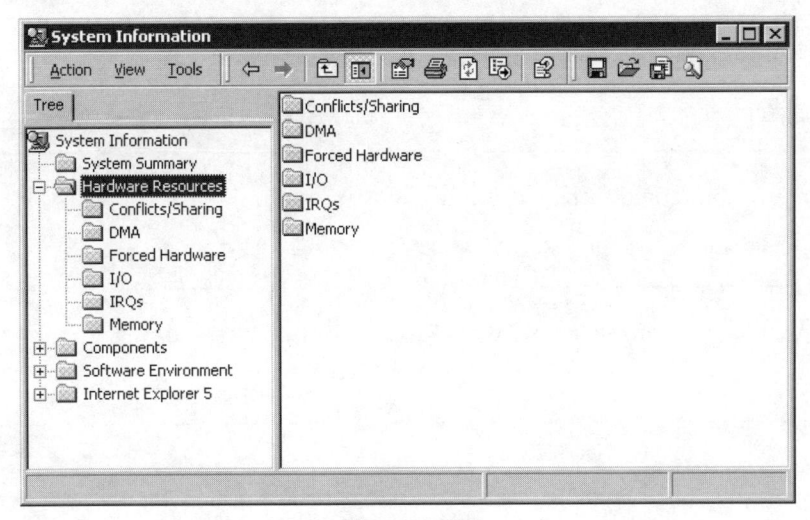

Figure 3.8.2

☐ What categories of system information are available under Hardware Resources?

_____

_____

_____

_____

_____

☐ Which Hardware Resources category will show manually configured hardware?

_____

_____

3. Explore the remaining system information options within the system information utility, and then answer the following questions:
   ☐ Which I/O address ranges are being used by your graphics adapter?

_____

_____

80 System Configuration

☐ What is the current baud-rate setting for your COM Port 1?

_____

☐ What is the PnP Device ID of your installed keyboard?

_____

☐ How many configured storage drives are on your system?

_____

☐ Which memory address ranges are assigned to your graphics adapter?

_____

_____

4. Close the System Information utility and return to Windows 2000 Professional.

End of Exercise

✓ Instructor Check _____

Student Notes

_____

_____

_____

_____

_____

_____

_____

_____

Lab 3.9 Using Windows 2000 Professional Device Manager

Introduction
In this lab you will use the Windows 2000 Professional Device Manager utility to manage devices.

Maps to the following CompTIA A+ Objectives

A+ Core Hardware Service Technician Objectives
- Objectives 1.3 and 1.7

A+ Operating System Technologies Objectives
- Objective 3.2

Required Materials
- Workstation with Windows 2000 Professional installed and configured

Lab Procedure
1. Right-click **My Computer** and select **Properties**. The system properties screen will open.
2. Choose the hardware tab and then select **Device Manager**. The Device Manager utility will open.
3. Expand the **Mice and Other Pointing Devices** category. Right-click the installed mouse device and select **Properties**. The properties for the mouse will be displayed. (Figure 3.9.1)

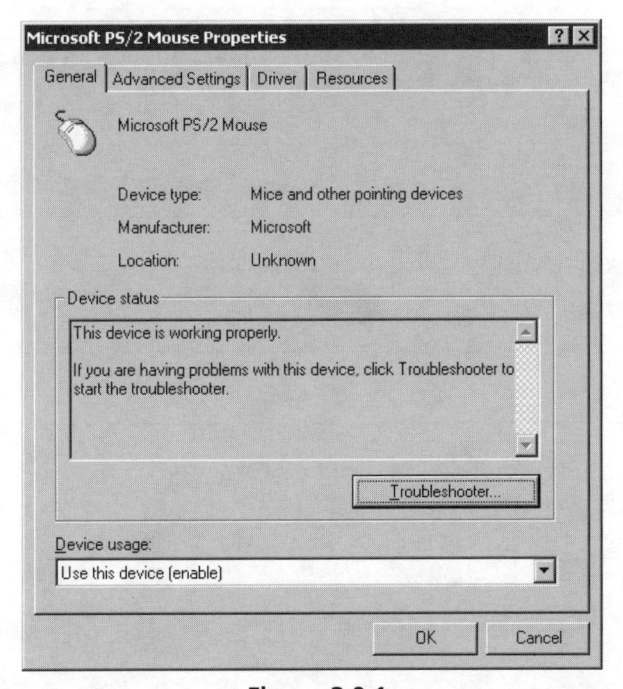

Figure 3.9.1

82 System Configuration

- What type of mouse is installed on your system?

_____

_____

- What version of device driver is installed?

_____

_____

- What resources are being used by your mouse?

_____

_____

4. Select cancel to return to the device manager window.
5. Explore the remaining **Device Manager** categories and then answer the following questions:
    - What type of display adapter is installed in your system?

    _____

    _____

    - What system resources are assigned to your standard floppy disk controller?

    _____

    _____

    - What type of LPT Port is installed in your system?

    _____

    _____

    - What is the Driver Date of the installed keyboard driver?

    _____

    _____

Lab 3.9 Using Windows 2000 Professional Device Manager 83

6. Expand the Network Adapter category, right-click your installed network adapter, then select properties. (Figure 3.9.2)

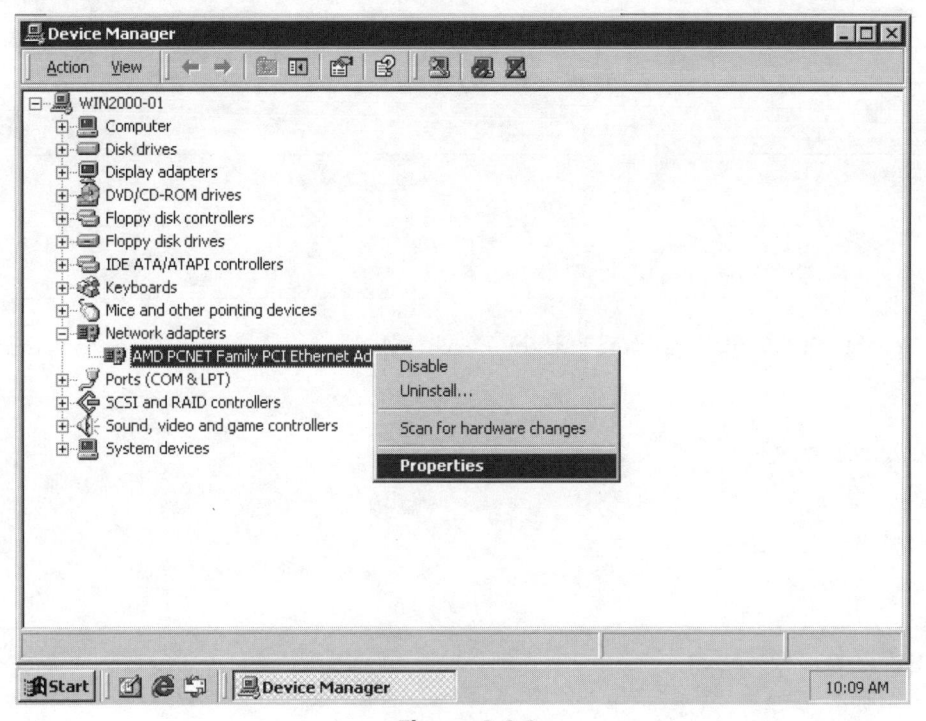

Figure 3.9.2

7. In the Device Usage drop-down menu, choose **Do not use this Device (Disable)**. Then click **OK**.
8. The network adapter should now appear as disabled in Device Manager window. (Figure 3.9.3)

Figure 3.9.3

84 System Configuration

☐ What will be the result of this configuration setting?

_____

_____

_____

_____

_____

9. Re-enable the network adapter, exit the Device Manager utility, and return to Windows 2000 Professional.

End of Exercise

✓ Instructor Check _____

Student Notes

CHAPTER 4
Disassembly and Assembly

4.1 Computer Disassembly and Assembly 86
4.2 System Module Identification 90

86 Disassembly and Assembly

Lab 4.1 Computer Disassembly and Assembly

Introduction

In this lab you will disassemble and reassemble your lab workstation.

Maps to the following CompTIA A+ Objectives

A+ Core Hardware Service Technician Objectives

- Objectives 1.2, 1.5, and 1.6

Required Materials

- Lab workstation

Part One: Computer Disassembly

1. Using proper "**ESD**" precautions, remove the workstation cover. (Figure 4.1.1)

Figure 4.1.1

2. Remove all ribbon cables, power connectors, switch leads, and LED leads.

> **Note:** Labeling all connectors before removal will help ensure proper reassembly.

3. Remove the hard drive, CD-ROM drive, and the floppy drive from the system. (Figure 4.1.2)

Figure 4.1.2

4. Remove all expansion cards from expansion slots by first removing the retaining screws, then applying even upward pressure to the cards.
5. Remove the system memory modules (RAM) from the system board.

> **Note:** Refer to lab 7.2 for specific RAM removal instructions.

6. Remove the Multiprocessor (CPU) from the system board.

> **Note:** Refer to lab 2.3 for specific CPU removal instructions.

88 Disassembly and Assembly

7. Remove the system board from the case. Your workstation is now disassembled. (Figure 4.1.3)

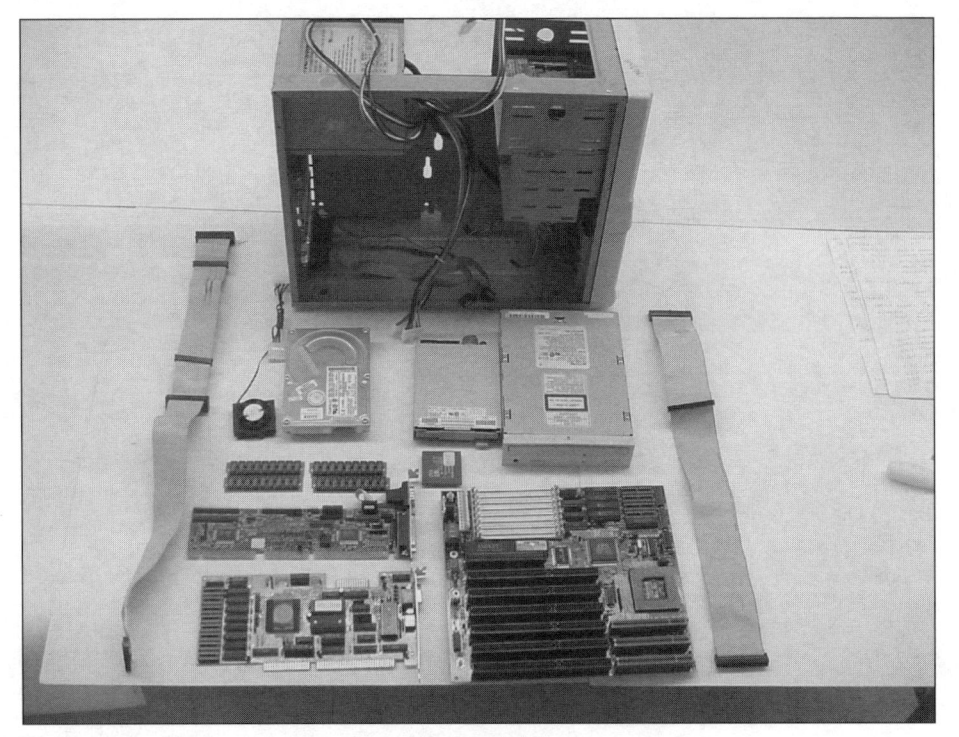

Figure 4.1.3

Part Two: Computer Reassembly

> **Note:** The reassembly procedure is basically a reversal of the disassembly procedure.

1. Install the system board into the case.
2. Install the CPU and RAM onto the system board.
3. Install the expansion cards into the expansion slots, and secure them with the retaining screws.
4. Install the hard drive, CD-ROM drive, and the floppy drive into the case.
5. Install all ribbon cables, power connectors, switch leads, and LED leads.

> **Note:** Pay close attention to the pin-one orientation on the ribbon cables.

6. Before installing the cover, start the workstation and ensure that it boots properly.
7. After verifying that the workstation boots properly, and that all components are working, replace the cover.

End of Exercise

✓ Instructor Check _____

Student Notes

Lab 4.2 System Module Identification

Introduction

In this lab you will identify the basic system modules in a workstation.

Maps to the following CompTIA A+ Objectives

A+ Core Hardware Service Technician Objectives
- Objective 1.1

Required Materials
- Lab manual

Lab Procedure

Study the following graphic and then match the letters with the system module description.

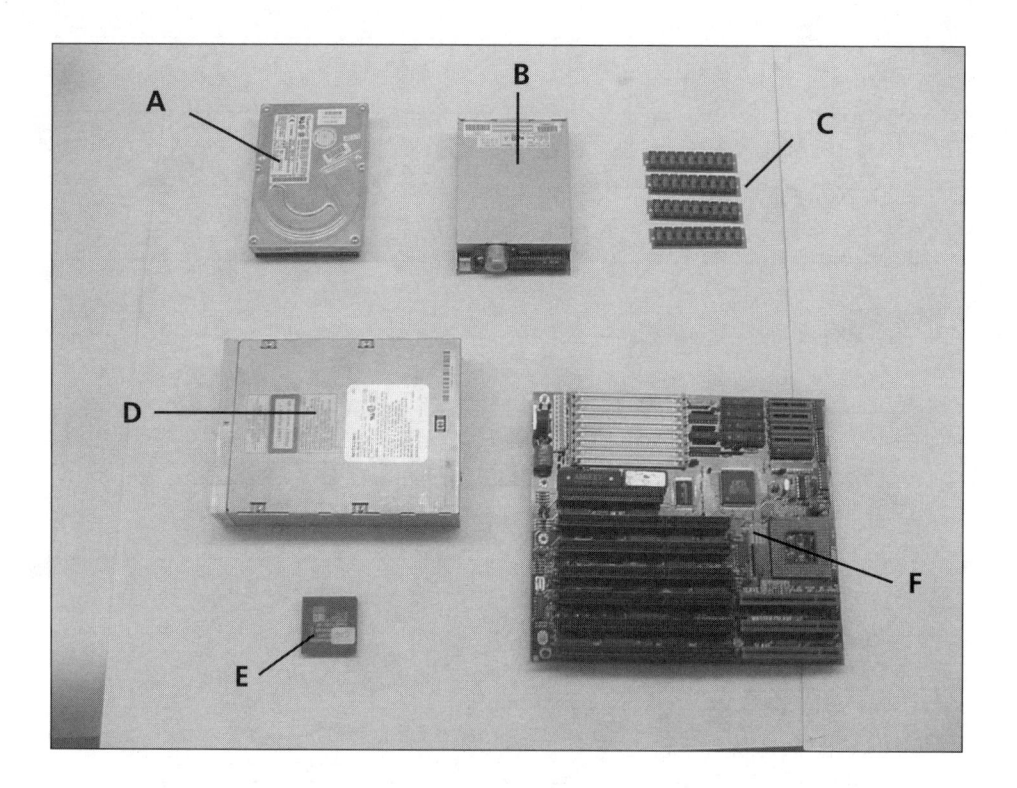

___ CD-ROM: (Compact Disk Read Only Memory)
___ CPU: (Central Processing Unit)
___ HDD: (Hard Disk Drive)
___ RAM: (Random Access Memory)
___ FDD: (Floppy Disk Drive)
___ System Board

End of Exercise

✓ Instructor Check _____

Student Notes

CHAPTER 5

Basic Electronics and Power

5.1 Volts, Amps, Ohms, and Watts   94

5.2 Power Supply Identification   95

5.3 Power Supply Removal and Installation   97

5.4 Calculating Power Supply Requirements for Your Workstation   100

5.5 Measuring Input Line Voltages   102

5.6 Measuring/Troubleshooting Internal System Voltages   108

5.7 Installing a Surge Suppressor   114

5.8 Installing a UPS   116

5.9 PC Shock Hazards   120

Lab 5.1 Volts, Amps, Ohms, and Watts

Introduction

In this lab you will review the terms electrical terminology and meanings.

Maps to the following CompTIA A+ Objectives

A+ Core Hardware Service Technician Objectives
- Objective 1.1

Required Materials
- Lab Textbook
- Lab Manual

Lab Procedure

1. Study the following electrical terms and match them with their corresponding definition:

VOLTS	A measure of the difference of potential between two points, also known as electrical pressure
AMPS	A unit of measurement for electrical current
OHMS	A unit of measurement for electrical resistance
WATTS	A unit measures power

End of Exercise

✓ Instructor Check _____

Student Notes

Lab 5.2 Power Supply Identification

Introduction

In this lab you will identify your lab workstation's power supply as to type and capacity.

Maps to the following CompTIA A+ Objectives

A+ Core Hardware Service Technician Objectives
- Objective 1.1

Required Materials
- Lab workstation

Lab Procedure

1. Using proper ESD precautions, remove your workstation's cover.
2. Study the following graphics and descriptions. (Figures 5.2.1 and 5.2.2)

AT-style power connectors
Figure 5.2.1

ATX-style power connetor
Figure 5.2.2

- **AT-style Power Supplies** use dual 6-pin connectors that connect side by side. They are usually labeled P8 and P9. When installing these connectors, it is important to remember the rule "Black-to-Black," i.e., the black wires on each connector should be adjacent to each other. (Figure 5.2.1)
- **ATX-Style Power Supplies** use a single 20-pin connector. This connector is "keyed" to prevent insertion in the wrong direction. (Figure 5.2.2)

3. Answer the following questions.
   - Which type of power supply is installed on your workstation?

   _____

   - What is the power rating (in watts) of your power supply?

   _____

Basic Electronics and Power

End of Exercise

✓ Instructor Check _____

Student Notes

Lab 5.3 Power Supply Removal and Installation

Introduction

In this lab you will remove and reinstall the power supply in your lab workstation.

Maps to the following CompTIA A+ Objectives

A+ Core Hardware Service Technician Objectives
- Objectives 1.2 and 1.8

Required Materials
- Lab workstation

Part One: Removing the Power Supply

1. Disconnect the power cable from your workstation.
2. Using proper ESD precautions, remove your workstation's cover.
3. Disconnect the power supply system board connectors, and disconnect all peripheral device power connectors. (Figure 5.3.1)

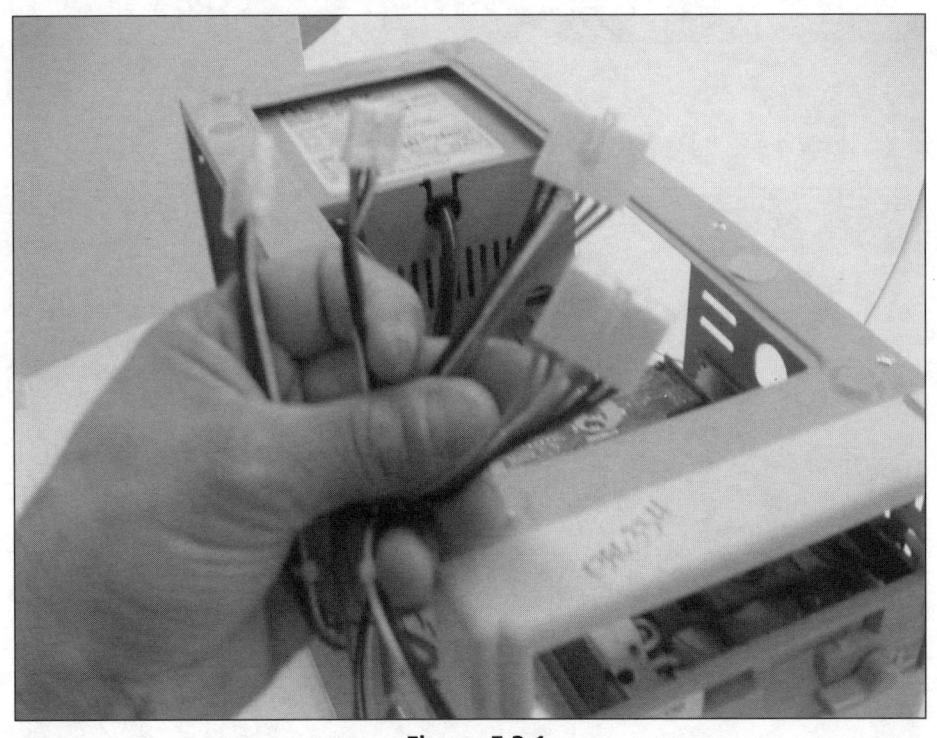

Figure 5.3.1

98 Basic Electronics and Power

4. Remove the power supply switch connector. (AT Power Supplies Only)
5. Locate and remove the power supply mounting screws. (Figure 5.3.2)

Figure 5.3.2

6. Remove the power supply from the case. (Figure 5.3.3)

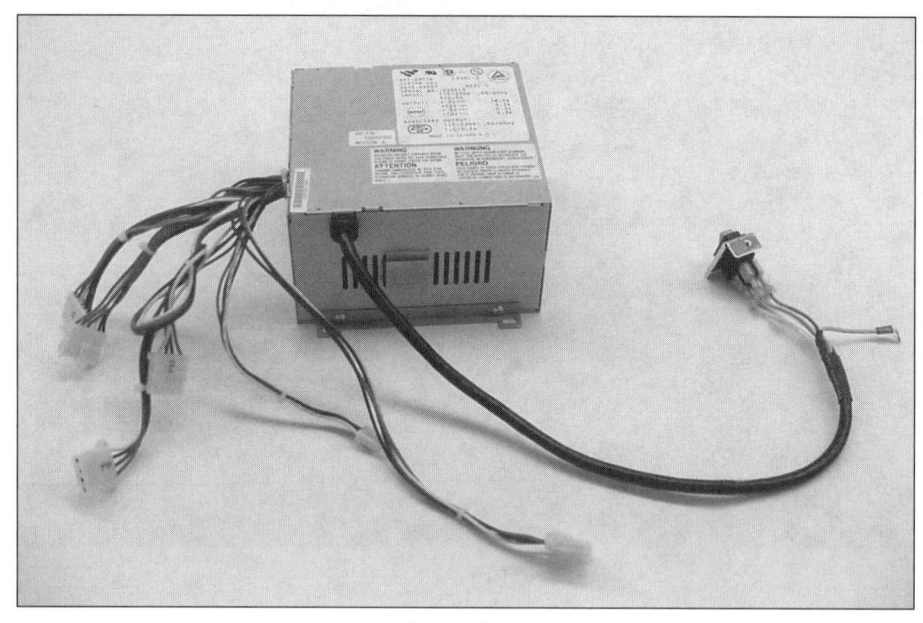

Figure 5.3.3

Part Two: Installing a Power Supply

1. Install the new power supply into the case, and secure it with the mounting screws.

   > **Note:** If you are replacing the power supply with a new one, ensure that the new power supply has a high enough wattage specification for your workstation.

2. Install the power supply switch connector, the peripheral device power connectors, and the system board power connector(s).
3. Replace the workstation cover, and start the workstation. Verify that the workstation boots properly, and that all peripherals are working properly.

End of Exercise

✓ Instructor Check _____

Student Notes

___
___
___
___
___
___
___
___
___
___
___
___

Lab 5.4 Calculating Power Supply Requirements for Your Workstation

Introduction

It is important that your power supply has a high enough wattage rating to meet the power requirements of your workstation. Also, if you add additional components, you will need to ensure that your power supply can accommodate the added load. In this exercise you will calculate the minimum power supply specification necessary for your workstation.

Maps to the following CompTIA A+ Objectives

A+ Core Hardware Service Technician Objectives
- Objectives 1.2, 1.7, and 1.8

Required Materials
- Lab workstation

Lab Procedure

1. Using proper ESD precautions, remove your workstation's cover.
2. In the following table, identify the components that are installed on your workstation. In the case of multiple PCI, ISA, etc., enter the number of devices installed. Multiply the number of each device by the maximum amp rating for that device and enter the total for both 5-volt and 12-volt usage.

   > **Note:** These amp ratings are considered MAXIMUM ratings. Your device may use less than the listed rating. If your device is not listed, refer to the manufacturer's documentation for power usage ratings.

#	DEVICE	+5 volt	+12 volt	+ 3.3 volt	Tot 5V	Tot12V	Tot 3.3V
	System Board	5.0 amps					
	Hard Disk Drive	0.5 amps					
	CD-ROM Drive	1.0 amp	1.0 amp				
	Floppy Disk	1.5 amps	1.0 amp				
	Cooling Fan	0.1 amp					
	PCI Slot Device	5.0 amps	0.5 amp	7.6 amps			
	ISA Slot Device	2.0 amps	0.2 amp				
	OTHER						
			TOTAL AMPS				

3. To calculate the maximum wattage usage for your workstation, multiply the total amps by volts. (e.g., 25 amps × 5 volts = 125 watts, etc.)

Lab 5.4 Calculating Power Supply Requirements for Your Workstation

- What is the maximum total wattage usage for your workstation?

  _____

- What is the maximum wattage rating for your power supply?

  _____

- Does the maximum wattage rating for your power supply exceed the maximum total usage for your workstation?

  _____

End of Exercise

✓ Instructor Check _____

Lab Notes

As a safety precaution, the maximum wattage rating for your power supply should exceed the maximum wattage usage by 20%. This gives a good buffer, and ensures that you will never exceed the maximum wattage rating for your power supply.

Student Notes

_____

_____

_____

_____

_____

_____

_____

Lab 5.5 Measuring Input Line Voltages

Introduction

In order to properly troubleshoot computer power problems, you need to be able to measure the input line voltage and verify that it is adequate for proper operation of the computer. In this lab you will follow the logical steps for measuring and troubleshooting input line voltages.

Maps to the following CompTIA A+ Objectives

A+ Core Hardware Service Technician Objectives
- Objectives 2.1 and 2.2

Required Materials
- Lab workstation
- Functional voltmeter or multitester

Lab Procedure

1. To begin the input voltage troubleshooting process, you must first check the voltage at the wall outlet. (Figure 5.5.1)

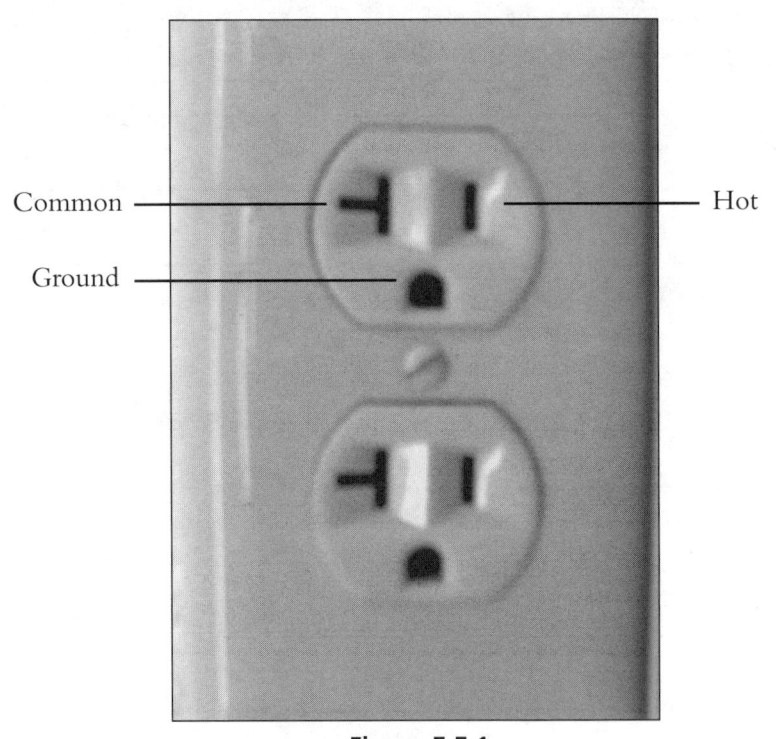

Figure 5.5.1

Lab 5.5   Measuring Input Line Voltages   103

2. Adjust your voltmeter to test AC voltage. Be sure to use a setting high enough to measure your voltage. (Figure 5.5.2)

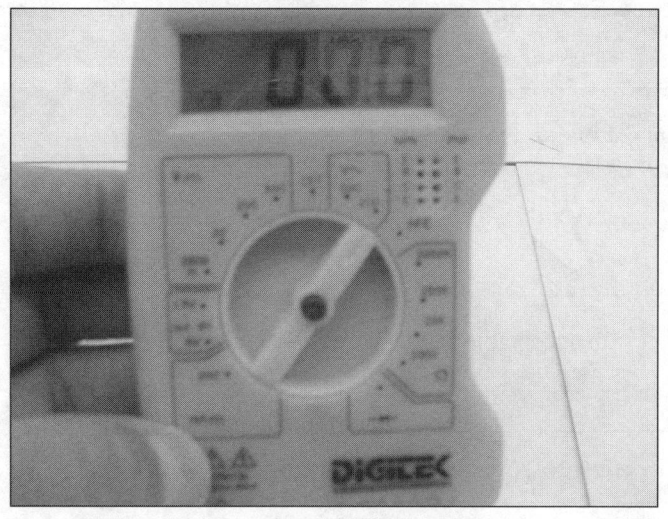

Figure 5.5.2

☐ What symbol is displayed on your voltmeter to indicate AC voltage?

_____

☐ What voltage should be present at the wall outlet?

_____

3. Insert the positive (usually red) lead into the HOT receptacle, and the negative (usually black) lead in the COMMON receptacle. (Figure 5.5.3)

Figure 5.5.3

104   Basic Electronics and Power

- Did you receive a voltage reading?

_____
_____

- What voltage reading did you receive?

_____
_____

- What would be an acceptable range for this voltage reading?

_____
_____

4. Insert the positive lead into the HOT receptacle, and the negative lead in the GROUND receptacle.
   - Did you receive a voltage reading?

_____
_____

5. Insert the positive lead into the COMMON receptacle, and the negative lead in the GROUND receptacle.
   - Did you receive a voltage reading?

_____

   - Why or Why Not?

_____
_____
_____
_____

Lab 5.5   Measuring Input Line Voltages   105

6. If the voltage at the wall outlet is acceptable, the next step is to check the power cord. Insert the power cord into the wall outlet and then check the voltage. (Figure 5.5.4)

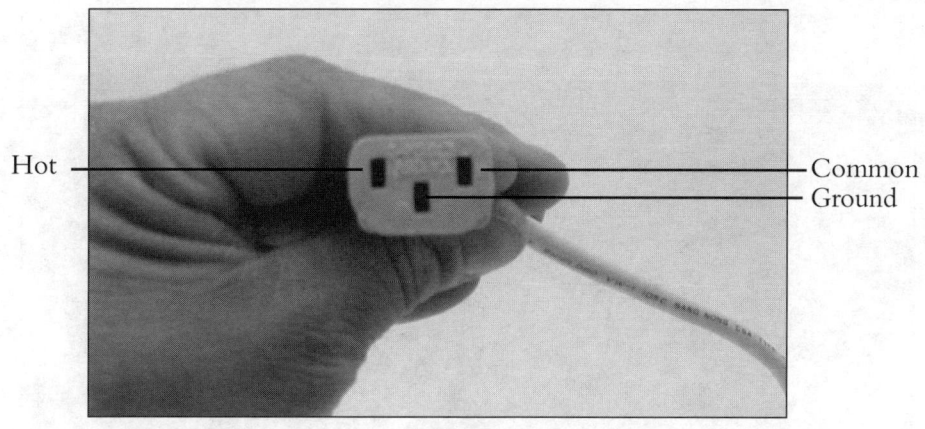

Figure 5.5.4

7. Insert the positive lead into the HOT receptacle, and the negative lead in the COMMON receptacle.
   - Did you receive a voltage reading?

   _____

   _____

   - What voltage reading did you receive?

   _____

   _____

8. Insert the positive lead into the HOT receptacle, and the negative lead in the GROUND receptacle.
   - Did you receive a voltage reading?

   _____

   _____

9. Insert the positive lead into the COMMON receptacle, and the negative lead in the GROUND receptacle.
   - Did you receive a voltage reading?

   _____

   _____

106 Basic Electronics and Power

10. If the voltage at the cable is acceptable, check the voltage setting on the power supply. (Figure 5.5.5)

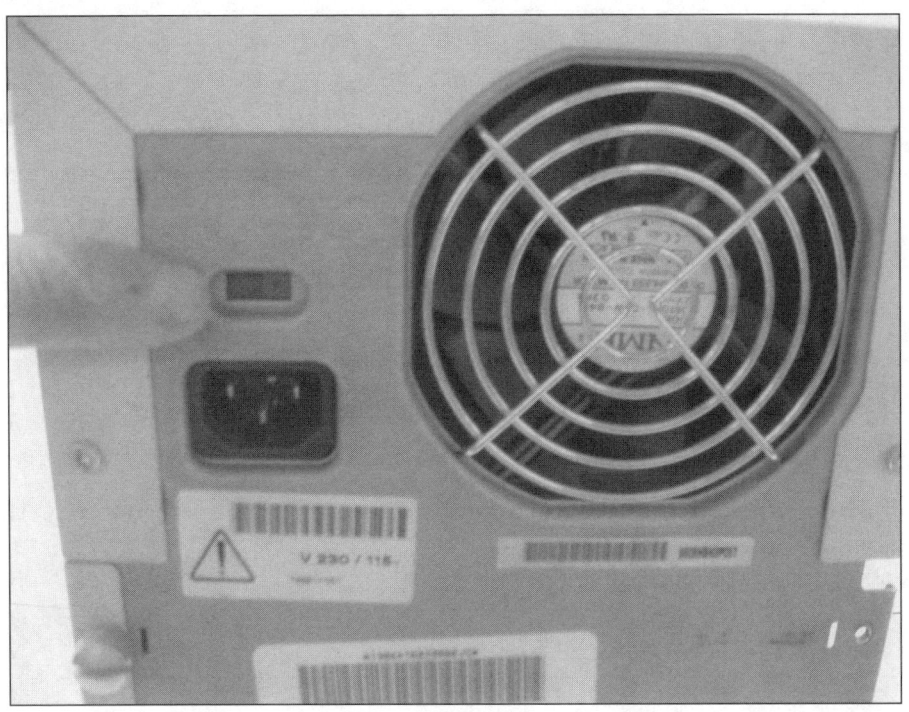

Figure 5.5.5

- What is the voltage setting on your power supply?

___

- Does this setting match your lab's electrical voltage?

___

- What would be the result if the power supply voltage setting DID NOT match your lab's electrical voltage?

___
___
___
___
___

End of Exercise

✓ Instructor Check _____

Student Notes

Lab 5.6 Measuring/Troubleshooting Internal System Voltages

Introduction

In order for your workstation to operate properly, it must have the proper combination of voltages available at the system board, and all internal components. In this exercise you will follow the logical steps for measuring and troubleshooting internal system voltages.

Maps to the following CompTIA A+ Objectives

A+ Core Hardware Service Technician Objectives
- Objectives 2.1 and 2.2

Required Materials
- Lab workstation
- Functional voltmeter or multitester

Lab Procedure

1. Using proper ESD precautions, remove your workstation's cover.
2. Adjust your voltmeter to test DC voltage. Be sure to use a setting high enough to measure your voltage. (Figure 5.6.1)

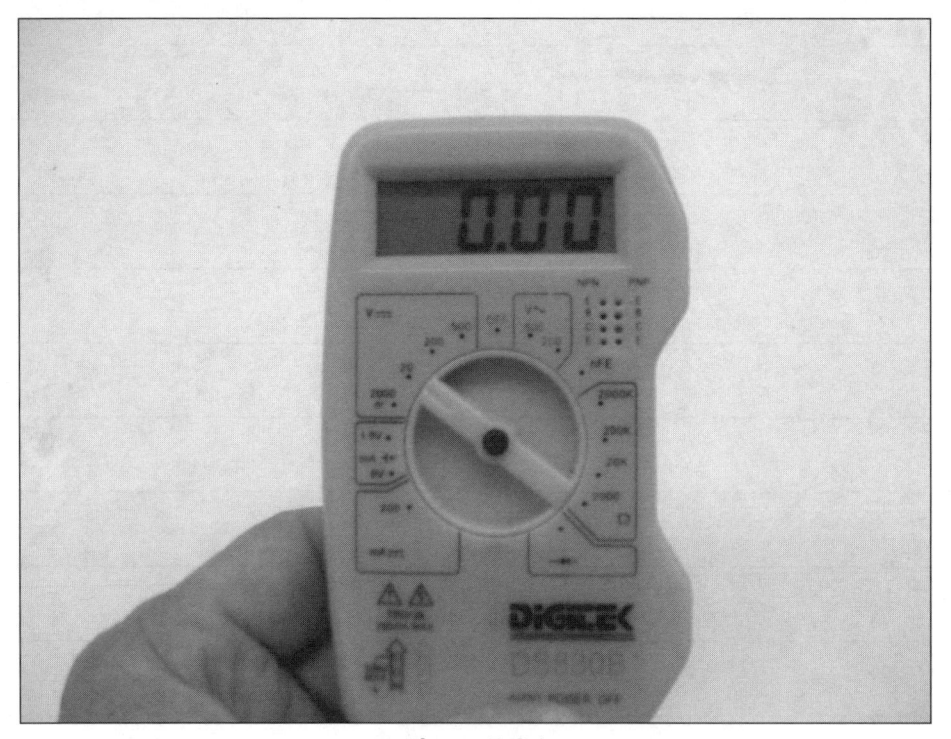

Figure 5.6.1

Lab 5.6 Measuring/Troubleshooting Internal System Voltages

❑ What symbol is displayed on your meter to indicate DC voltage?

3. Depending on which type of system board your workstation has (AT or ATX), refer to the following tables.

AT-Style

Pin	Wire Color	Standard Voltage	Your Voltage
P8-1	Orange	+5V	
P8-2	Red	+5V	
P8-3	Yellow	+12V	
P8-4	Blue	–12V	
P8-5	Black	Ground	
P8-6	Black	Ground	
P9-1	Black	Ground	
P9-2	Black	Ground	
P9-3	White	–5V	
P9-4	Red	+5V	
P9-5	Red	+5V	
P9-6	Red	+5V	

ATX-Style

Pin	Wire Color	Standard Voltage	Your Voltage
1	Orange	+3.3V	
2	Orange	+3.3V	
3	Black	Ground	
4	Red	+5V	
5	Black	Ground	
6	Red	+5V	
7	Black	Ground	
8	Gray	+5V	

ATX-Style (continued)

9	Purple	+5V	
10	Yellow	+12V	
11	Orange	+3.3V	
12	Blue	−12V	
13	Black	Ground	
14	Green	Power Signal	
15	Black	Ground	
16	Black	Ground	
17	Black	Ground	
18	White	-5V	
19	Red	+5V	
20	Red	+5V	

Note: These are standard color codings. Some power supply manufacturers may change the wire colors. If this is the case with your workstation, refer to the pin numbers for the voltage assignments.

4. Start your workstation, and ensure that it boots properly.
5. Locate the system board power connector.

Lab 5.6 Measuring/Troubleshooting Internal System Voltages 111

6. With the negative (black) lead on your voltmeter grounded, touch each power connector pin with the Red lead, and enter the voltage readings in the tables above under **Your Voltage**. (Figure 5.6.2)

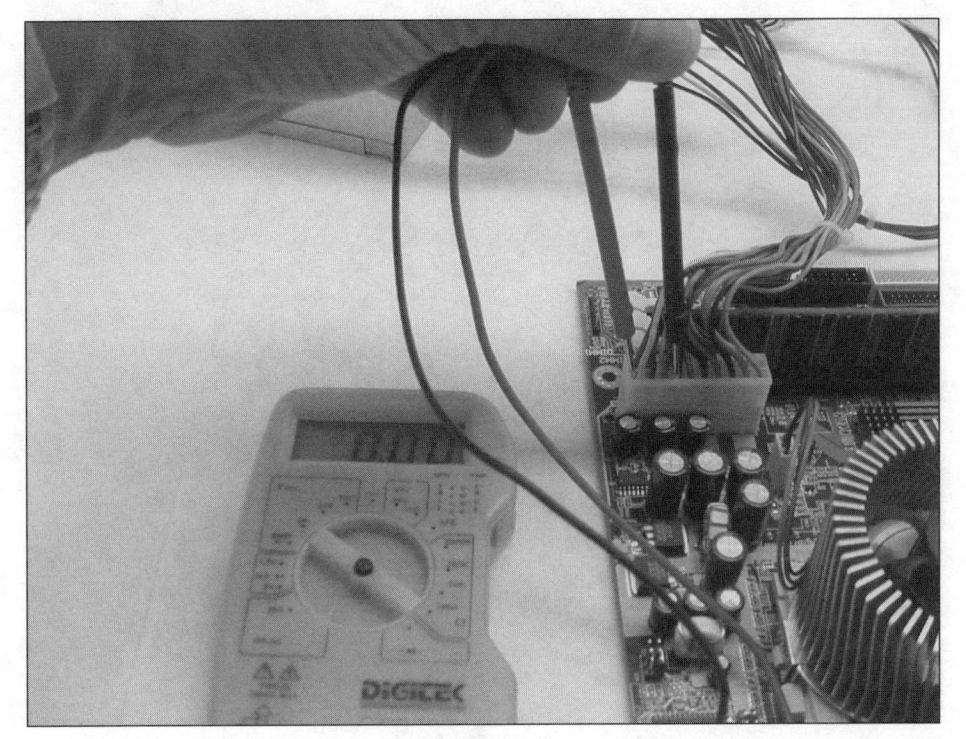

Figure 5.6.2

☐ Are any of the voltage readings more than three volts different than the standard voltage?

_____

7. Refer to the table below.

MOLEX Power Connectors

Pin	Wire Color	Standard Voltage	Your Voltage
1	Yellow	+12V	
2	Black	Ground	
3	Black	Ground	
4	Red	+5V	

112 Basic Electronics and Power

8. With the negative (black) lead on your voltmeter grounded, touch each MOLEX power connector pin with the Red lead, and enter the voltage readings in the tables above under **Your Voltage**. (Figure 5.6.3)

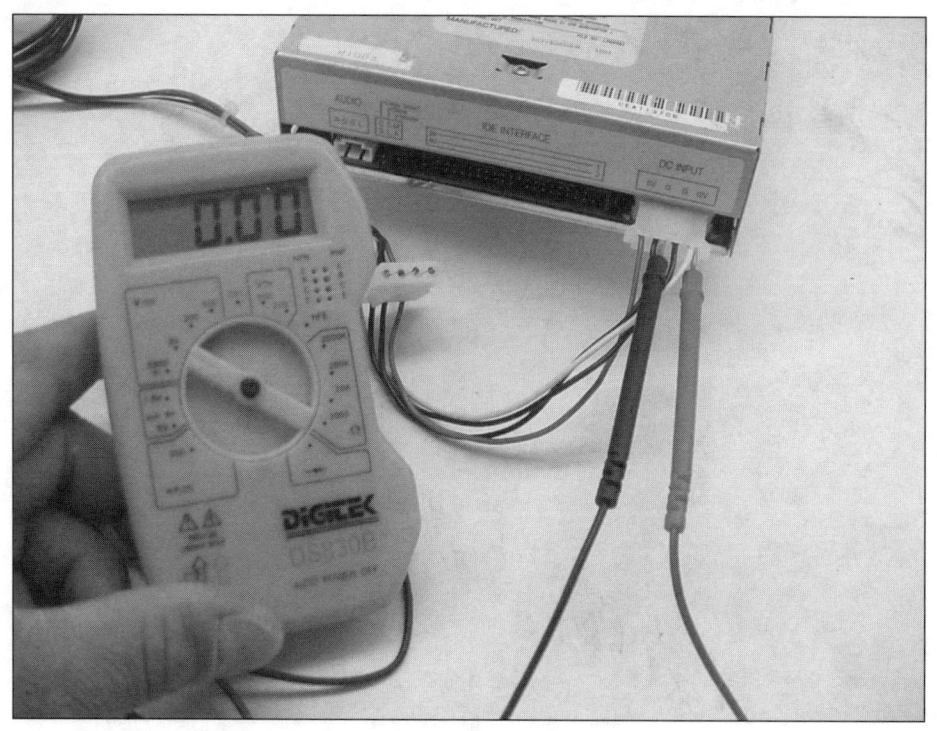

Figure 5.6.3

☐ Are any of the voltage readings more than three volts different than the standard voltage?

_____

☐ Based on your readings, do you think your system's power supply is working adequately?

_____

_____

9. Shut down your workstation, replace the cover, and ensure that the workstation boots properly.

End of Exercise

✓ Instructor Check _____

Lab 5.6 Measuring/Troubleshooting Internal System Voltages

Student Notes

Lab 5.7 Installing a Surge Suppressor

Introduction

Voltage problems such as blackouts, brownouts, sags, and spikes can damage the internal circuitry in your workstation. In this lab you will install a surge suppressor on your workstation.

Maps to the following CompTIA A+ Objectives

A+ Core Hardware Service Technician Objectives
- Objectives 3.1 and 3.2

Required Materials
- Lab workstation
- Surge suppressor

Lab Procedure

1. With the workstation turned off, remove the power cables from the wall outlet.
2. Plug the surge suppressor into the wall outlet, and plug the workstation power cables into the surge suppressor. (Figure 5.7.1)

Figure 5.7.1

3. Ensure that the surge suppressor is turned on, and start the workstation.
    - Three common voltage problems are brownouts, sags, and spikes. Against which of these does a surge suppressor protect?

☐ Should surge suppressors be replaced, or will they continue to offer protection indefinitely?

_____
_____
_____
_____
_____

End of Exercise

✓ Instructor Check _____

Lab Notes

Key Terms

Brownout: A condition where the overall voltage on a circuit drops for an extended time

Sag: A condition where the voltage on a circuit drops briefly, then recovers

Spike: A condition where the voltage on a circuit rises sharply, then drops back to normal levels

Blackout: A condition of complete input power failure

Student Notes

_____
_____
_____
_____
_____
_____
_____

Lab 5.8 Installing a UPS

Introduction

Voltage problems such as blackouts, brownouts, sags, and spikes can damage the internal circuitry in your workstation. In this lab you will install and configure a UPS (Uninterruptible Power Supply) in Windows 2000 Pro.

Maps to the following CompTIA A+ Objectives

A+ Core Hardware Service Technician Objectives
- Objectives 3.1 and 3.2

Required Materials
- Lab workstation with Windows 2000 Pro installed and configured
- UPS with workstation/server shutdown capability

Lab Procedure

1. With the workstation turned off, remove the power cables from the wall outlet.
2. Plug the UPS into the wall outlet. Plug the workstation power cables into the UPS. Connect the UPS control cable to a serial port on your workstation. Start the workstation and ensure that Windows 2000 loads properly.
3. From the **Start Menu** choose **Settings**, **Control Panel**, and then double-click **Power Options**. (Figure 5.8.1)

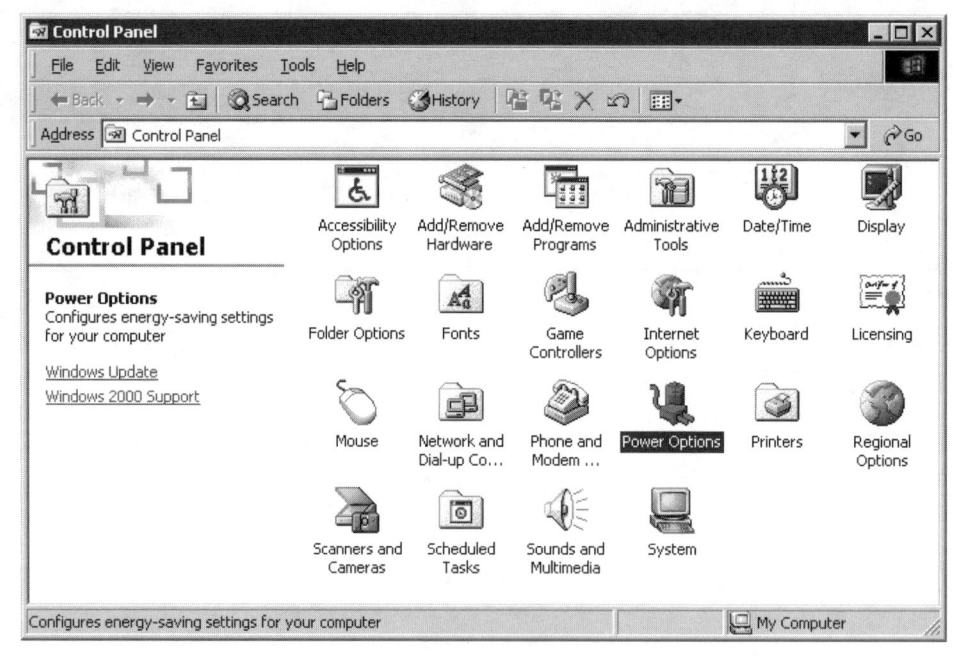

Figure 5.8.1

Lab 5.8 Installing a UPS 117

4. Select the **UPS** tab. From the **Details** pane, click the **Select** button.
5. Choose the manufacturer and model of your UPS, select the COM port your UPS is connected to, then click **Finish**. (Figure 5.8.2)

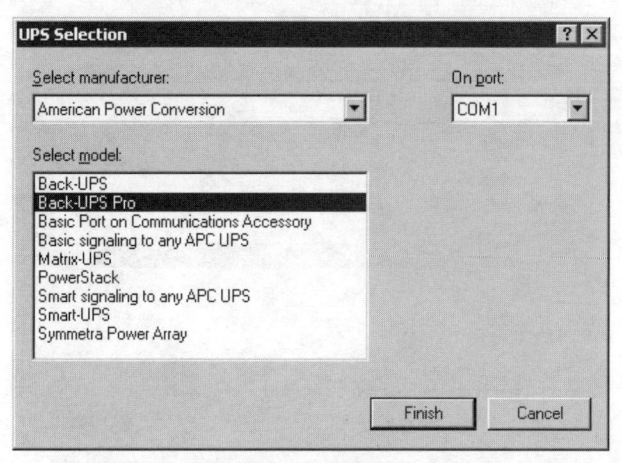

Figure 5.8.2

6. To configure the workstation shutdown parameters for your UPS, from the **Details** pane, click **Configure**. (Figure 5.8.3)

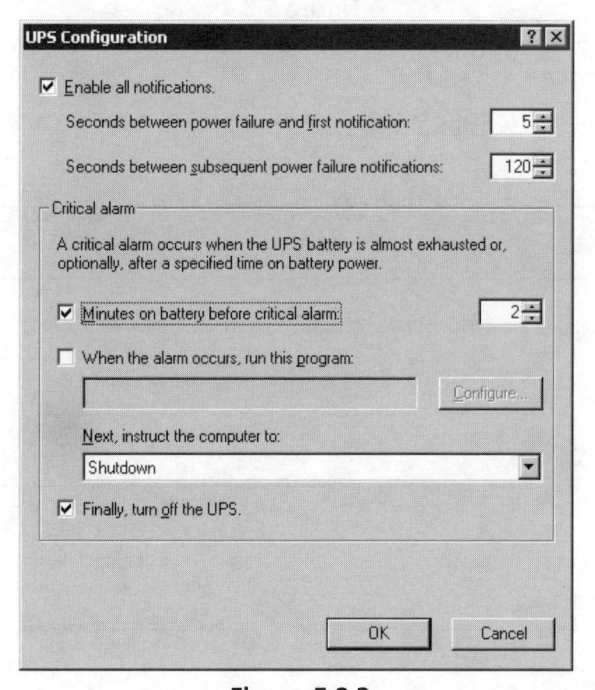

Figure 5.8.3

7. To start the UPS service, from the **Start Menu**, choose **Programs**, **Administrative Tools**, and then select **Services**.
8. Scroll to and double-click **Uninterruptible Power Supply**.

Basic Electronics and Power

9. In the Startup Type field, select **Automatic**. To start the service, click **Start**. (Figure 5.8.4)

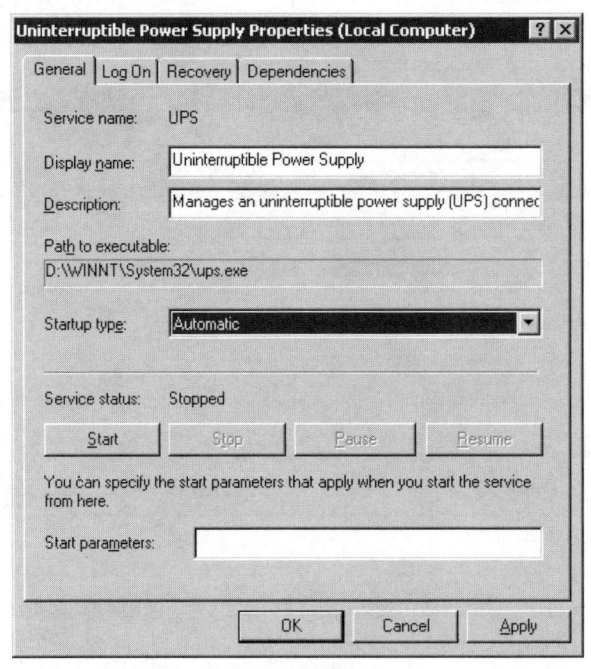

Figure 5.8.4

10. When the service starts, click **OK**.

    ☐ Of the four common voltage problems, which are corrected by using a UPS?

    _____
    _____

    ☐ What is the purpose of connecting the UPS control cable to your workstation's COM port?

    _____
    _____
    _____
    _____
    _____

End of Exercise

✓ Instructor Check _____

Student Notes

Lab 5.9 PC Shock Hazards

Introduction
In this lab you will review procedures to avoid PC shock hazards.

Maps to the following CompTIA A+ Objectives

A+ Core Hardware Service Technician Objectives
- Objective 3.2

Required Materials
- Lab textbook
- Lab manual

Lab Procedure

General Guidelines
- Before working inside a workstation's case, always unplug all input power cables.
- When working inside a workstation, work with only one hand if possible. This prevents your body from becoming a ground path for electrical discharge.

Power Supply
- When working inside a PC power supply, avoid touching exposed wires and connections. Capacitors inside the power supply remain energized even when the power is off, and can present a serious shock hazard.
- When working inside a power supply, avoid using a static grounding wrist strap. In case of a capacitor discharge, the wrist strap acts as a direct ground.

Display Monitor
- In most cases you will have no reason to open a monitor's case. Display monitors have capacitors that remain energized even when the power is off. They can deliver a charge of up to 30,000 volts.
- If it becomes necessary to work inside a monitor, avoid using a static grounding wrist strap. In case of a capacitor discharge, the wrist strap acts as a direct ground.

End of Exercise

✓ Instructor Check _____

Student Notes

CHAPTER 6

Logical Troubleshooting

6.1 Troubleshooting Fundamentals   124

6.2 Practical Troubleshooting   128

6.3 CMOS Beep Codes and Error Codes   129

6.4 Diagnostic Utilities   131

6.5 P.O.S.T. Cards (Power On Self-Test Cards)   134

6.6 Basic Maintenance Procedures   136

6.7 Creating a Preventive Maintenance Plan   139

6.8 Backing Up Data in Windows 98 and Windows 2000   141

6.9 Installing Virus Protection   146

6.10 Creating an ERD in Windows NT Workstation   149

6.11 Creating an ERD in Windows 2000 Professional   151

6.12 Using Regedit to Backup the Windows 98 Registry   153

6.13 Restoring Your Data from a Backup in Windows 98 and 2000 Pro   155

6.14 Using an ERD to Recover Windows NT Workstation   159

6.15 Using Recovery Console to Recover Windows 2000   161

6.16 Using an ERD to Recover Windows 2000 Pro   163

6.17 Using Regedit to Restore the Windows 98 Registry   165

124 Logical Troubleshooting

Lab 6.1 Troubleshooting Fundamentals

Introduction

In order to troubleshoot workstation problems efficiently, it is important to follow a logical step-by-step troubleshooting procedure. In this exercise you will review the recommended steps for practical troubleshooting.

Maps to the following CompTIA A+ Objectives

A+ Core Hardware Service Technician Objectives
- Objectives 2.1 and 2.2

Required Materials
- Lab textbook
- Lab manual

Lab Procedure

There are six steps in the logical troubleshooting procedure. Follow these six steps to complete this exercise:

1. Recreate the problem
2. Divide the problem into hardware or software
3. Divide and conquer—divide the problem into logical areas
4. Repair the problem or test another theory
5. Test the solution
6. Provide feedback to the user

Step One: Recreate the problem
- Ask creative questions to isolate possible causes.
  - What seems to be the general problem?

_____

_____

_____

_____

_____

- Ask the user to demonstrate the problem.
  - ☐ Could this problem be due to user error?

  _____

  _____

  _____

  _____

Step Two: Divide the problem into hardware or software
- Will the computer boot?
  - ☐ If not, check power and peripheral cables.
  - ☐ If the computer will not boot, did you receive any CMOS beep codes or error codes?

  _____

  _____

  _____

  _____

  - ☐ If the computer will boot, can you access any applications?

  _____

  _____

  _____

  _____

Step Three: Divide and Conquer

- Using the information in the above steps, can you isolate this problem to a general area? List the possible areas below:

  _____
  _____
  _____
  _____
  _____
  _____

- For each of the problem areas, list a possible solution to the problem.

  _____
  _____
  _____
  _____
  _____
  _____

Step Four: Repair the problem or go back and test another theory

- Try each of the possible solutions, one at a time.
  - Did any of the solutions seem to fix the problem?

  _____
  _____

Step Five: Test the Solution

- Can you recreate the problem?

  _____

- If yes, go back to Step Three.

Step Six: Provide Feedback to the User

- Show the user that the workstation is operating properly.
- If the problem was caused by user error, demonstrate the proper procedure.
- Document the service call for future reference.

End of Exercise

✓ Instructor Check _____

Student Notes

Lab 6.2 Practical Troubleshooting

Introduction

In this lab you will use the troubleshooting steps you practiced in Lab 6.1 to diagnose and repair your lab workstation.

Maps to the following CompTIA A+ Objectives

A+ Core Hardware Service Technician Objectives
- Objectives 2.1 and 2.2

Required Materials
- Lab workstation

> **Instructor Note:** This lab is a practical troubleshooting lab. As such, you will need to "BUG" the student workstations. In order to provide a good troubleshooting experience, place at least three to four "Bugs" on each workstation.

Lab Procedure

1. At the Instructor's direction, all students should leave the lab. The Instructor will place "Bugs" on each workstation.
2. When the student reenters the lab, he/she will play the part of the PC technician. The Instructor will play the part of the user complaining of the problem.
3. Use the troubleshooting steps from Lab 6.1 to diagnose and repair the workstation.

End of Exercise

✓ Instructor Check _____

Student Notes

___
___
___
___
___

Lab 6.3 CMOS Beep Codes and Error Codes

Introduction

In this lab you will create CMOS Beep and Error codes, and then verify their meanings.

Maps to the following CompTIA A+ Objectives

A+ Core Hardware Service Technician Objectives
- Objectives 2.2 and 4.4

Required Materials
- Workstation with operating system installed and configured

Part One: CMOS Error Codes

1. Unplug the keyboard connector from your workstation and restart the system.
   - Did this cause any CMOS errors?

   _____

   - If a CMOS error was displayed on your screen, refer to Appendix F and list the number and meaning of the CMOS error below:

   _____

   _____

2. Plug the keyboard connector in and ensure that the workstation starts correctly.

Part Two: CMOS Beep Codes

1. Using proper ESD precautions, open the workstation case and remove the video adapter. Restart the workstation and observe the boot process.
   - Did this cause any CMOS Beep errors?

   _____

   - If a CMOS Beep error was heard, refer to Appendix F and list the Beep error and its meaning below:

   _____

   _____

2. Shut down the workstation, and reinstall the video adapter.

3. Remove the memory modules from the workstation. Restart the workstation and observe the boot process.
    - Did this cause any CMOS Beep errors?

    _____

    - If a CMOS Beep error was heard, refer to Appendix F and list the Beep error and its meaning below:

    _____

    _____

4. Shut down the workstation and reinstall the memory modules. Restart the workstation and ensure that it boots properly.

End of Exercise

✓ Instructor Check _____

Student Notes

_____

_____

_____

_____

_____

_____

_____

_____

Lab 6.4 Diagnostic Utilities

Introduction

There are many different diagnostic utilities available that will help you to diagnose problems with your workstation. In this lab you will download, install, and use a shareware diagnostic utility.

Maps to the following CompTIA A+ Objectives

A+ Core Hardware Service Technician Objectives
- Objective 2.2

Required Materials
- Workstation with Windows 2000 Professional installed and configured
- Internet Access

Lab Procedure

1. From a workstation with Internet access, browse to the following URL: http://www.hwinfo.com.
2. There are two versions of the HWINFO utility. HWINFO is for use with 16-bit operating systems such as DOS, and HWINFO32 is for use with 32-bit operating systems such as Windows 98, NT, and 2000.
3. Browse to and download the HWINFO32 installation executable.

> **Note:** HWINFO is a shareware program. It can be freely distributed. It comes with a 14-day evaluation license only! After 14 days you must either register it, or discontinue using it!

4. After the download completes, double-click the installation executable and follow the on-screen prompts to install HWINFO32.

132 Logical Troubleshooting

5. When the installation completes, start the HWINFO32 utility. The utility will scan your system hardware and display the results on-screen. (Figure 6.4.1)

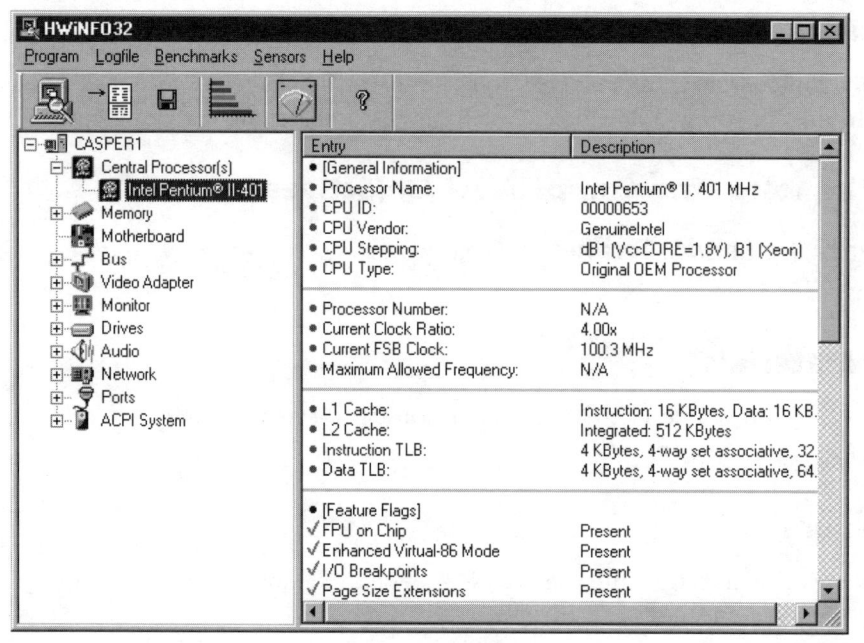

Figure 6.4.1

6. Browse through the available system information then answer the following questions:
   ☐ What is your CPU ID number?

   _____

   ☐ What is your video BIOS version number?

   _____

   ☐ What model motherboard and chipset is in your workstation?

   _____

   _____

End of Exercise

✓ Instructor Check _____

Student Notes

Lab 6.5 P.O.S.T. Cards (Power On Self-Test Cards)

Introduction

Most diagnostic utilities require a workstation that will operate, or at least can be booted from, a boot disk. For systems that are completely dead, a POST Card may be able to provide information to diagnose the problem.

Maps to the following CompTIA A+ Objectives

A+ Core Hardware Service Technician Objectives
- Objective 2.2

Required Materials
- Lab workstation
- POST card

Lab Procedure

1. Using proper ESD procedures, remove the workstation case.
2. Following the POST Card manufacturer's directions, install the card into the workstation. (Figure 6.5.1)

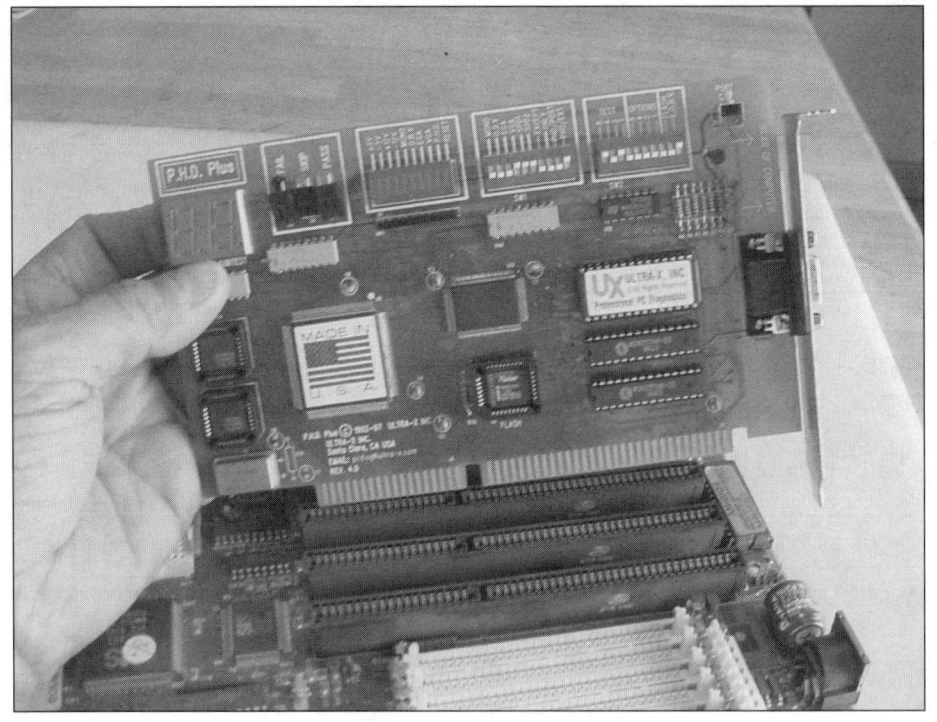

Figure 6.5.1

3. Following the POST Card manufacturer's directions, start the workstation and allow the card to perform the diagnostic procedures.

End of Exercise

✓ Instructor Check _____

> ### 💡 Lab Notes
>
> 1. Some POST cards come with special diagnostic ROM-BIOS chips. You may need to replace your system BIOS with one of these to get full diagnostic functionality.
> 2. POST cards have various types of diagnostic output. Your card may use LED lights, a video output to a monitor, a digital readout, or a combination of these.

Student Notes

Lab 6.6 Basic Maintenance Procedures

Introduction

In this lab you will review basic workstation maintenance procedures.

Maps to the following CompTIA A+ Objectives

A+ Core Hardware Service Technician Objectives
- Objectives 3.1 and 3.2

Required Materials
- Lab textbook
- Lab manual

Lab Procedure

Following a comprehensive preventive maintenance plan will prevent many workstation problems and failures. Study the following recommended preventive maintenance guidelines, then answer the following questions:

Activity	Description	Who is responsible
Daily Maintenance Activities		
Back up user data	Back up user generated files by copying them to the network or floppy disks.	User
Check work area	Ensuring that no books, papers, or other materials are blocking the PC or monitor ventilation ports.	User
Back up Network Data	Daily backups of all data stored on network servers.	Technician
Weekly Maintenance Activities		
Disk Maintenance	Run scandisk, checkdisk, and defrag utilities.	User
Clean and dust PC and monitor	Remove dust from the monitor screen, PC case, and the keyboard.	User
Monthly Maintenance Activities (every one to six months)		
External cleaning	Cleaning the case and monitor	Technician
Internal cleaning	Brush and vacuum inside the PC case. Ensure that all internal components are secure	Technician
Check cables and connections	Ensure that all external and internal cables are connected securely	Technician
Mouse and keyboard	Clean and vacuum the keyboard, clean the mouse ball and rollers	Technician

Activity	Description	Who is responsible
Virus Update	Download and install new virus signatures	Technician
Yearly Maintenance Activities		
Clean floppy drives	Clean the heads in the floppy drives with an alcohol swab or floppy cleaning disk.	Technician
Clean CD-ROM drives	Clean the laser	Technician
Voltage checks	Ensure that power supply output is within specs.	Technician

> **Note:** The previous guidelines are standard recommendations for maintenance. The actual operating environment at your site will dictate how often the maintenance procedures are performed.

- What type of condition might dictate that you clean the inside of the case more often?

___

- When might it become necessary to download and apply additional virus signature updates?

___

- What should you use to clean your monitor screen?

___

138 Logical Troubleshooting

☐ Why should you NOT use compressed air to blow the dust out of a computer case?

_____

_____

_____

_____

End of Exercise

✓ Instructor Check _____

Student Notes

Lab 6.7 Creating a Preventive Maintenance Plan

Introduction
In this lab you will create a preventive maintenance plan for a fictitious company.

Maps to the following CompTIA A+ Objectives

A+ Core Hardware Service Technician Objectives
- Objectives 3.1 and 3.2

Required Materials
- Lab textbook
- Lab manual

Lab Procedure

1. Study the following scenario:

   > You are the Computer Service Center manager for a company called Compu-Mine. This company specializes in computer-controlled hardrock mining for gold and other precious metals. The data that is produced each day has a direct effect on precious metals pricing worldwide. As such, it is imperative that no data be lost. The onsite computers operate in an extremely dusty and dirty environment. There is also an extreme amount of vibration and movement generated from the mining operations.

2. Based on the above scenario, how often should each of the following preventive maintenance procedures be completed?

Activity	How Often
Backup user data	
Check work area	
Backup Network Data	
Disk Maintenance	
Clean and dust PC and monitor	
External cleaning	
Internal cleaning	
Check cables and connections	
Mouse and keyboard	

Logical Troubleshooting

Activity	How Often
Virus Update	
Clean floppy drives	
Clean CD-ROM drives	
Voltage checks	

End of Exercise

✓ Instructor Check _____

Student Notes

_____
_____
_____
_____
_____
_____
_____
_____
_____
_____
_____
_____

Lab 6.8   Backing Up Data in Windows 98 and Windows 2000

Introduction

Performing data backups is the single most important step you can take toward protecting your important data. In this exercise you will practice backing up data in Windows 98 and Windows 2000 Professional.

Maps to the following CompTIA A+ Objectives

A+ Core Hardware Service Technician Objectives
- Objective 3.1

A+ Operating System Technologies Objectives
- Objective 1.2

Required Materials
- Workstation with Windows 98 and Windows 2000 installed and configured
- Blank formatted floppy disk

Part One: Creating a File To Backup

1. From the **Start Menu**, choose **Programs**, **Accessories**, and then select **Notepad**.
2. In Notepad, type "**This is a test file**." From the File menu, choose **Save As** and save the file as "**Testfile**" in **C:\My Documents**.
3. Close the Notepad utility.

Part Two: Backing Up Data in Windows 98

1. Start your workstation and ensure that Windows 98 loads properly.
2. From the **Start Menu**, choose **Accessories**, **System Tools**, and then select **Backup**. The Windows 98 backup utility will start. (Figure 6.8.1)

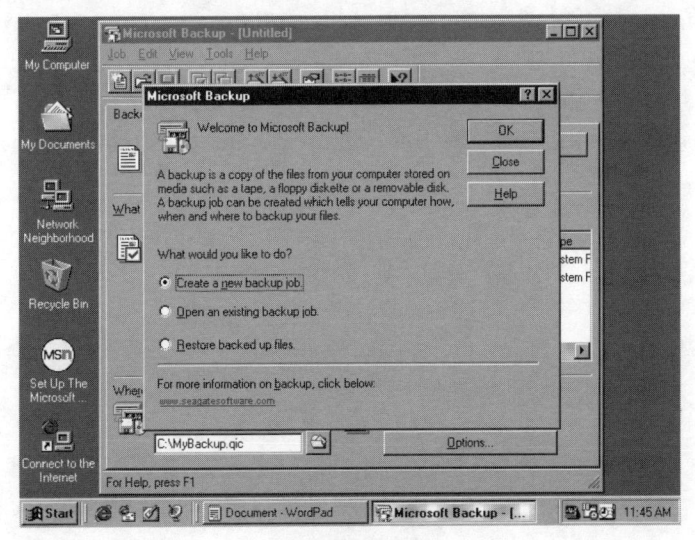

Figure 6.8.1

142   Logical Troubleshooting

> **Note:** If the backup utility is not available under System Tools, from the **Start Menu** choose Settings, then select Control panel. Double-click Add/Remove Programs then select Windows Setup. Under System Tools, choose **Backup** then click **OK** twice. The Backup utility will install. Restart your computer and continue with the exercise.

3. If prompted that **No Backup Devices Were Found On Your Computer**, choose **NO** to continue.
4. From the Microsoft Backup screen, choose **Create a New Backup Job**, and then click **OK**.
5. From the **Backup Wizard** screen choose **Backup Selected Files**, **Folders**, and **Drives**, then select **Next**.
6. Browse to and select the **Testfile.txt file** you created (**C:\My Documents\Testfile.txt**) and then click **Next**. (Figure 6.8.2)

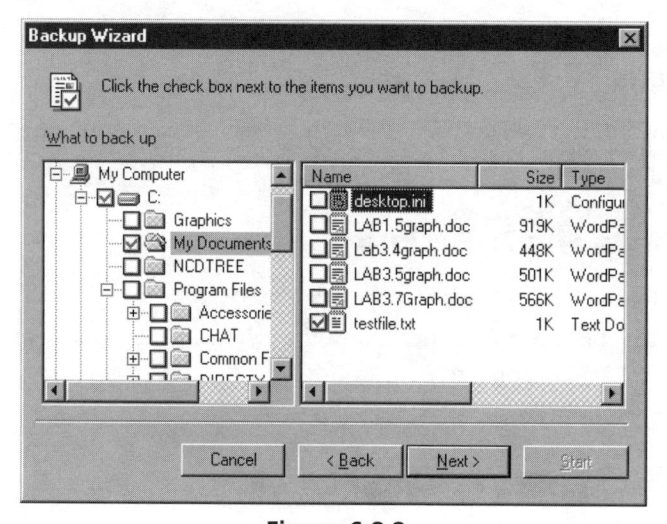

Figure 6.8.2

7. From the **What to Backup** screen, ensure that **All Selected Files** is marked, and then click **Next**.
8. From the **Where to Backup** screen, ensure that **File** is selected and **A:\mybackup.qic** appears as the destination, then click **Next**.
9. At the **How to Backup** screen click **Next**.
10. Enter **Test Backup** as the name for this backup job, and then select **Start**.

Lab 6.8 Backing Up Data in Windows 98 and Windows 2000

11. When Windows 98 Backup completes the backup job, a progress report will be displayed. (Figure 6.8.3)

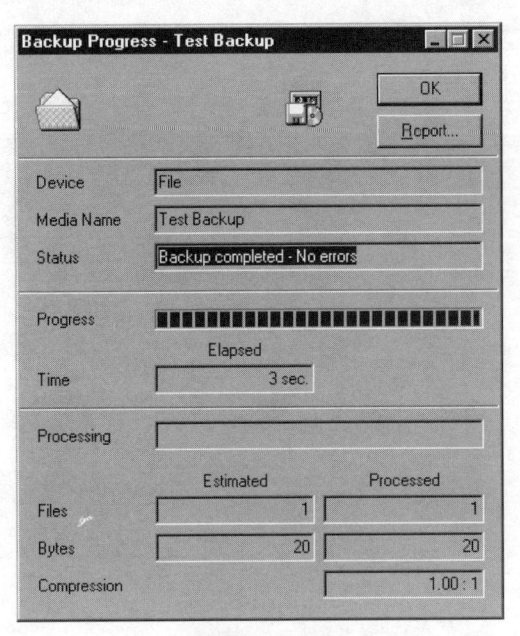

Figure 6.8.3

12. After viewing the Backup progress report, click **OK**, then exit the Windows 98 Backup utility.

Part Three: Backing Up Data in Windows 2000

1. Start your workstation and ensure that Windows 2000 workstation starts properly.
2. From the **Start Menu** choose **Programs**, **Accessories**, **System Tools**, and then select **Backup**.
3. Select the **Backup Wizard** button to start the **Backup Wizard**. Click **Next**.
4. At the **What to Backup**, screen choose **Backup Selected Files**, **Drives**, **or Network Data**, then select **Next**.

144 Logical Troubleshooting

5. Browse to and select the **testfile.txt** file at **C:\MYDOCUMENTS**, then click **Next**. (Figure 6.8.4)

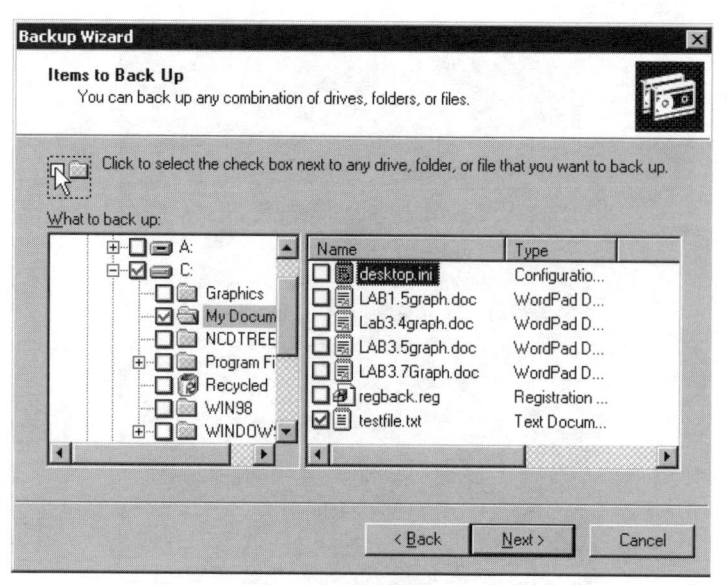

Figure 6.8.4

6. At the **Where to Backup** screen, ensure that **File** appears as the Backup Media Type and **A:\Backup.dkf** appears as the backup file name. Click **Next** to continue.
7. At the **Completing the Backup Wizard** screen, ensure that the backup settings are correct, then click **Finish**. Windows Backup will begin backing up the selected file.
8. When the backup completes, a **Backup Progress** screen will be displayed.
9. After viewing the **Backup Progress** screen, click **Close** and exit the backup utility.

End of Exercise

✓ Instructor Check _____

Lab Notes

The backup utility that ships with Windows NT Workstation requires a tape drive to operate. If your workstation is equipped with a tape drive, perform a Windows NT Backup by going to the **Start Menu**, **Programs**, **Administrative Tools**, and then select **Backup**. The Windows NT Backup utility operates much the same as the Windows 2000 Backup utility.

Student Notes

Student Notes

Lab 6.9 Installing Virus Protection

Introduction

With so many destructive viruses loose on the Internet, it is imperative that a good hardware/software technician be able to install and configure virus protection.

Maps to the following CompTIA A+ Objectives

A+ Core Hardware Service Technician Objectives
- Objective 3.2

Required Materials
- Workstation with Windows 98 installed and configured
- Anti-Virus installation CD

Part One: Installing Anti-Virus Software

1. Start the workstation and ensure that Window 98 loads properly.
2. Insert the Anti-Virus CD into the CD-ROM drive. If your system is configured for autorun, the Anti-Virus installation program will start automatically. If your system is not configured for autorun, use **My Computer** to browse the CD. Double-click the Installation executable (i.e., *install.exe* or *setup.exe*).
3. Follow the on-screen prompts to complete the installation program.
4. If prompted, restart your workstation.

Part Two: Performing a Virus Scan

1. From the **Start Menu**, browse to and open your anti-virus application. (Figure 6.9.1)

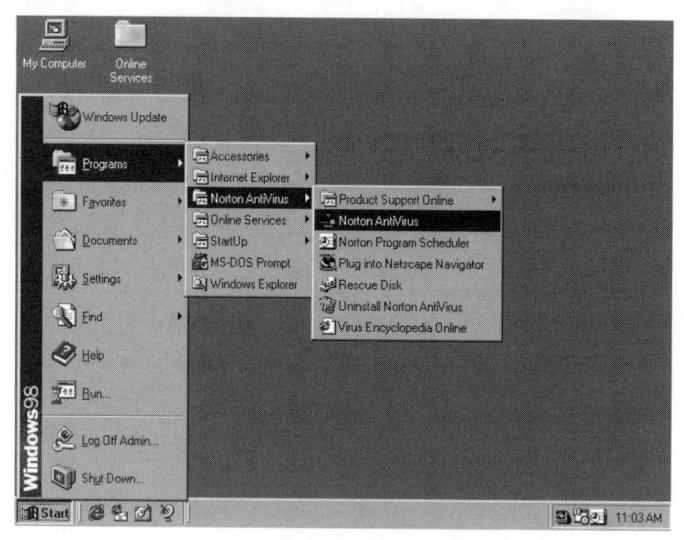

Figure 6.9.1

2. Select the drives you wish to scan, then start the scan process. The anti-virus software will begin scanning the selected drives. (Figure 6.9.2)

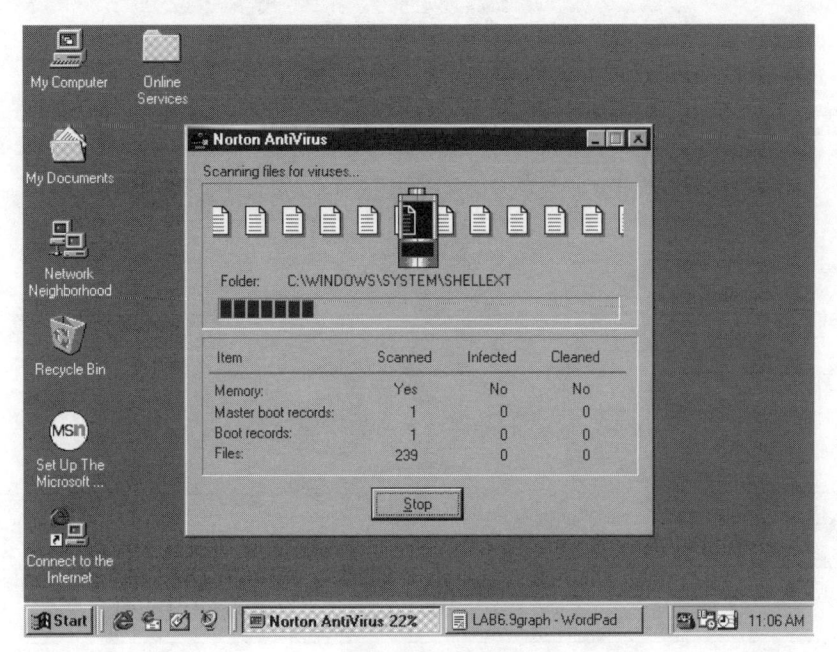

Figure 6.9.2

3. When the anti-virus scan is completed, exit the anti-virus utility.

Part Three: Creating Anti-Virus Rescue Disks

1. From the **Start Menu**, browse to and open your anti-virus rescue disk application. (Figure 6.9.3)

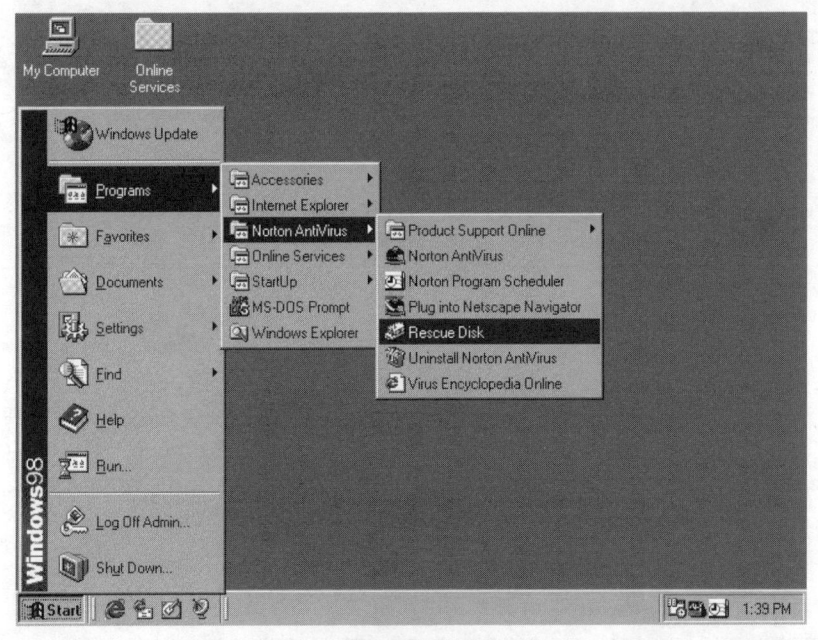

Figure 6.9.3

148 Logical Troubleshooting

2. Follow the on-screen prompts to create your anti-virus rescue disks. (Figure 6.9.4)

Figure 6.9.4

End of Exercise

✓ Instructor Check _____

Student Notes

_____
_____
_____
_____
_____
_____
_____
_____
_____
_____
_____

Lab 6.10 Creating an ERD in Windows NT Workstation

Introduction

In this lab you will create an ERD (emergency repair disk) for your Windows NT Workstation.

Maps to the following CompTIA A+ Objectives

A+ Core Hardware Service Technician Objectives
- Objective 3.2

A+ Operating System Technologies Objectives
- Objective 2.3

Required Materials
- Workstation with Windows NT Workstation installed and configured

Lab Procedure

1. From the **Start Menu**, choose **Run**, type **RDISK**, then click **OK**. The **Repair Disk Utility** will start. (Figure 6.10.1)

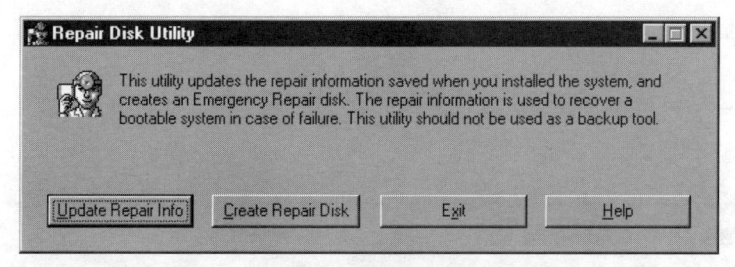

Figure 6.10.1

2. Choose **Create Repair Disk**. When prompted, insert a floppy disk into drive "A" and click **OK**.

150 Logical Troubleshooting

3. The Repair Disk Utility will format the disk and copy the necessary files. (Figure 6.10.2)

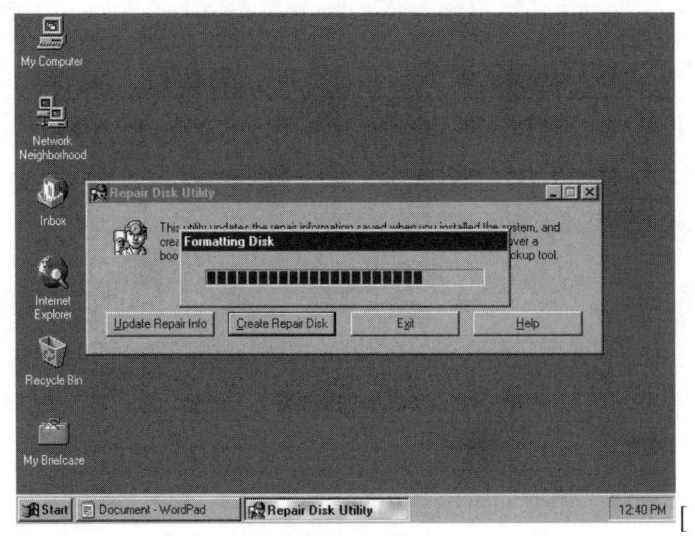

Figure 6.10.2

4. When prompted, click **OK** and exit the Repair Disk Utility.

End of Exercise

✓ Instructor Check _____

Student Notes

_____
_____
_____
_____
_____
_____
_____
_____

Lab 6.11 Creating an ERD in Windows 2000 Professional

Introduction

In this lab you will create an ERD (emergency repair disk) for your Windows 2000 Professional Workstation.

Maps to the following CompTIA A+ Objectives

A+ Core Hardware Service Technician Objectives
- Objective 3.2

A+ Operating System Technologies Objectives
- Objective 2.3

Required Materials
- Workstation with Windows 2000 Professional installed and configured.

Lab Procedure

1. From the **Start Menu**, choose **Programs**, **Accessories**, **System Tools**, and then select **Backup**. The Windows 2000 Backup Utility will open. (Figure 6.11.1)

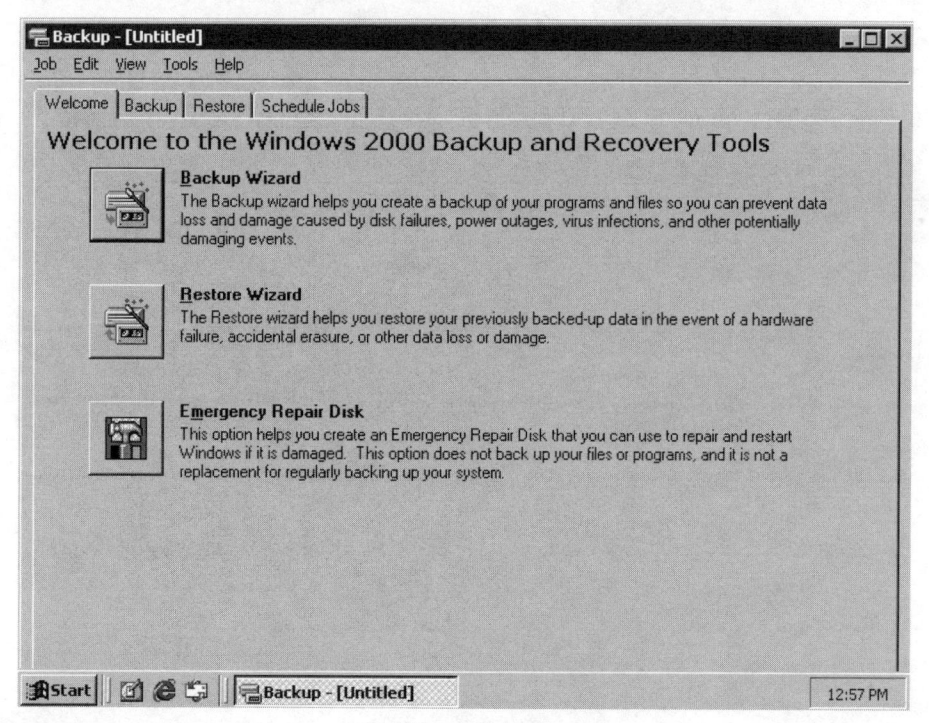

Figure 6.11.1

2. From the Backup Utility, select Emergency Repair Disk.

152 Logical Troubleshooting

3. Insert a blank formatted floppy disk into drive "A," select **Also Backup the Registry to the Repair Directory**, then click OK. (Figure 6.11.2)

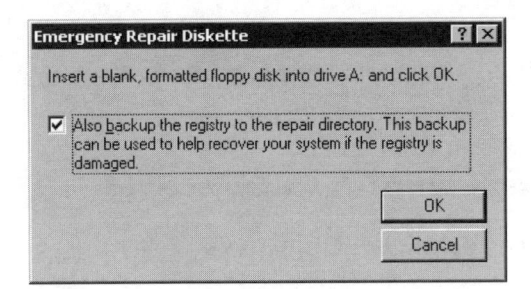

Figure 6.11.2

4. The Windows 2000 ERD Utility will format the floppy disk and copy the necessary files. (Figure 6.11.3)

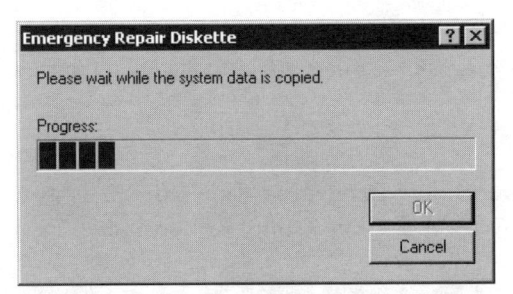

Figure 6.11.3

5. When prompted, remove the ERD from the drive, click OK, and exit the Backup Utility.

End of Exercise

✓ Instructor Check _____

Student Notes

Lab 6.12 Using Regedit to Backup the Windows 98 Registry

Introduction

The registry holds the primary configuration information for the Windows operating system. In this lab you will create a backup copy of your Windows 98 registry.

Maps to the following CompTIA A+ Objectives

A+ Core Hardware Service Technician Objectives
- Objective 3.2

A+ Operating System Technologies Objectives
- Objective 2.3

Required Materials
- Workstation with Windows 98 installed and configured

Lab Procedure

1. From the **Start Menu**, choose **Run**, type **Regedit**, then click OK. The Windows 98 Registry Editor utility will open. (Figure 6.12.1)

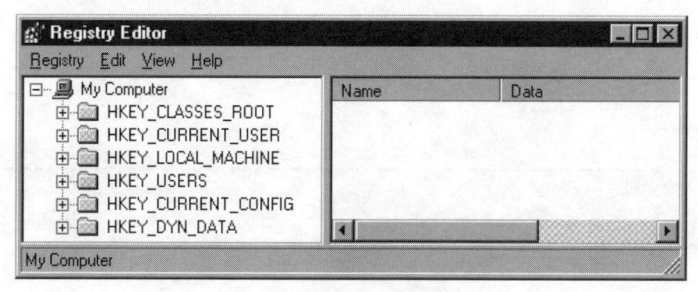

Figure 6.12.1

2. From the Registry menu, select **Export Registry File**.

154 Logical Troubleshooting

3. From the **Save In** screen, select C:\My Documents, type **Regback** in the file name field, then click **Save**. (Figure 6.12.2)

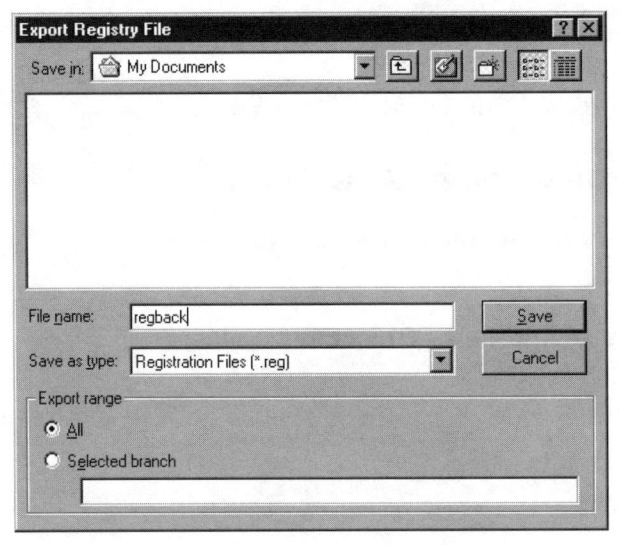

Figure 6.12.2

4. **Regedit** will copy the registry to the specified location. When finished, close the registry editor utility.

End of Exercise

✓ Instructor Check _____

Student Notes

___
___
___
___
___
___
___

Lab 6.13 Restoring Your Data from a Backup in Windows 98 and 2000 Pro

Introduction

In this lab you will restore the data backups you created in Lab 6.8.

Maps to the following CompTIA A+ Objectives

A+ Core Hardware Service Technician Objectives
- Objective 3.1

A+ Operating System Technologies Objectives
- Objective 1.2

Required Materials
- Workstation with Windows 98 and 2000 Pro installed and configured.

Part One: Restoring Your Data From a Backup in Windows 98

1. Start your workstation and ensure that Windows 98 loads properly.
2. From the **Start Menu**, choose **Accessories**, **System Tools**, and then select **Backup**. The Windows 98 backup utility will start.
3. Select **Restore Backed Up Files**, then click OK. (Figure 6.13.1)

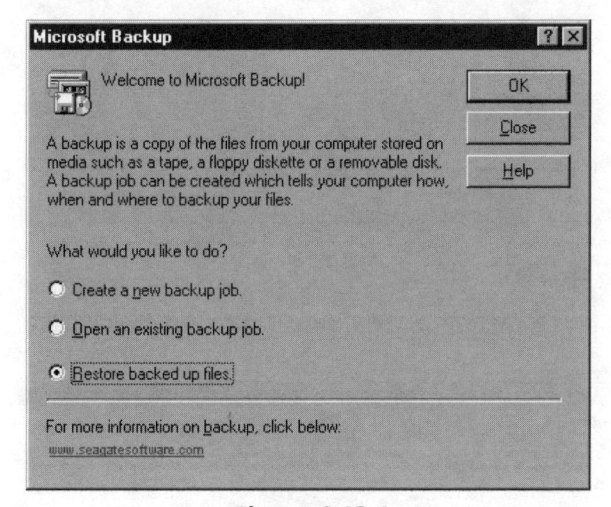

Figure 6.13.1

156 Logical Troubleshooting

4. Verify that **Restore From File** appears, and that **A:\My Backup.QIC** appears as the backup file. Insert the disk containing the backup into the A: drive, then click **Next**. (Figure 6.13.2)

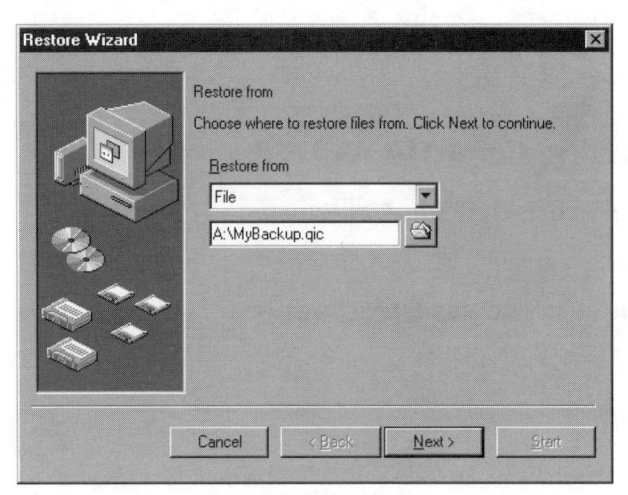

Figure 6.13.2

5. Click OK to select the backup set. (Figure 6.13.3)

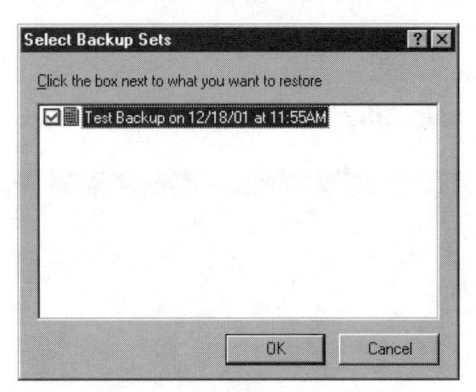

Figure 6.13.3

6. Browse to and select **C:\My Documents\Testfile.txt**, then click **Next**. (Figure 6.13.4)

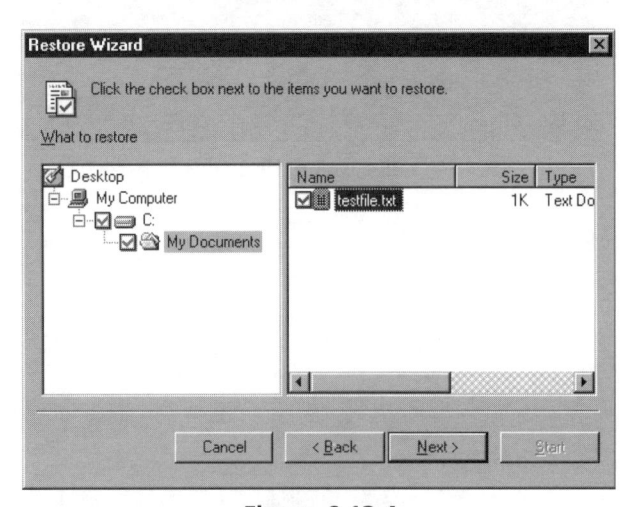

Figure 6.13.4

Lab 6.13 Restoring Your Data from a Backup in Windows 98 and 2000 Pro

7. Choose to restore the file to the **Original Location**, then click **Next**.
8. Choose to **Always Replace the File on my Computer**, then select **Start**.
9. When asked for required media, click OK. The restore process will begin.
10. When the restore process completes, a progress report will be displayed. (Figure 6.13.5)

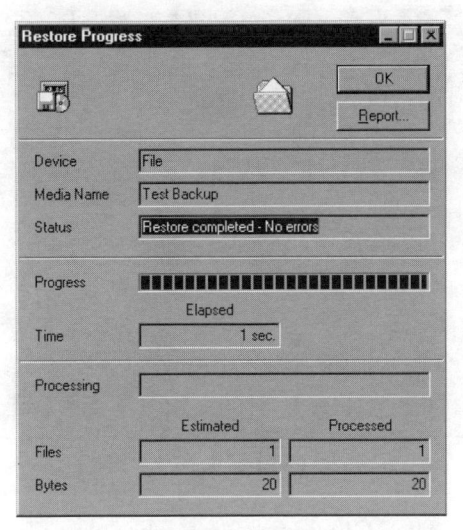

Figure 6.13.5

11. After viewing the report, click OK and exit the backup utility.

Part Two: Restoring Your Data From a Backup in Windows 2000 Pro

1. Start your workstation and ensure that Windows 2000 Pro loads properly.
2. Insert the disk containing the backup into the "A" drive.
3. From the **Start Menu**, choose **Programs**, **Accessories**, **System Tools**, then select **Backup**.
4. Select the **Restore Wizard** button. The restore wizard will start. Click **Next**.
5. From the **What to Restore** screen, browse to and select the **C:\My Documents\testfile.txt** file, then click **Next**. (Figure 6.13.6)

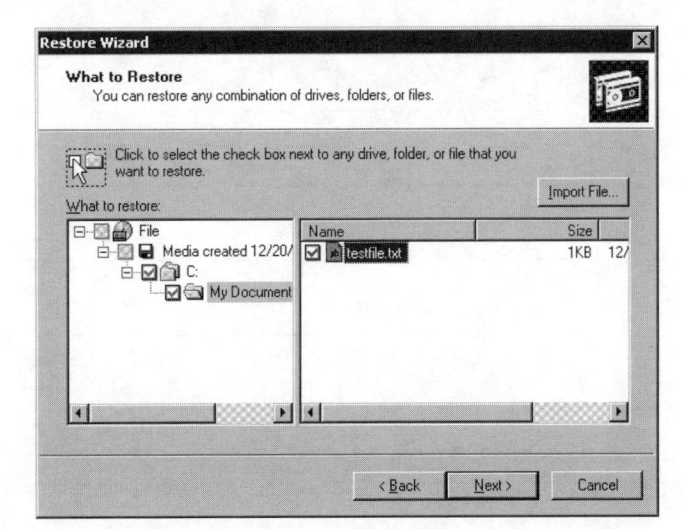

Figure 6.13.6

158 Logical Troubleshooting

6. Review the restore wizard settings, then select **Finish**.
7. Ensure that **A:\Backup.bkf** appears in the **Backup File** name field, then click OK. The restore process will begin.
8. When the restore process completes, a progress report will be displayed. (Figure 6.13.7)

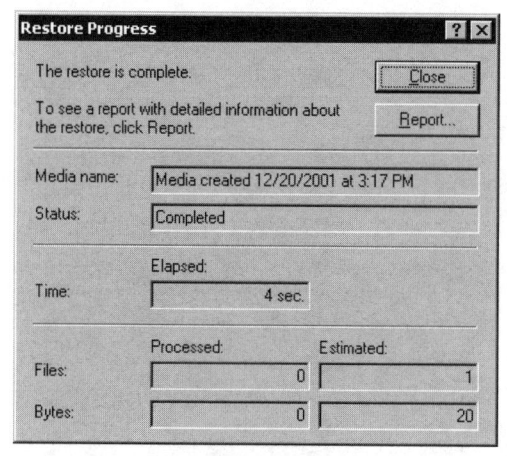

Figure 6.13.7

9. After viewing the report, click **Close** and exit the backup utility.

End of Exercise

✓ Instructor Check _____

Student Notes

_____
_____
_____
_____
_____
_____
_____
_____

Lab 6.14 Using an ERD to Recover Windows NT Workstation

Introduction

This lab will take you through the process of using a previously created ERD (Emergency Repair Disk) to recover a failed Windows NT Workstation.

Maps to the following CompTIA A+ Objectives

A+ Core Hardware Service Technician Objectives
- Objective 3.2

A+ Operating System Technologies Objectives
- Objective 2.3

Required Materials
- Workstation with Windows NT Workstation installed and configured
- Windows NT Workstation ERD
- Windows NT Setup floppy Disks

Lab Procedure

1. Start the Windows NT Workstation installation process using the Windows NT setup floppy disks. Windows NT setup will enter the file copy phase of setup.

   > **Note:** To create the Windows NT setup floppies, from your Windows NT Workstation command prompt, browse to the I386 directory on the Windows NT installation CD-ROM. Type the command **WINNT32 /OX** and press enter. You will be prompted to label and insert three floppy disks. Windows NT setup will copy the necessary files to the disks.

2. Insert and remove the Windows NT Setup disks as prompted.
3. At the **Welcome to Setup** screen, press **R** to **Repair a Damaged Windows NT Version 4.0 Installation**.
4. At the **Repair Process Tasks** screen, ensure that all repair tasks are selected, highlight **Continue**, and press **Enter**.
5. Press **Enter** to allow setup to detect your workstation's mass storage devices. When detection completes, press **Enter** to continue.
6. At the **Emergency Repair Disk** screen, press **Enter** to verify that you have an **ERD**. When prompted, insert the ERD into drive "A," then press **Enter**.
7. Press **Enter** to allow setup to verify your hard disk.
8. If prompted, insert the Windows NT install CD-ROM and press **Enter**.
9. When the repair process completes, remove all disks from disk drives and restart the workstation.

End of Exercise

✓ Instructor Check _____

Student Notes

Lab 6.15 Using Recovery Console to Recover Windows 2000

Introduction

In this lab you will use the Windows 2000 Recovery Console to recover a failed Windows 2000 Professional installation.

Maps to the following CompTIA A+ Objectives

A+ Core Hardware Service Technician Objectives
- Objective 3.2

A+ Operating System Technologies Objectives
- Objectives 2.3 and 3.2

Required Materials
- Workstation with Windows 2000 installed and configured
- Windows 2000 Installation CD-ROM
- Windows 2000 Setup floppy Disks

Lab Procedure

1. Start the Windows 2000 Pro Installation process using the setup floppy disks. Windows 2000 setup will begin the file copy phase of setup.

   > **Note:** To create the setup boot floppies, from within Windows 2000, browse to the **BOOTDISK** directory on the Windows 2000 installation CD-ROM. Execute **MAKEBOOT32.EXE**. You will be prompted to label and insert four floppy disks. Windows 2000 setup will copy the necessary files to the disks.

2. Insert the Windows 2000 Pro setup disks as prompted.
3. At the **Welcome to Setup** screen, Press **R** to repair a Windows 2000 installation.
4. At the **Windows 2000 Repair Options** screen, press **C** to start the recovery console.
5. Enter the number of the Windows 2000 installation you wish to log on to.
6. When prompted, type the administrator password and press **Enter**.
7. From the recovery console, you can repair the MBR, copy system files that are missing or corrupted, and reconfigure services.
8. To view a list of available recovery console commands, type **Help** and press **Enter**. To view information about a specific command, type *command* **/?** and press **Enter**. Explore the commands, then answer the following questions:
   - Which command sets the current directory to Systemroot?

Logical Troubleshooting

    ☐ Which command writes a new boot sector onto the system partition?

___

    ☐ Which command repairs the master boot record of the boot partition?

___

9. Type **Exit** and press **Enter** to quit the recovery console and restart the workstation.

End of Exercise

✓ Instructor Check _____

Student Notes

Lab 6.16 Using an ERD to Recover Windows 2000 Pro

Introduction

In this lab you will use the Windows 2000 ERD (Emergency Repair Disk) to repair a failed Windows 2000 Professional installation.

Maps to the following CompTIA A+ Objectives

A+ Core Hardware Service Technician Objectives
- Objective 3.2

A+ Operating System Technologies Objectives
- Objectives 2.3 and 3.2

Required Materials
- Workstation with Windows 2000 Professional installed and configured.

Lab Procedure

1. Start the Windows 2000 Pro Installation process using the setup floppy disks. Windows 2000 setup will begin the file copy phase of setup.

   > **Note:** To create the setup boot floppies, from within Windows 2000, browse to the **BOOTDISK** directory on the Windows 2000 installation CD-ROM. Execute **MAKEBOOT32.EXE**. You will be prompted to label and insert four floppy disks. Windows 2000 setup will copy the necessary files to the disks.

2. Insert the Windows 2000 Professional setup disks as prompted.
3. At the **Welcome to Setup** screen, Press **R** to repair a Windows 2000 installation.
4. At the **Windows 2000 Repair Options** screen, press **R** to repair a Windows 2000 installation using the ERD.
5. Press **F** to allow the emergency repair process to perform all repair options.
6. Press **Enter** to indicate that you have the emergency disk. Insert the ERD into drive "A" and press **Enter**.
7. The emergency repair process will run. When the process completes, remove the ERD from the floppy drive and allow the workstation to boot normally.
   - What three things can the ERD repair if you choose to do a manual repair?

   _____

   _____

   _____

164 Logical Troubleshooting

☐ What four things can the ERD repair if you choose fast repair?

___

End of Exercise

✓ Instructor Check _____

Student Notes

Lab 6.17 Using Regedit to Restore the Windows 98 Registry

Introduction

In this lab you will restore the registry on your Windows 98 workstation using the registry backup you created in lab 6.12.

Maps to the following CompTIA A+ Objectives

A+ Core Hardware Service Technician Objectives
- Objective 3.2

A+ Operating System Technologies Objectives
- Objective 2.3

Required Materials
- Workstation with Windows 98 installed and configured

Lab Procedure

1. From the **Start Menu**, choose **Run**, type **Regedit**, then click OK. The Widows 98 Registry Editor utility will open. (Figure 6.17.1)

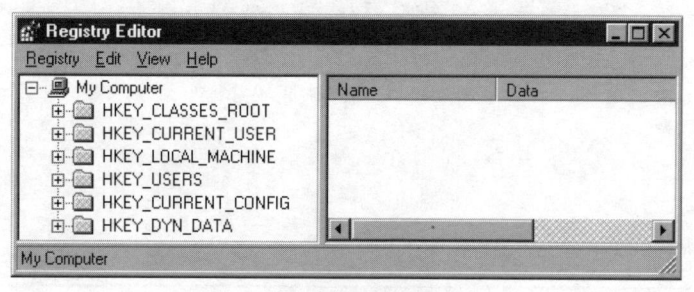

Figure 6.17.1

2. From the Registry menu, select **Import Registry File**.

166 Logical Troubleshooting

3. From the **Look In** screen, select C:\My Documents, highlight the **Regback** file, then click **Open**. (Figure 6.17.2)

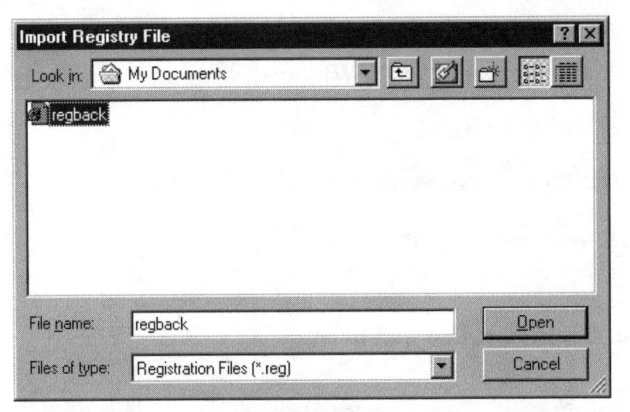

Figure 6.17.2

4. **Regedit** will import the backup registry file into the registry. (Figure 6.17.3)

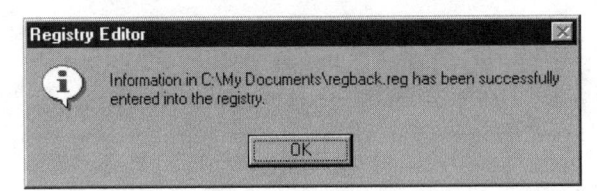

Figure 6.17.3

End of Exercise

✓ Instructor Check _____

Student Notes

Student Notes

CHAPTER 7
Memory

7.1 Memory Module Identification   170

7.2 Installing/Upgrading System RAM   173

170 Memory

Lab 7.1 Memory Module Identification

Introduction
In this lab you will identify the memory modules installed on your workstation, and identify different types of memory modules.

Maps to the following CompTIA A+ Objectives

A+ Core Hardware Service Technician Objectives
- Objectives 1.8 and 4.2

Required Materials
- Lab manual
- Lab workstation

Lab Procedure
1. Using proper ESD precautions, remove the workstation cover.
2. Locate the memory module(s) on your system board. (Figure 7.1.1)

Figure 7.1.1

- What type of memory modules are installed on your system?

_____

_____

Lab 7.1 Memory Module Identification

- How much total RAM is installed on your system?

_____

3. There are three basic types of RAM in use today.
   - **30-pin SIMM** (single inline memory module)
   - **72-pin SIMM** (single inline memory module)
   - **168-pin DIMM** (double inline memory module)

   Study the figures below. Label the figures as to type, (e.g., 30-pin SIMM, 72-pin SIMM, and 168-pin DIMM) and then answer the following questions:

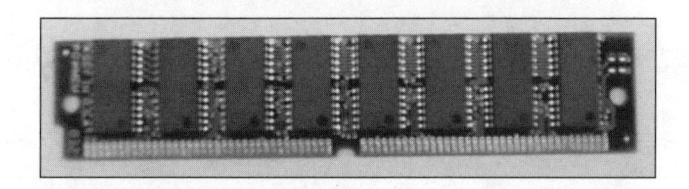

   _____

   _____

   _____

   - In a normal configuration, how many 72-pin SIMMs are required per bank?

   _____

   - In a normal configuration, how many 30-pin SIMMs are required per bank?

   _____

   - True or False: You must always install 168-pin DIMMs in sets of two.

   _____

End of Exercise

✓ Instructor Check _____

Student Notes

Lab 7.2 Installing/Upgrading System RAM

Introduction

In this lab you will remove and replace the RAM in your workstation.

Maps to the following CompTIA A+ Objectives

A+ Core Hardware Service Technician Objectives
- Objectives 1.8 and 4.2

Required Materials
- Lab manual
- Lab workstation

Lab Procedure

1. Using proper ESD precautions, remove the workstation cover.
2. Locate the memory module(s) on your system board. (Figure 7.2.1)

Figure 7.2.1

Memory

3. Depending on the type of memory module in your system, release and remove the memory modules. (Figure 7.2.2)

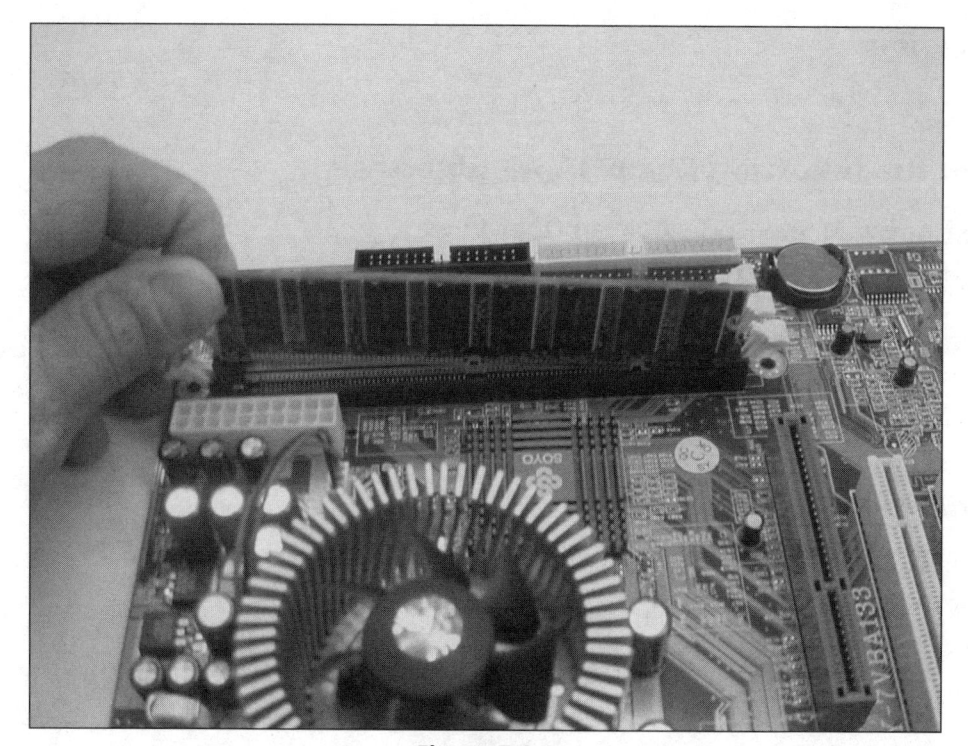

Figure 7.2.2

4. Reinstall the memory modules in the slots and/or install upgraded memory modules.
5. Start the workstation and verify that setup detects all installed RAM.

End of Exercise

✓ Instructor Check _____

> ### 💡 Lab Notes
>
> The method for removing and installing memory modules depends on the type of memory module.
> - To remove a 168-pin DIMM, follow these steps:
>   - Push outward on the retaining clips on each end of the DIMM
>   - Pull straight up on the DIMM to remove it from the slot
> - To remove 30- or 72-pin SIMMs, follow these steps:
>   - Push outward on the retaining clips on each end of the SIMM
>   - Pull the SIMM out until it releases from the slot
> - To reinstall a SIMM or DIMM, reverse the above steps.

Student Notes

CHAPTER 8

Floppy Drives

8.1　Installing a Second Floppy Drive　178

8.2　Formatting a Floppy Disk Using Windows 98, NT Workstation, and 2000 Professional　180

8.3　Creating a Bootable Floppy　184

Lab 8.1 Installing a Second Floppy Drive

Introduction

In this lab you will install a second floppy drive in your workstation.

Maps to the following CompTIA A+ Objectives

A+ Core Hardware Service Technician Objectives
- Objectives 1.2 and 1.5

Required Materials

- Workstation with operating system installed and configured
- Extra 3.5" or 5.25" floppy drive

Lab Procedure

1. Using proper ESD precautions, remove the PC cover.
2. Select an unused 3.5" external bay. Insert the second floppy drive into the bay until it is flush with the front of the case.
3. Connect the "B" floppy ribbon connector to the back of the floppy drive. Pay close attention to proper pin-one orientation.
   - Which floppy ribbon connector is the "B" connector?

   _____

   - How can you identify pin one on the ribbon cable?

   _____

   _____

   _____

   _____

   _____

4. Attach the power connector to the floppy drive.
5. Start the workstation and enter the CMOS setup utility. Enter the new floppy drive's configuration information, save the new settings, then exit the CMOS setup utility.
6. Allow the workstation to boot normally. The new "B" floppy drive should now be accessible.

End of Exercise

✓ Instructor Check _____

Student Notes

180　Floppy Drives

Lab 8.2　Formatting a Floppy Disk Using Windows 98, NT Workstation, and 2000 Professional

Introduction

Before a floppy disk can be used for data storage it must be formatted. In this exercise you use the built-in utilities in Windows 98, NT, and 2000 to format a floppy disk.

Maps to the following CompTIA A+ Objectives

A+ Operating System Technologies Objectives
- Objectives 1.1 and 1.2

Required Materials
- Workstation with Windows 98, NT Workstation, and 2000 Professional installed and configured
- Blank floppy disks

Part One: Formatting with Windows 98

1. Start your workstation and ensure that Windows 98 loads properly.
2. Insert a floppy disk into the floppy drive.
3. From **My Computer**, right-click the 3.5″ floppy drive and select **Format**. (Figure 8.2.1)

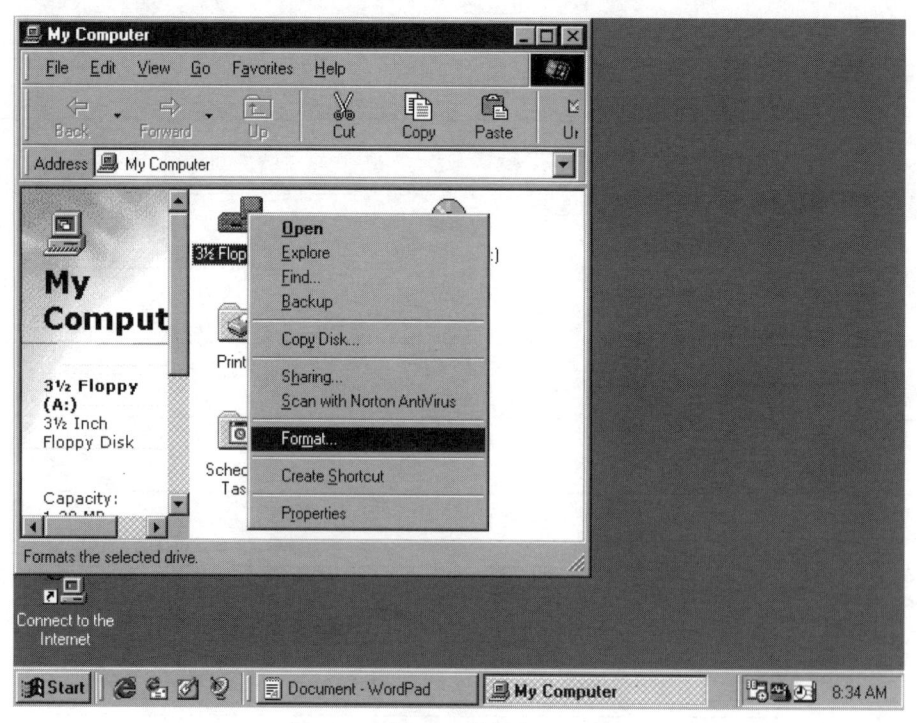

Figure 8.2.1

4. From the format window, ensure that the capacity setting is correct, choose **Full** as the format type, then click **Start**. (Figure 8.2.2)

Lab 8.2   Formatting a Floppy Disk Using Windows   **181**

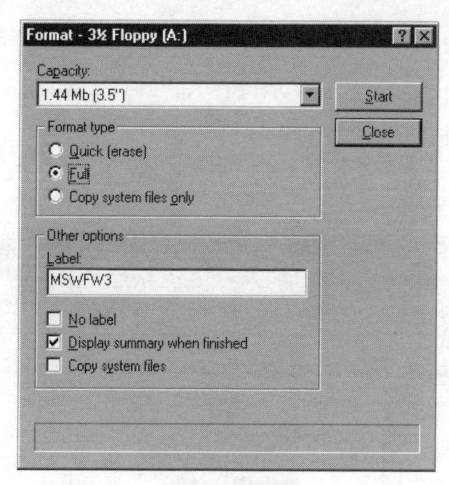

Figure 8.2.2

5. When the format is finished, a format results screen will be displayed. Click **Close** twice to exit the format utility.

Part Two: Formatting with Windows NT Workstation

1. Start the workstation and ensure that Windows NT Workstation loads properly.
2. Insert a floppy disk into the floppy drive.
3. From **My Computer**, right-click the 3.5″ floppy and select **Format**.
4. From the format window, ensure that the capacity setting is correct, choose **FAT** for the file system, then click **Start**. At the format warning screen, click **OK**. The format process will begin. (Figure 8.2.3)

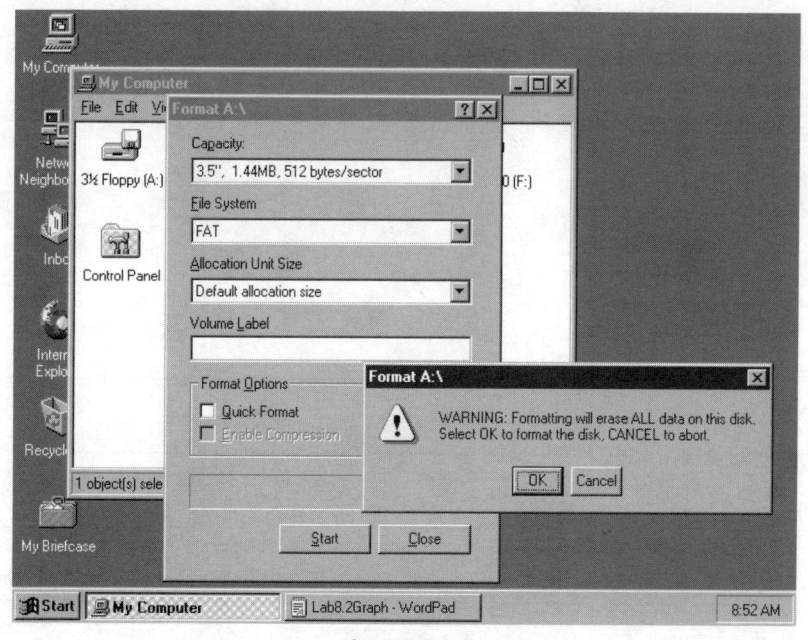

Figure 8.2.3

5. When the format is finished, click OK, then click **Close** to exit the format utility.

182 Floppy Drives

Part Three: Formatting with Windows 2000 Professional

1. Start the workstation and ensure that Windows 2000 Professional loads properly.
2. Insert a floppy disk into the floppy drive.
3. From **My Computer**, right-click the 3.5" floppy and select **Format**. (Figure 8.2.4)

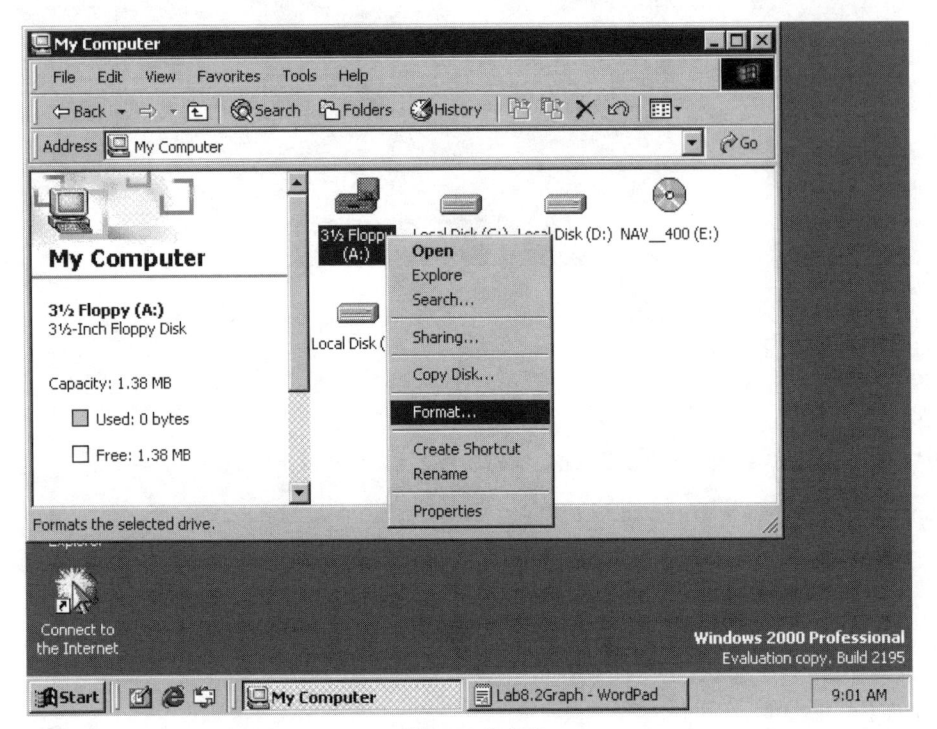

Figure 8.2.4

4. From the format window, ensure the capacity setting is correct, choose **FAT** for the file system, then click **Start**. At the format warning screen, click **OK**. The format process will begin.
5. When the format is finished, click **OK**, then click **Close** to exit the format utility.

End of Exercise

✓ Instructor Check _____

Student Notes

Student Notes

Lab 8.3 Creating a Bootable Floppy

Introduction
There are times when a computer may be unable to boot properly. By using a boot disk you will be able to access the computer to replace files, run utilities, or copy needed files from the hard drive. In this lab you will create a Windows 98 boot disk.

Maps to the following CompTIA A+ Objectives

A+ Operating System Technologies Objectives
- Objectives 1.1 and 1.2

Required Materials
- Workstation with Windows 98 installed and configured
- Blank floppy disk

Lab Procedure

1. Start your workstation and ensure that Windows 98 loads properly.
2. Insert a blank floppy disk into the floppy drive.
3. From **My Computer**, right-click the 3.5" floppy and then select **Format**.
4. From the format window, ensure that the capacity is correct, select **Full** for the format type, under **Other Options**, select **Display Summery When Finished**, and also select **Copy system files**. Click **Start** to begin the format process. (Figure 8.3.1)

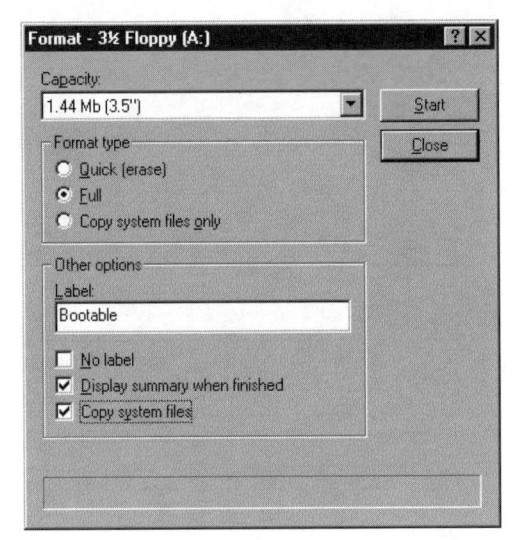

Figure 8.3.1

5. The format utility will format the disk and copy the system files to the disk's MBR.

6. When the format process is complete, a format results window will be displayed. Click **Close** twice to close the format utility. (Figure 8.3.2)

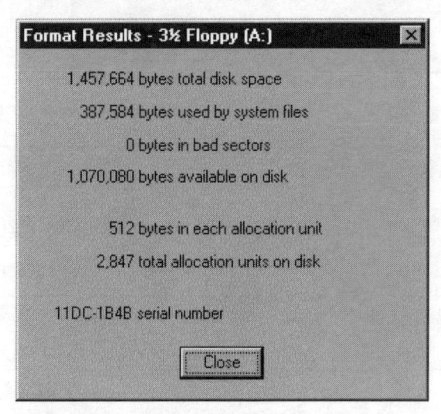

Figure 8.3.2

7. To test your new boot disk, check CMOS settings to ensure that the system tries to boot from the "A" drive first, insert the boot disk into the "A" drive, and restart the workstation. The workstation should boot from the boot disk.

   ☐ What files are copied to the floppy disk in order to make it bootable?

   _____

   _____

   ☐ On which track is the boot sector located?

   _____

End of Exercise

✓ Instructor Check _____

Student Notes

_____

_____

_____

_____

Student Notes

CHAPTER 9
Hard Drives

9.1 Installing an EIDE Hard Drive   188

9.2 Installing a SCSI Hard Drive   190

9.3 Creating and Formatting Disk Partitions   193

9.4 Using Windows 98, NT, and 2000 Disk Utilities   199

Lab 9.1 Installing an EIDE Hard Drive

Introduction

In this lab you will install and configure a second EIDE Hard Drive in your workstation.

Maps to the following CompTIA A+ Objectives

A+ Core Hardware Service Technician Objectives
- Objectives 1.2 and 1.5.

Required Materials
- Workstation with operating system installed and configured
- EIDE hard drive

Lab Procedure

1. Using proper ESD precautions, remove the workstation case.
2. Set the configuration jumpers to the proper Master/Slave or Cable Select configuration depending on how the drive will be installed.
   - What jumper setting did you use?

   _____

3. Insert the hard drive in an unused 3.5″ internal bay, and secure with mounting screws.
4. Attach the 40-pin ribbon cable and the power connector. (Figure 9.1.2)

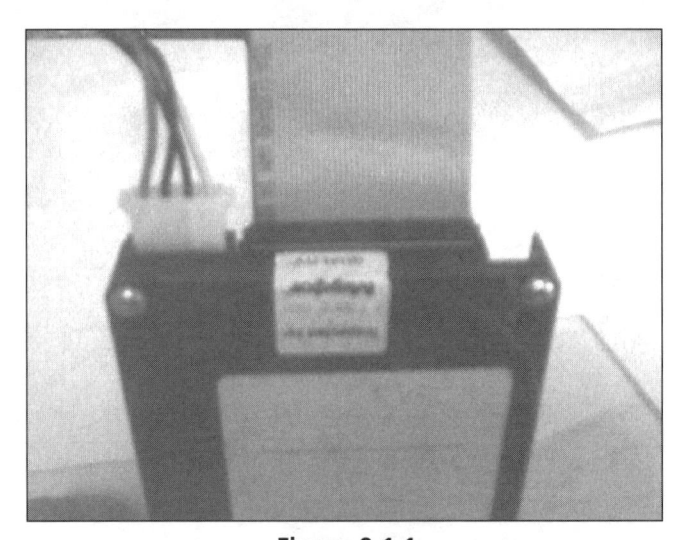

Figure 9.1.1

> **Note:** Ensure that pin one on the cable connects to pin one on the drive.

5. Start the workstation, and enter the CMOS Setup utility.

6. Ensure that the proper hard drive configuration parameters are entered for the hard drive. Save the settings and exit the CMOS Setup utility.

End of Exercise

✓ Instructor Check _____

Student Notes

___
___
___
___
___
___
___
___
___
___
___
___
___
___
___
___
___

Lab 9.2 Installing a SCSI Hard Drive

Introduction

In this lab you will install and configure a SCSI adapter and a SCSI hard drive.

Maps to the following CompTIA A+ Objectives

A+ Core Hardware Service Technician Objectives
- Objectives 1.2 and 1.6

Required Materials
- Workstation with Windows 2000 installed and configured
- SCSI hard drive
- SCSI adapter
- SCSI ribbon cable

Part One: Installing the SCSI Adapter

1. Using proper ESD precautions, remove the workstation case.
2. Insert the SCSI adapter into the proper expansion slot and secure with a retaining screw. (Figure 9.2.1)

Figure 9.2.1

> **Note:** Most newer SCSI Adapters come preconfigured with a SCSI ID of 7 and automatic termination enabled. If you are using an older adapter, you may have to set the SCSI ID and apply manual termination.

3. Start the workstation, and ensure that Windows 2000 loads properly. Windows 2000 should detect and autoload the drivers for the SCSI adapter. (Figure 9.2.2)

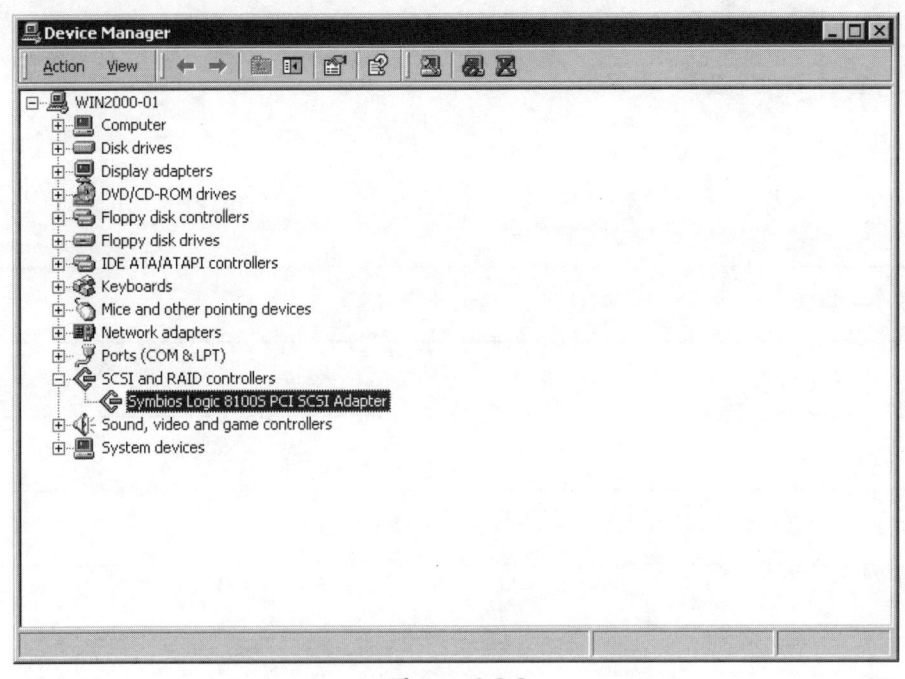

Figure 9.2.2

4. Shut down your workstation.

Part Two: Installing the SCSI Hard Drive

1. Set the SCSI ID number and the termination jumpers on the hard drive.
   - What SCSI ID number did you set for your hard drive?

   _____

2. Install the SCSI drive into an empty device bay.
3. Attach the SCSI ribbon cable and the power connector. (Figure 9.2.3)

Figure 9.2.3

Hard Drives

4. Start the workstation and ensure that Windows 2000 loads properly.

End of Exercise

✓ Instructor Check _____

Student Notes

Lab 9.3 Creating and Formatting Disk Partitions

Introduction

Before a hard disk can be used for data storage it must be partitioned and formatted. This lab introduces you to partitioning and formatting operations in Windows 98, Windows NT Workstation, and Windows 2000 Professional.

Maps to the following CompTIA A+ Objectives

A+ Operating System Technologies Objectives
- Objectives 1.1 and 1.2

Required Materials
- Workstation with Windows 98, Windows NT, and Windows 2000 installed and configured
- Second hard drive installed and configured

Part One: Partitioning and Formatting in Windows 98

1. Start the workstation and ensure that Windows 98 loads properly.
2. From the **Start Menu**, choose **Run**, type **FDISK**, and click **OK**.
3. When prompted to **Enable Large Disk Support**, press "**Y**" then press **Enter**. The **FDISK Options** screen will open. (Figure 9.3.1)

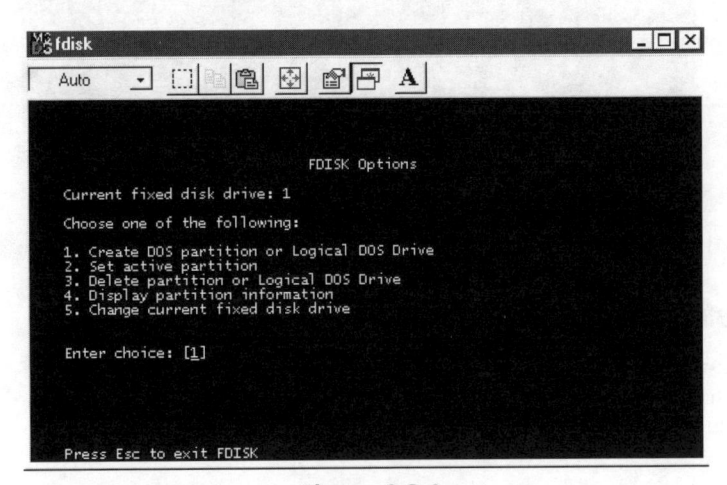

Figure 9.3.1

4. From the **FDISK Options** screen, enter "**5**" to **Change the Current Fixed Disk Drive**, then press **Enter**.
5. Enter the number of the second disk drive, and press **Enter**.
6. From the **FDISK Options** screen, enter "**4**" to **Display Partition Information** and then press **Enter**.

Hard Drives

☐ Are any partitions defined on this drive?

> **Note:** If any partitions are defined, return to the **FDISK Options** screen and delete those partitions before continuing.

7. Press **ESC** to return to the **FDISK Options** screen. Enter "**1**" to **Create DOS Partition** then press **Enter**.
8. Enter "**1**" to create primary DOS partition, then press enter.
9. When asked if you wish to use the maximum available size for the partition, press "**N**" and then press **Enter**.
10. Enter **100** for the partition size, then press **Enter**. (Figure 9.3.2)

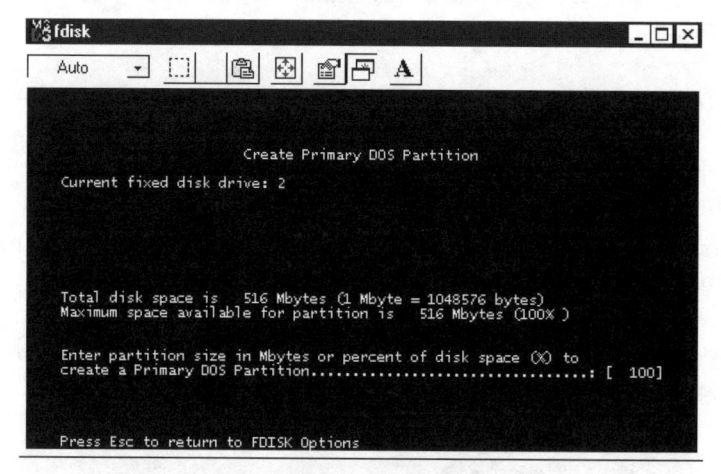

Figure 9.3.2

11. Press **ESC** three times to exit the FDISK utility then restart Windows 98.
12. When Window 98 loads, double-click **My Computer**. The newly created partition should appear as drive "**D**." Right-click drive "D" and select **Format**.
13. From the **Format** window choose **Full** as the format type, and then click **Start**. Click **OK** to allow Windows 98 to format the drive.

Lab 9.3 Creating and Formatting Disk Partitions 195

14. When the format is finished, **the Format Results** screen will be displayed. (Figure 9.3.3)

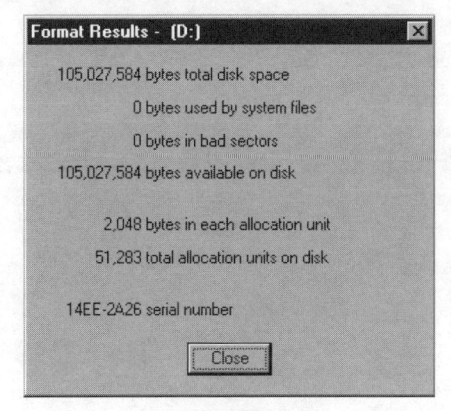

Figure 9.3.3

15. Close the **Format Results** screen and exit the format utility.

Part Two: Partitioning and Formatting in Windows NT

1. Start the workstation and ensure that Windows NT loads properly.
2. From the **Start Menu**, choose **Programs**, **Administrative Tools**, and then **select Disk Administrator**. (Figure 9.3.4)

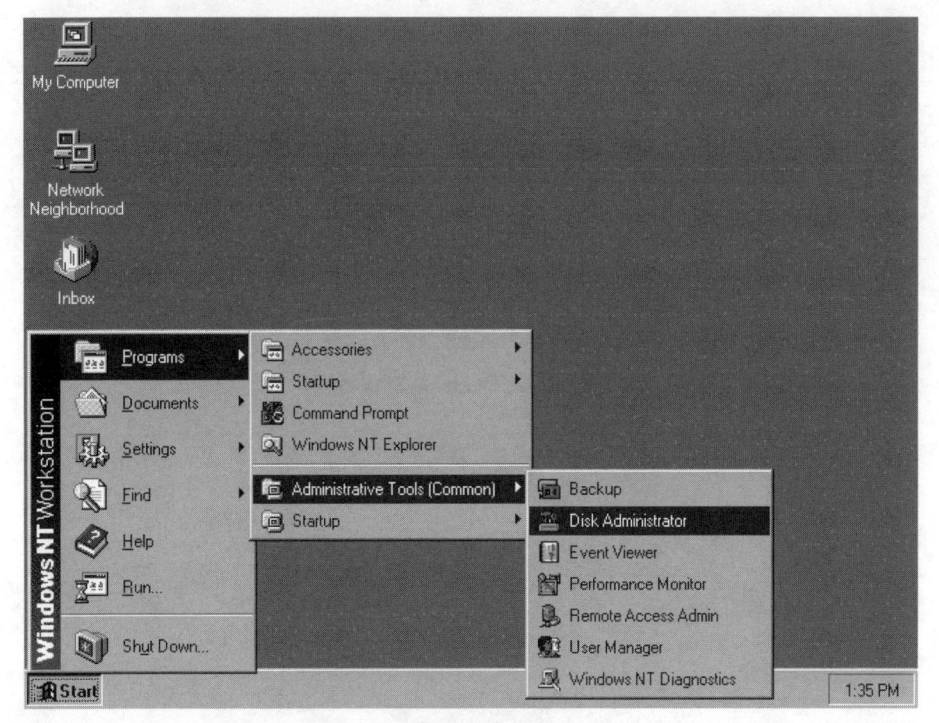

Figure 9.3.4

3. From **Disk Administrator**, select the free space on the second hard disk.
4. From the **Partition** drop-down menu, select **Create**. If prompted to confirm, click **Yes**.

196 Hard Drives

5. Type **100** in the **Create Partition of Size** field, and then click **OK**. The disk partition will be created. (Figure 9.3.5)

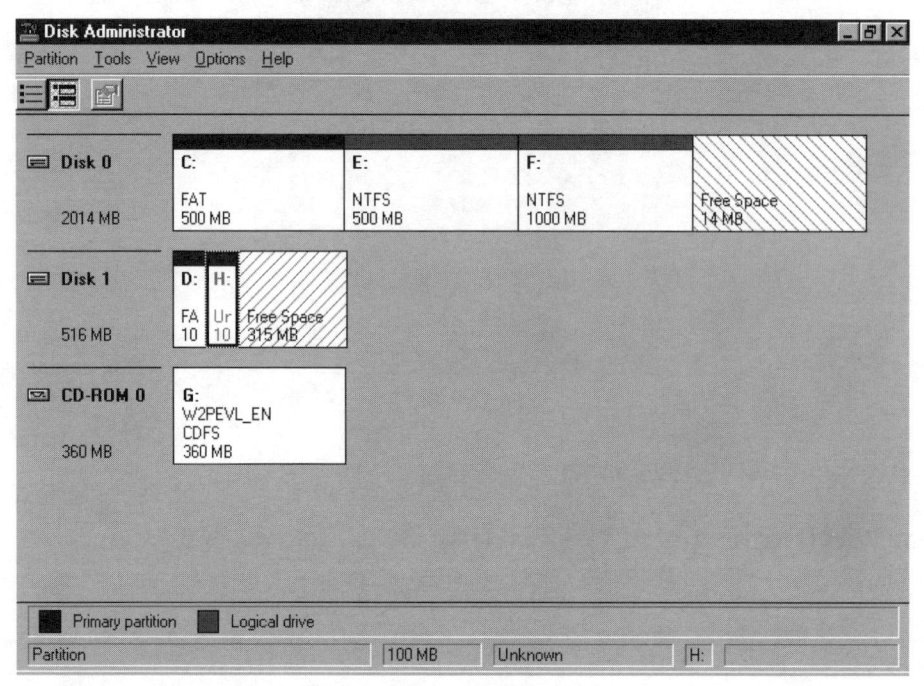

Figure 9.3.5

6. **Right-click** the new partition and select **Commit Changes Now**. Click **Yes** to confirm the change.
7. To format the new partition, **right-click** the partition and choose **Format**. Select **NTFS** as the file system, and then click **start**. Click **OK** to confirm the format. (Figure 9.3.6)

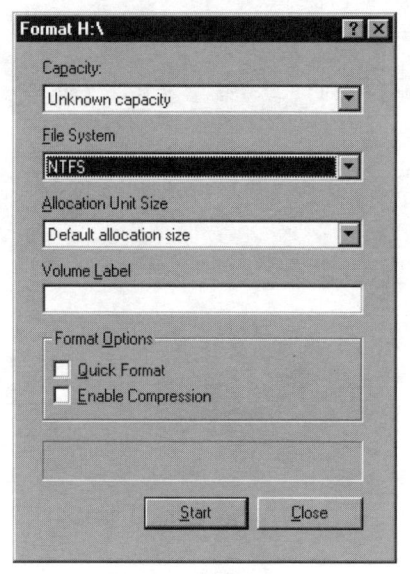

Figure 9.3.6

Lab 9.3 Creating and Formatting Disk Partitions 197

8. When the format completes, click **OK**. Close the format utility, and exit the **Disk Administrator**.

Part Three: Partitioning and Formatting in Windows 2000

1. Start the workstation and ensure that Windows 2000 loads properly.
2. From the **Start Menu**, choose **Setting**, and then select **Control Panel**.
3. From **Control Panel**, double-click the **Administrative Tools** folder, and then double-click **Computer Management**. (Figure 9.3.7)

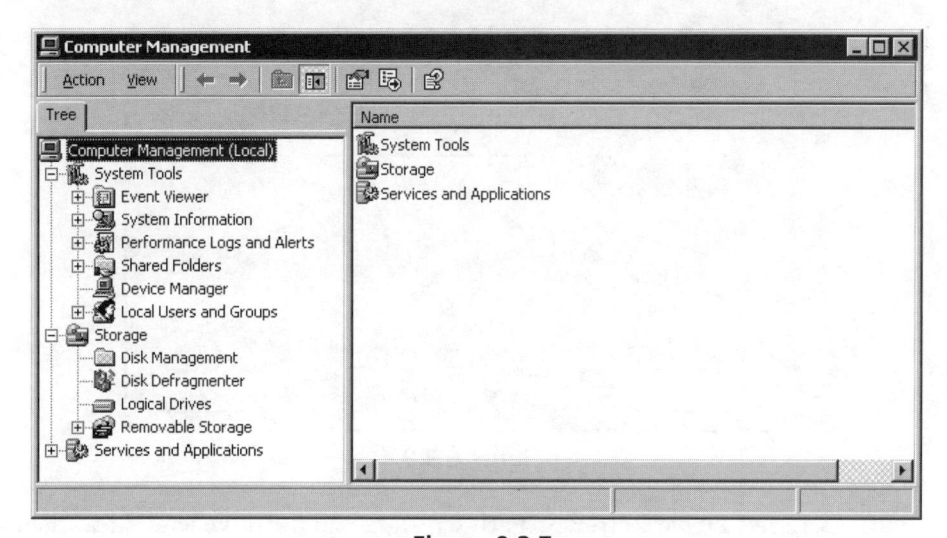

Figure 9.3.7

4. From **Computer Management**, select the **Disk Management** folder. (Figure 9.3.8)

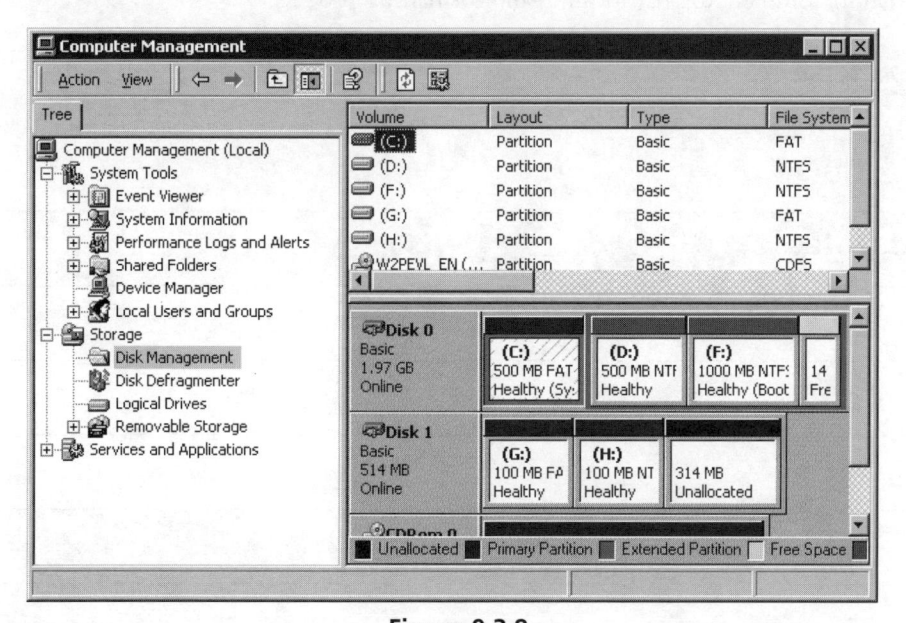

Figure 9.3.8

5. Right-click the unallocated space on the second hard disk, and choose **Create Partition**. The **Create Partition Wizard** will start. To continue, click **Next**.
6. From the **Select Partition Type** screen choose **Primary Partition**, then select **Next**.
7. From the **Specify Partition Size** screen, type **100** then select **Next**. (Figure 9.3.9)

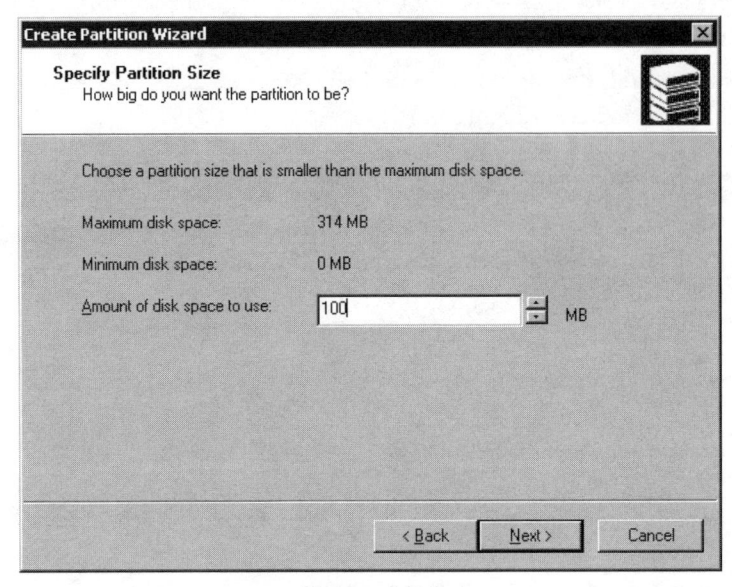

Figure 9.3.9

8. From the **Assigned Drive Letter of Path** screen, assign the drive letter "**M**," then select **Next**.
9. From the **Format Partition** screen, choose **NTFS** as the file system then select **Next**. Click **Finish** to complete the partitioning and formatting process.

End of Exercise

✓ Instructor Check _____

Student Notes

Lab 9.4 Using Windows 98, NT, and 2000 Disk Utilities

Introduction

In this lab you will use the built-in Windows disk utilities to analyze and perform maintenance on your hard disks.

Maps to the following CompTIA A+ Objectives

A+ Operating System Technologies Objectives
- Objectives 1.1 and 1.2

Required Materials
- Workstation with Windows 98, NT, and 2000 installed and configured

Part One: Window 98 Disk Utilities

1. Start your workstation and ensure that Windows 98 loads properly.
2. From **My Computer**, right-click the "**C**" drive, choose **Properties** then select the **Tools** tab. (Figure 9.4.1)

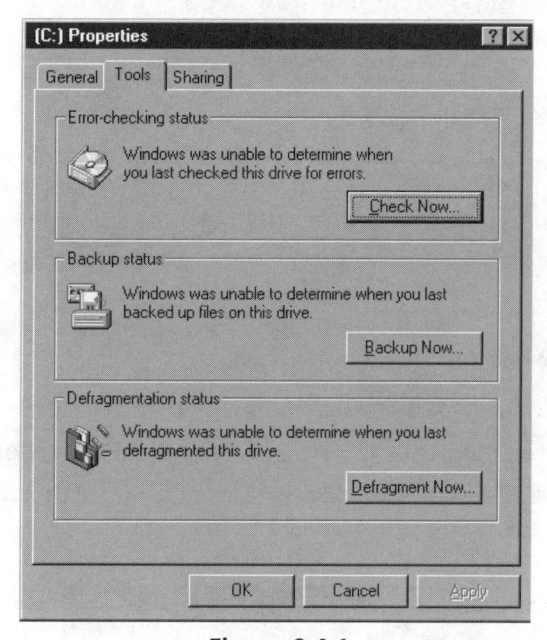

Figure 9.4.1

200 Hard Drives

3. To run **Scan Disk** click the **Check now** button. Click **Start** to perform a standard disk scan. (Figure 9.4.2)

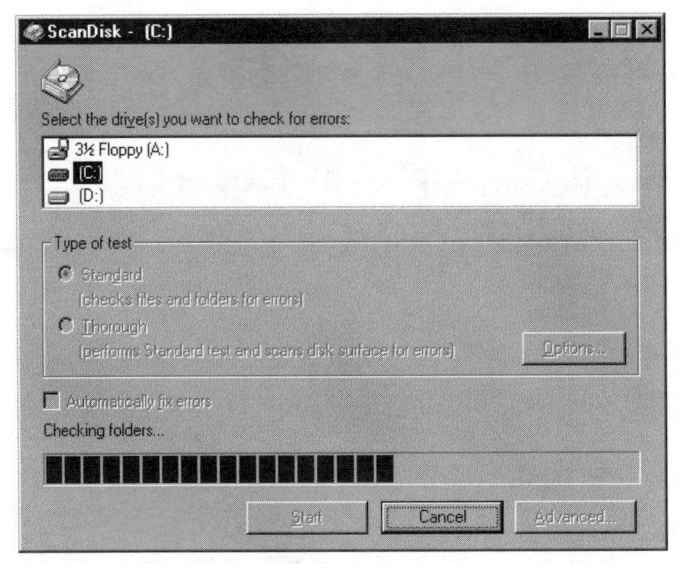

Figure 9.4.2

4. To run **Defrag**, click the **Defragment now** button. (Figure 9.4.3)

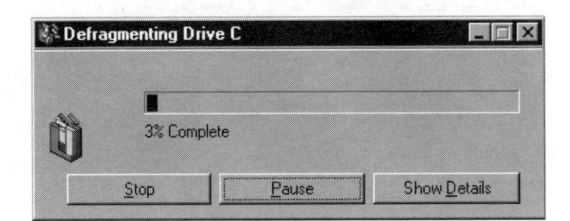

Figure 9.4.3

Part Two: Windows NT Workstation Disk Utilities

1. Start your workstation and ensure that Windows NT loads properly.
2. From **My Computer**, right-click the "C" drive, choose **Properties** then select the **Tools** tab.
3. To run **Check Disk**, click the **Check now** button. Select **Automatically Fix File System Errors** then click **Start**. (Figure 9.4.4)

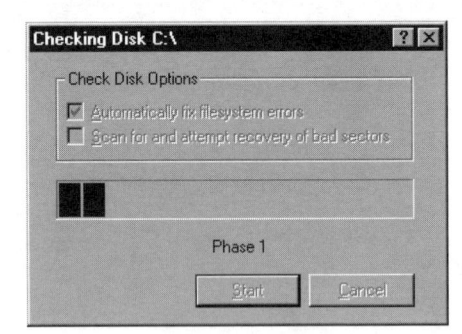

Figure 9.4.4

Lab 9.4 Using Windows 98, NT, and 2000 Disk Utilities 201

Part Three: Windows 2000 Disk Utilities

1. Start your workstation and ensure that Windows 2000 loads properly.
2. From **My Computer**, right-click the "**C**" drive, choose **Properties** then select the **Tools** tab.
3. To run **Check Disk** click the **Check now** button. Select **Automatically Fix File System Errors** then click **Start**.
4. To run **Defrag**, click the **Defragment now** button.
5. From the **Disk Defragmenter** screen, highlight the "C" drive and click **Defragment**. The utility will analyze and defragment the drive. (Figure 9.4.5)

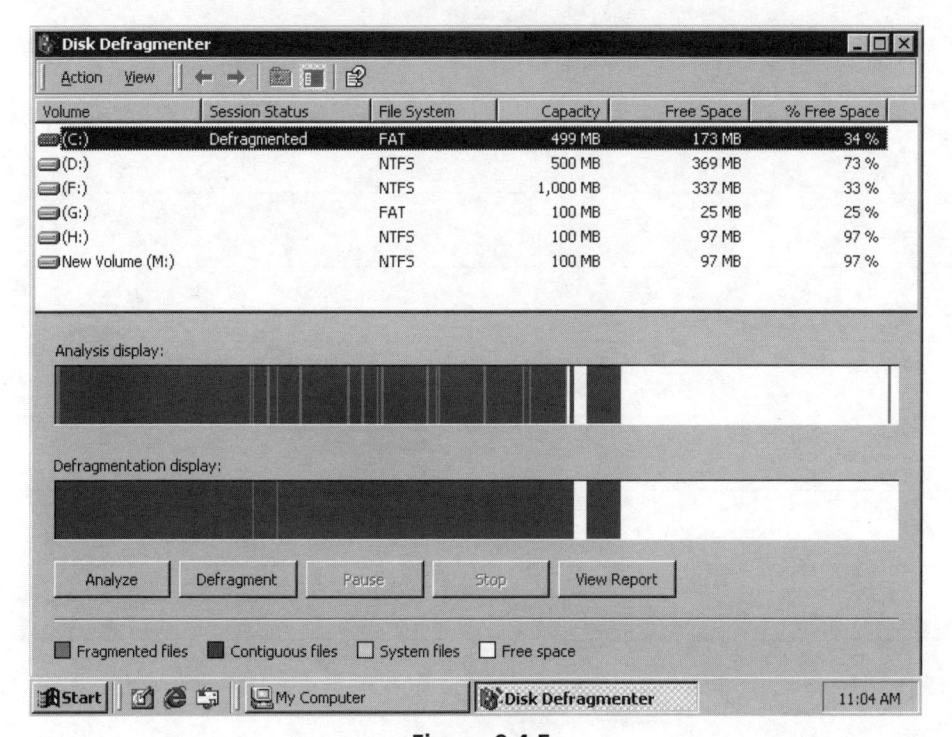

Figure 9.4.5

End of Exercise

✓ Instructor Check _____

> ### Lab Notes
>
> **Note:** Two common disk maintenance utilities are **Scan Disk** for checking disk errors such as cross link files, lost clusters, and bad sectors, and **Defrag** for defragmentation of files.
>
> The only disk maintenance utility available in **Windows NT** is **Check Disk**. Check disk checks for lost clusters, cross linked files, and bad disk sectors.

Student Notes

CHAPTER 10
Multimedia Devices

10.1 Installing an EIDE CD-ROM   204

10.2 Installing a SCSI CD-ROM Drive   207

10.3 Installing a Sound Card in Windows 98, NT, and 2000   209

Lab 10.1   Installing an EIDE CD-ROM

Introduction

In this lab you will install and configure an EIDE CD-ROM drive.

Maps to the following CompTIA A+ Objectives

A+ Core Hardware Service Technician Objectives
- Objectives 1.2, 1.5, 1.7 and 1.8

A+ Operating System Technologies Objectives
- Objective 2.4

Required Materials
- Workstation with Windows 98 installed and configured
- EIDE CD-ROM Drive

Lab Procedure

1. Using proper ESD precautions, remove the workstation cover.
2. Set the jumpers on the CD-ROM for the proper Master-Slave or Cable Select configuration. (Figure 10.1.1)

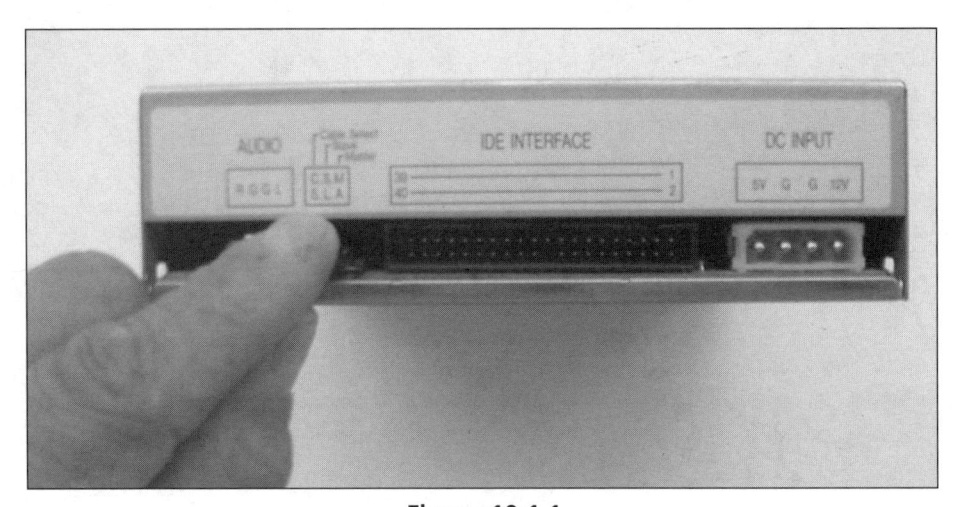

Figure 10.1.1

Lab 10.1   Installing an EIDE CD-ROM   205

3. Install the CD-ROM into an empty 5.25" bay. (Figure 10.1.2)

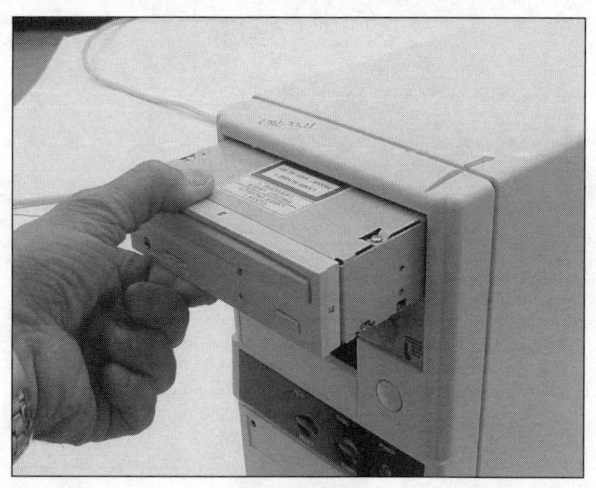

Figure 10.1.2

4. Attach the EIDE ribbon cable and power connector to the CD-ROM.
5. Start the workstation and ensure that Window 98 loads properly.
6. Double-click **My Computer** and verify that the new CD-ROM drive appears. (Figure 10.1.3)

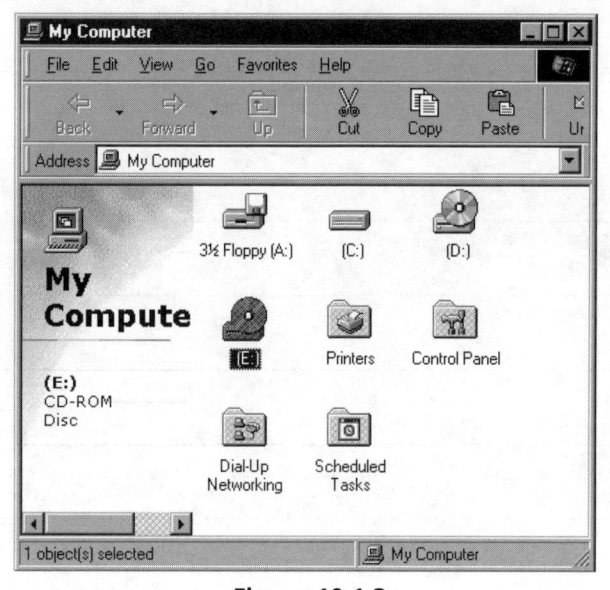

Figure 10.1.3

End of Exercise

✓ Instructor Check _____

Student Notes

Lab 10.2 Installing a SCSI CD-ROM Drive

Introduction
In this lab you will configure and install a SCSI adapter and SCSI CD-ROM.

Maps to the following CompTIA A+ Objectives

A+ Core Hardware Service Technician Objectives
- Objectives 1.2, 1.6, 1.7, and 1.8

A+ Operating System Technologies Objectives
- Objective 2.4

Required Materials
- Workstation with Windows 2000 installed and configured
- SCSI CD-ROM
- SCSI adapter
- SCSI ribbon cable

Part One: Installing the SCSI Adapter

1. Using proper ESD precautions, remove the workstation case.
2. Following the SCSI adapter manufacturers instructions, set the SCSI ID and termination configuration.

> **Note:** Most newer SCSI Adapters come preconfigured with a SCSI ID of 7 and automatic termination enabled. If you are using an older adapter, you may have to set the SCSI ID and termination manually.

3. Insert the SCSI Adapter into the proper expansion slot and secure with a retaining screw. (Figure 10.2.1)

Figure 10.2.1

208 Multimedia Devices

4. Start the workstation, and ensure that Windows 2000 loads properly. Windows 2000 should detect and autoload the drivers for the SCSI adapter. (Figure 10.2.2)

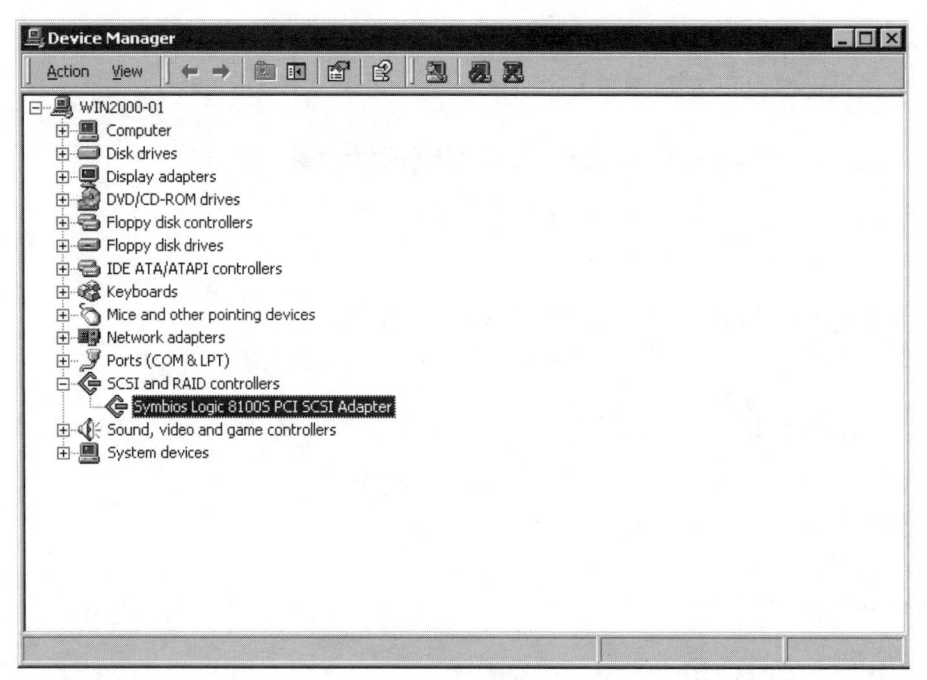

Figure 10.2.2

5. Shut down your workstation.

Part Two: Installing the SCSI CD-ROM

1. Set the SCSI ID number and the termination jumpers on the CD-ROM.
2. Install the SCSI drive into an empty device bay.
3. Attach the SCSI ribbon cable and the power connector.
4. Start the workstation and ensure that Windows 2000 loads properly.
5. Double-click **My Computer** and verify that the new CD-ROM appears.

End of Exercise

✓ Instructor Check _____

Student Notes

Lab 10.3 Installing a Sound Card in Windows 98, NT, and 2000

Introduction

In this lab you will install and configure a sound card in Windows 98, Windows NT Workstation, and Windows 2000.

Maps to the following CompTIA A+ Objectives

A+ Core Hardware Service Technician Objectives
- Objectives 1.2, 1.7, and 1.8

A+ Operating System Technologies Objectives
- Objective 2.4

Required Materials
- Workstation with Windows 98, NT, and 2000 installed and configured
- Plug and Play sound card
- Speakers
- CD-ROM audio cable

Part One: Installing a Sound Card in Windows 98

1. Using proper ESD precautions, remove the workstation cover.
2. Insert and secure the sound card in the proper bus slot. (Figure 10.3.1)

Figure 10.3.1

3. Plug the speakers into the proper port on the sound card, and attach the CD-ROM audio cable between the CD-ROM and the sound card.
4. Start the workstation and ensure that Windows 98 loads properly.

210 Multimedia Devices

5. During the Windows 98 boot process, the Plug and Play sound card should be detected and the driver should be installed. If Windows 98 does not have the proper drivers, insert the driver disk and enter the proper path to the driver files. (Figure 10.3.2)

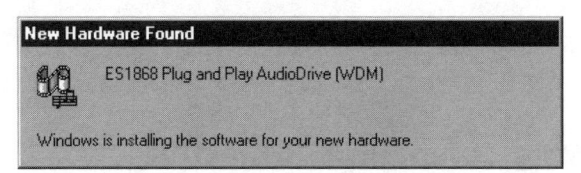

Figure 10.3.2

6. From the **Start Menu**, choose **Settings**, choose **Control Panel**, then double-click **System**. Expand the **Sound, Video and Game Controllers** category. The new sound card should appear. (Figure 10.3.3)

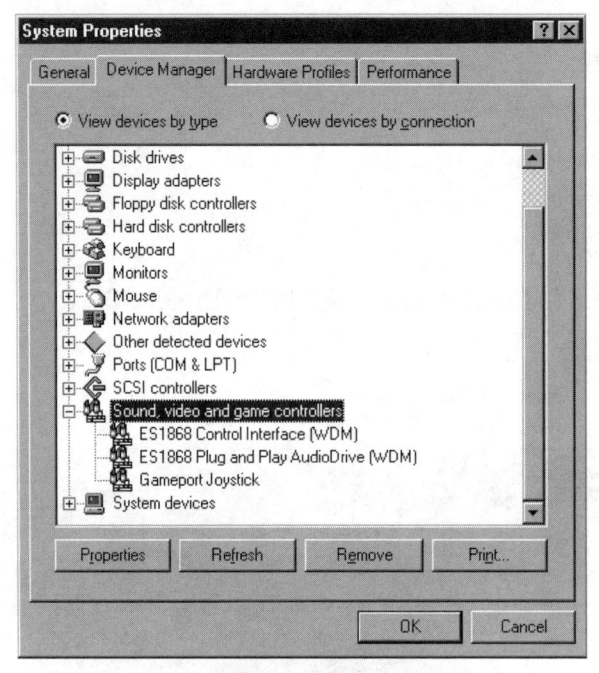

Figure 10.3.3

Part Two: Installing a Sound Card in Windows NT

1. Using proper ESD precautions, remove the PC cover.
2. Insert and secure the sound card in the proper bus slot.
3. Plug the speakers into the proper port on the sound card, and attach the CD-ROM audio cable between the CD-ROM and the sound card.
4. Start the workstation and ensure that Windows NT loads properly.
5. From the **Start Menu** choose **Settings**, choose **Control Panel**, then double-click **Multimedia**.

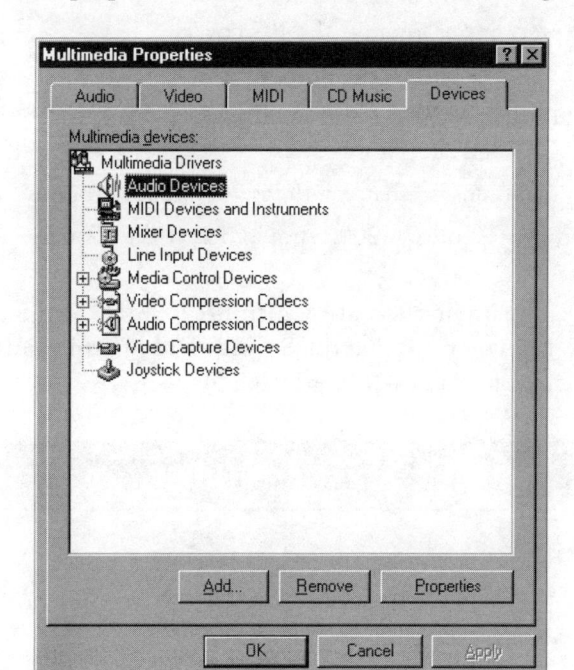

6. From the **Multimedia** properties box, select the **Devices** tab. (Figure 10.3.4)

Figure 10.3.4

7. Highlight **Audio Devices** then click **Add**.
8. Choose your sound card from the available list of drivers. If prompted, insert the Windows NT CD-ROM.

> **Note:** If your sound card is not listed, choose **Unlisted or Updated Driver,** and click **OK**. Browse to the location of the needed driver, then click **OK**.

9. If prompted, enter configuration information for your sound card. (Figure 10.3.5)

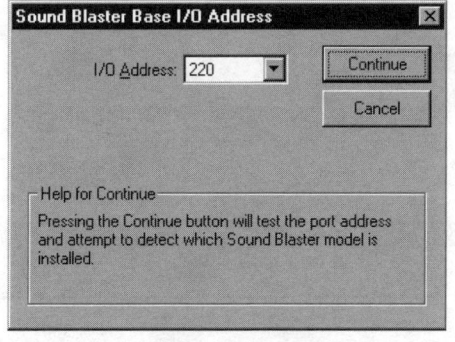

Figure 10.3.5

10. If prompted, restart your system for the new setting to take effect.

Multimedia Devices

Part Three: Installing a Sound Card in Windows 2000

1. Using proper ESD precautions, remove the PC cover.
2. Insert and secure the sound card in the proper bus slot.
3. Plug the speakers into the proper port on the sound card, and attach the CD-ROM audio cable between the CD-ROM and the sound card.
4. Start the workstation and ensure that Windows 2000 loads properly.
5. During the boot process, Windows 2000 should detect the sound card and install the drivers automatically.
6. To check the installation, right-click **My Computer**, choose **Properties**, choose **Hardware** then select **Device Manager**. Expand the **Sound, Video and Game Controllers** category. The new sound card should appear. (Figure 10.3.6)

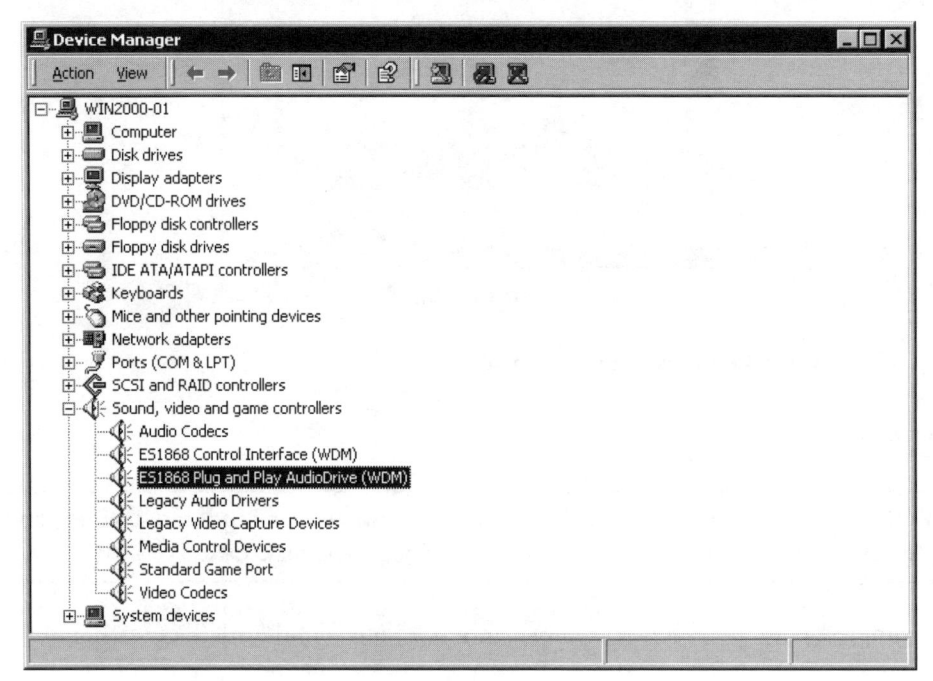

Figure 10.3.6

End of Exercise

✓ Instructor Check _____

Student Notes

CHAPTER 11

Serial Devices, Mice, and Keyboards

11.1 Installing an Internal Modem in Windows 98, NT, and 2000   214

11.2 Installing an External Modem in Windows 98, NT, and 2000   218

11.3 Installing a Serial Mouse   222

11.4 Installing a PS2 Mouse   224

Lab 11.1 Installing an Internal Modem in Windows 98, NT, and 2000

Introduction

In this lab you will install and configure an internal modem on Windows 98, Windows NT, and Windows 2000 workstations.

Maps to the following CompTIA A+ Objectives

A+ Core Hardware Service Technician Objectives
- Objectives 1.2, 1.3, and 1.7

A+ Operating System Technologies Objectives
- Objective 2.4

Required Materials
- Workstation with Window 98, NT, and 2000 installed and configured
- Internal Plug and Play modem

Part One: Installing an Internal Modem in Windows 98

1. Using proper ESD precautions, remove the PC cover.
2. Insert and secure the internal modem in the proper bus slot.
3. Start the workstation and ensure that Windows 98 loads properly.
4. During the boot process, Windows 98 should detect the Plug and Play modem. The **Add New Hardware Wizard** should start. (Figure 11.1.1)

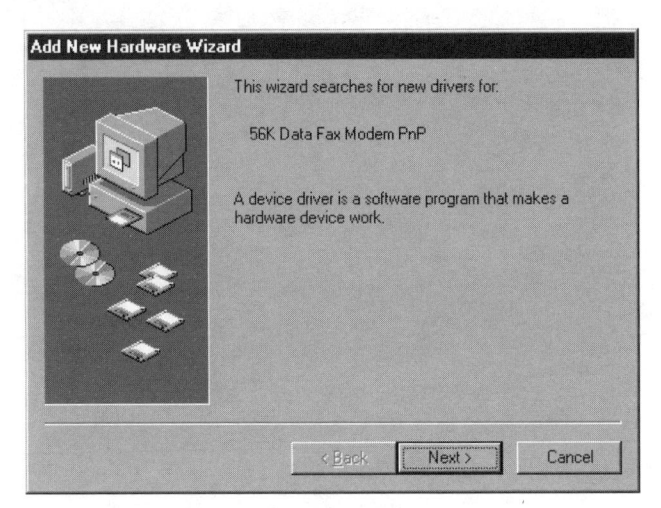

Figure 11.1.1

5. Select **Search for the best driver for your device**, then click **Next**.
6. If you have a vendor-supplied driver for the modem, insert the driver into the proper drive, specify the location of the driver, then click **Next**.

Lab 11.1 Installing an Internal Modem in Windows 98, NT, and 2000   215

7. When Windows 98 finds the appropriate driver, select **Next**, then click **Finish** to install the driver.
8. To check the modem installation, from the **Start Menu**, choose **Settings**, **Control Panel**, then double-click **Modems**. (Figure 11.1.2)

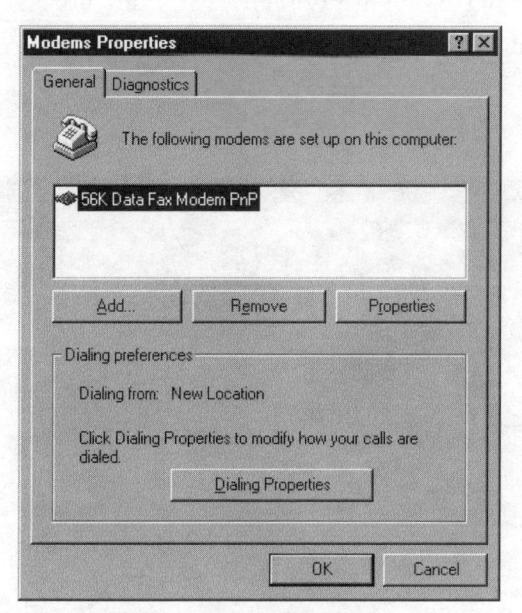

Figure 11.1.2

> **Note:** If prompted for location information, enter your area code, then select **Close**.

9. From the diagnostics tab, highlight the installed modem, then select **More Info**. The results of the modem test will be displayed. (Figure 11.1.3)

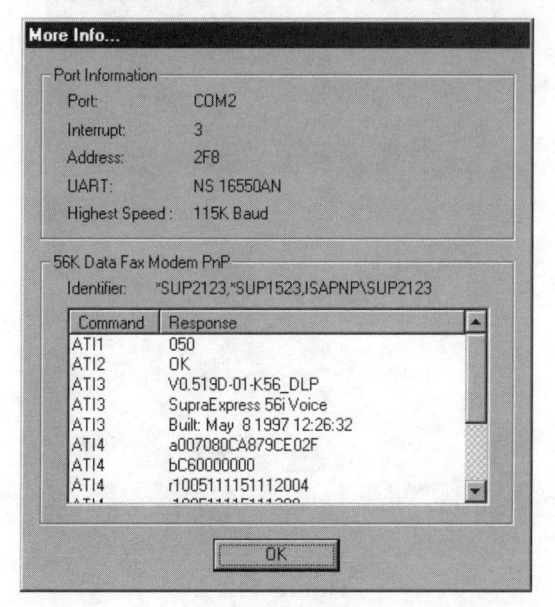

Figure 11.1.3

216 Serial Devices, Mice, and Keyboards

Part Two: Installing an Internal Modem in Windows NT

1. Using proper ESD precautions, remove the PC cover.
2. Insert and secure the internal modem in the proper bus slot.
3. Start the workstation and ensure that Windows NT loads properly.
4. From the **Start Menu**, choose **Settings**, **Control Panel**, then double-click **Modems**.
5. From the **Install New Modem Screen**, click **Next** to allow Windows NT to detect your new modem. (Figure 11.1.4)

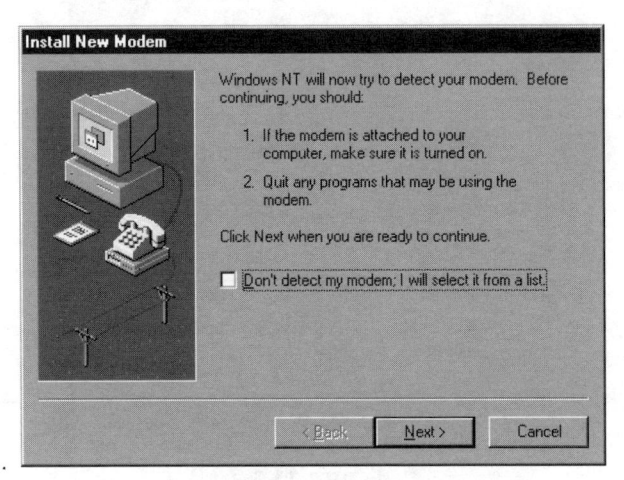

Figure 11.1.4

6. Windows NT will query your COM ports in an attempt to detect a modem. If a modem is detected, the modem's type will be displayed on the screen. If the modem type is correct, select **Next**, then click **Finish**. The new modem will now appear as installed. (Figure 11.1.5)

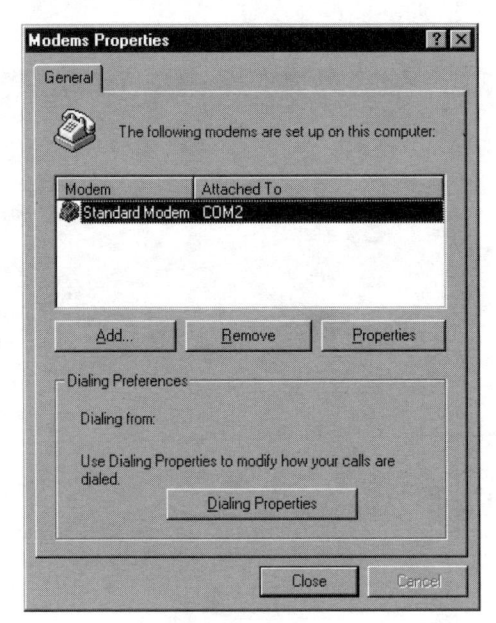

Figure 11.1.5

Lab 11.1   Installing an Internal Modem in Windows 98, NT, and 2000   217

Part Three: Installing an Internal Modem in Windows 2000

1. Using proper ESD precautions, remove the PC cover.
2. Insert and secure the internal modem in the proper bus slot.
3. Start the workstation and ensure that Windows 2000 loads properly.
4. During the boot process, Windows 2000 should detect the modem and automatically install the drivers.
5. To check the installation, right-click **My Computer**, choose **Properties**, **Hardware**, then select **Device Manager**. Expand the **Modems** category. The new modem should appear. (Figure 11.1.6)

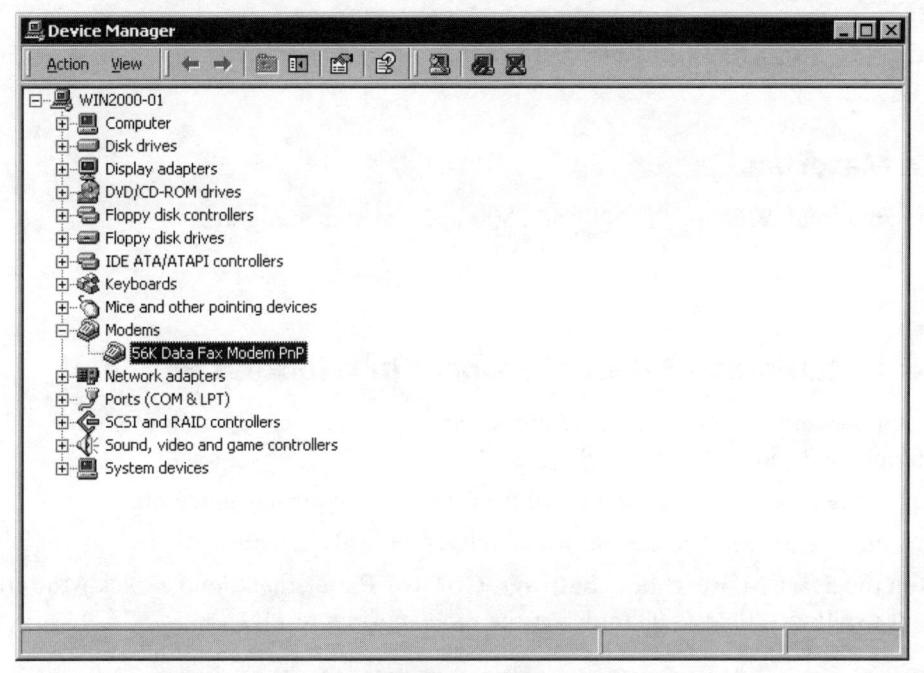

Figure 11.1.6

End of Exercise

✓ Instructor Check _____

Student Notes

218   Serial Devices, Mice, and Keyboards

Lab 11.2   Installing an External Modem in Windows 98, NT, and 2000

Introduction

In this lab you will install and configure an external modem on Windows 98, Windows NT, and Windows 2000 workstations.

Maps to the following CompTIA A+ Objectives

A+ Core Hardware Service Technician Objectives
- Objectives 1.2, 1.3, and 1.7

A+ Operating System Technologies Objectives
- Objective 2.4

Required Materials
- Workstation with Window 98, NT, and 2000 installed and configured
- External modem
- Serial cable

Part One: Installing an External Modem in Windows 98

1. Attach one end of your serial cable to the external modem, and attach the other end to the appropriate 9-pin or 25-pin COM port.
2. Plug in the modem power supply, and turn the modem power switch on.
3. Start the workstation and ensure that Windows 98 loads properly.
4. From the **Start Menu**, choose **Settings**, **Control Panel**, then double-click **Modems**. Click **Next** to allow Windows 98 to detect the modem. (Figure 11.2.1)

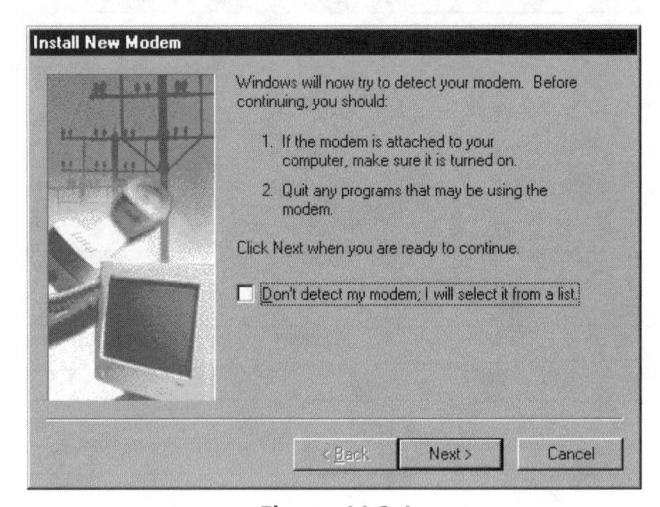

Figure 11.2.1

Lab 11.2 Installing an External Modem in Windows 98, NT, and 2000

5. Windows will query each COM port and attempt to detect a modem. When the modem is detected, verify the proper modem type is displayed, then click **Next**.

> **Note:** If the proper modem type is not displayed, click **Change** and then select the proper type from a list, or select **Have Disk** and enter a path to the modem driver file.

6. Click **Finish** to complete the Modem installation.
7. To check the modem installation, from the **Start Menu**, choose **Settings**, **Control Panel**, then double-click **Modems**.

> **Note:** If prompted for location information, enter your area code, then select **Close**.

8. From the diagnostics tab, highlight the installed modem then select **More Info**. The results of the modem test will be displayed.

Part Two: Installing an External Modem in Windows NT

1. Attach one end of your serial cable to the external modem, and attach the other end to the appropriate 9-pin or 25-pin COM port.
2. Plug in the modem power supply, and turn the modem power switch on.
3. Start the workstation and ensure that Windows NT loads properly.
4. From the **Start Menu**, choose **Settings**, **Control Panel**, then double-click **Modems**.
5. From the **Install New Modem Screen**, click **Next** to allow Windows NT to detect your new modem.
6. Windows NT will query your COM ports in an attempt to detect a modem. If a modem is detected, the modem type will be displayed on the screen. If the modem type is correct, select **Next**, then click **Finish**. The new modem will now appear as installed.

> **Note:** If the proper modem type is not displayed, click **Change** and then select the proper type from a list, or select **Have Disk** and enter a path to the modem driver file.

Part Three: Installing an External Modem in Windows 2000

1. Attach one end of your serial cable to the external modem, and attach the other end to the appropriate 9-pin or 25-pin COM port.
2. Plug in the modem power supply, and turn the modem power switch on.
3. Start the workstation and ensure that Windows 2000 loads properly.
4. From the **Start Menu**, choose **Settings**, **Control Panel**, then double-click **Phone and Modem Options**.
5. From the **Phone and Modem Options** screen, Choose the **Modems** tab, then select **Add**. Click **Next** to allow Windows 2000 to detect the new modem. (Figure 11.2.2)

220　Serial Devices, Mice, and Keyboards

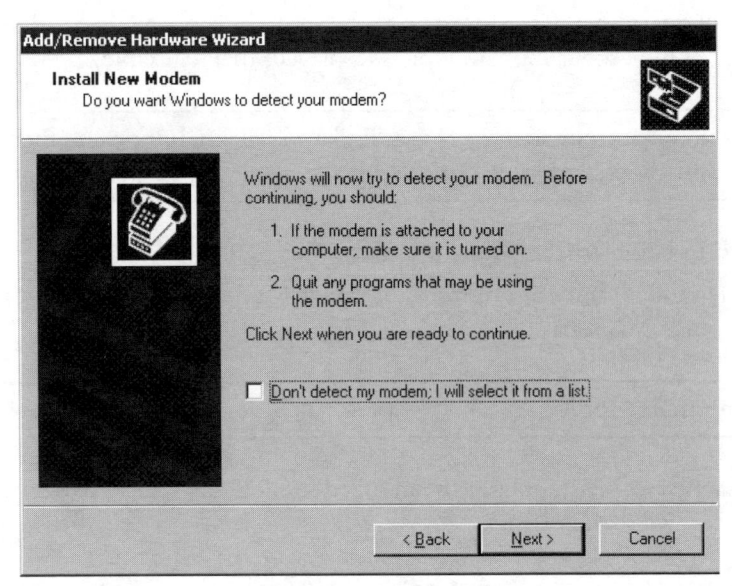

Figure 11.2.2

6. Windows 2000 will first attempt to detect any Plug and Play modems, and then will query each COM port. When the modem is detected the modem type will be displayed on the screen. If the modem type is correct, select **Next**, then click **Finish**. The new modem will now appear as installed. (Figure 11.2.3)

> **Note:** If the proper modem type is not displayed, click **Change** and then select the proper type from a list, or select **Have Disk** and enter a path to the modem driver file.

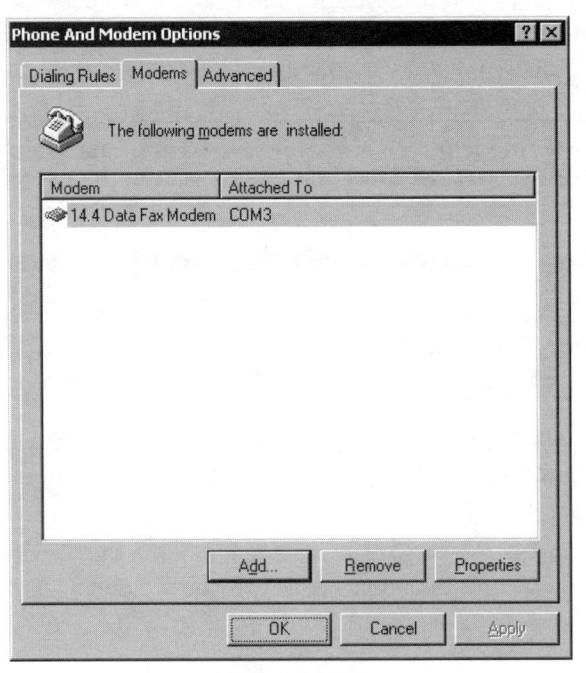

Figure 11.2.3

7. To check the installation, right-click **My Computer**, choose **Properties**, **Hardware** then select **Device Manager**. Expand the **Modems** category. The new modem should appear.

End of Exercise

✓ Instructor Check _____

Student Notes

Lab 11.3 Installing a Serial Mouse

Introduction

In this lab you will install and configure a serial mouse in Windows 98, NT Workstation, and 2000 Professional.

Maps to the following CompTIA A+ Objectives

A+ Core Hardware Service Technician Objectives
- Objectives 1.2 and 1.4

A+ Operating System Technologies Objectives
- Objective 2.4

Required Materials
- Workstation with Windows 98, NT Workstation, and 2000 Professional installed and configured
- Serial mouse

Part One: Installing a Serial Mouse in Windows 98

1. With the workstation off, remove the existing PS2 mouse, and install the serial mouse into the proper COM port.
2. Start the workstation and ensure that Windows 98 loads properly.
3. Windows 98 should detect the mouse and load the drivers.

Part Two: Installing a Serial Mouse in Windows NT

1. With the workstation off, remove the existing PS2 mouse, and install the serial mouse into the proper COM port.
2. Start the workstation and ensure that Windows NT loads properly.
3. Windows NT should detect the mouse and load the drivers.

Part Three: Installing a Serial Mouse in Windows 2000

1. With the workstation off, remove the existing PS2 mouse, and install the serial mouse into the proper COM port.
2. Start the workstation and ensure that Windows 2000 loads properly.
3. Windows 2000 should detect the mouse and load the drivers.
   - Which COM Port did you use to attach the serial mouse?

   - How many pins does a standard serial mouse connector have?

- Can you use a 25-pin COM Port for a serial mouse?

End of Exercise

✓ Instructor Check _____

Student Notes

Lab 11.4 Installing a PS2 Mouse

Introduction

In this lab you will install and configure a PS2 mouse in Windows 98, NT Workstation, and 2000 Professional.

Maps to the following CompTIA A+ Objectives

A+ Core Hardware Service Technician Objectives
- Objectives 1.2, 1.3, and 1.7

A+ Operating System Technologies Objectives
- Objective 2.4

Required Materials
- Workstation with Windows 98, NT Workstation, and 2000 Professional installed and configured
- PS2 mouse

Part One: Installing a PS2 Mouse in Windows 98

1. With the workstation off, remove the existing serial mouse and install the PS2 mouse into the proper port.
2. Start the workstation and ensure that Windows 98 loads properly.
3. Windows 98 should detect the mouse and load the drivers.

Part Two: Installing a PS2 Mouse in Windows NT

1. With the workstation off, remove the existing serial mouse and install the PS2 mouse into the proper port.
2. Start the workstation and ensure that Windows NT loads properly.
3. Windows NT should detect the mouse and load the drivers.

Part Three: Installing a PS2 Mouse in Windows 2000

1. With the workstation off, remove the existing serial mouse and install the PS2 mouse into the proper port.
2. Start the workstation and ensure that Windows 2000 loads properly.
3. Windows 2000 should detect the mouse and load the drivers.
4. If prompted, restart the workstation.
    - How many PS2-style ports are available on your workstation?

Lab 11.4 Installing a PS2 Mouse

- What would the result be if you plug the PS2 mouse into the wrong port?

___

- Can you use a PS2 mouse in a serial port?

___

End of Exercise

✓ Instructor Check _____

Student Notes

___

CHAPTER 12

Video

12.1 Installing a Video Adapter in Windows 98, NT Workstation, and 2000   228

12.2 Updating a Video Driver in Windows 98, NT Workstation, and 2000   231

12.3 Installing a Second Video Adapter and Monitor in Windows 2000   236

228 Video

Lab 12.1 Installing a Video Adapter in Windows 98, NT Workstation, and 2000

Introduction

In this lab you will install and configure a video adapter and the appropriate driver for Windows 98, NT Workstation, and 2000 Professional.

Maps to the following CompTIA A+ Objectives

A+ Core Hardware Service Technician Objectives
- Objectives 1.2 and 1.8

A+ Operating System Technologies Objectives
- Objectives 2.2 and 2.4

Required Materials
- Workstation with Windows 98, NT Workstation, and 2000 Professional installed and configured
- Video Adapter and driver
- Windows 98, NT and 2000 installation CD-ROMs

Part One: Installing a Video Adapter in Windows 98

1. Using proper ESD precautions, remove the PC cover.
2. Remove the old video adapter (if applicable) and install the new video adapter in the proper bus slot.
3. Start the workstation and ensure that Windows 98 loads properly.
4. During the boot process, Windows 98 should detect the new video adapter and load the proper drivers. (Figure 12.1.1)

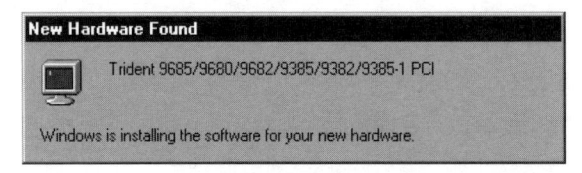

Figure 12.1.1

> **Note:** If Windows 98 cannot find the proper driver, insert the driver disk and/or enter the path to the driver files.

Part Two: Installing a Video Adapter in Windows NT

1. Using proper ESD precautions, remove the PC cover.
2. Remove the old video adapter, and install the new video adapter in the proper slot.
3. Start the workstation and ensure that Windows NT loads properly.

Lab 12.1 Installing a Video Adapter in Windows 98, NT Workstation, and 2000

> **Note:** If Windows does not start properly with the new video adapter, restart the workstation and, when prompted, choose to start the workstation in VGA mode.

4. If prompted that your current video display resolution is invalid, click OK to change the display settings. (Figure 12.1.2)

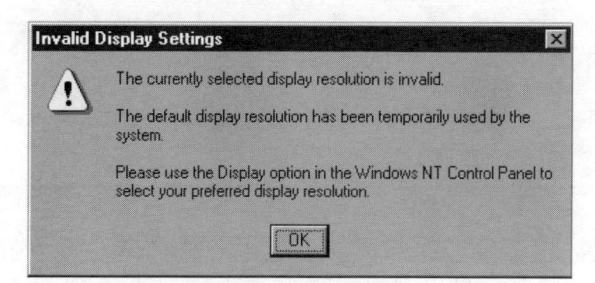

Figure 12.1.2

> **Note:** If no prompt was received, right-click the desktop and select properties.

5. From the **Display Properties Screen**, select **Display Type**, then click **Change**.
6. Select your video adapter from the list. If your adapter does not appear on the list, choose **Have Disk** and browse to the driver files. (Figure 12.1.3)

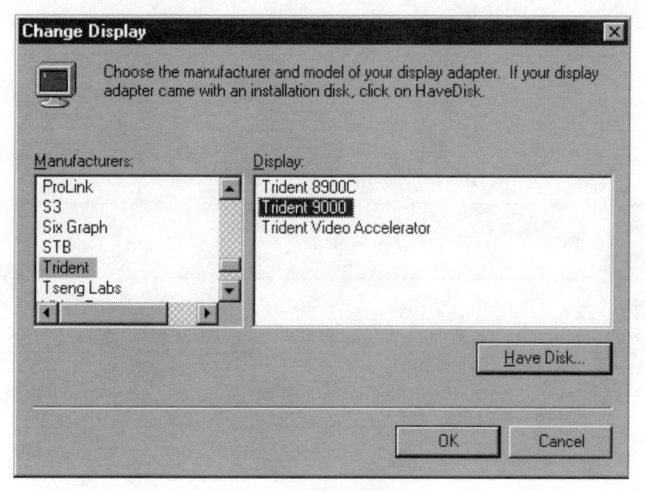

Figure 12.1.3

7. When the proper driver has been selected, click OK. If prompted, insert the Windows NT Workstation CD-ROM.
8. Windows NT will load the driver files for your new video adapter.

Part Three: Installing a Video Adapter in Windows 2000 Professional

1. Using proper ESD precautions, remove the PC cover.
2. Remove the old video adapter, and install the new video adapter in the proper bus slot.
3. Start the workstation and ensure that Windows 2000 Professional loads properly.

4. During the boot process, Windows 2000 Professional should detect the new video adapter and load the proper drivers.

> **Note:** If Windows 2000 Professional cannot find the proper driver, insert the driver disk and/or enter the path to the driver files.

End of Exercise

✓ Instructor Check _____

Student Notes

Lab 12.2 Updating a Video Driver in Windows 98, NT Workstation, and 2000

Introduction

In this lab you will install an updated video driver for Windows 98, NT Workstation, and 2000 Professional.

Maps to the following CompTIA A+ Objectives

A+ Core Hardware Service Technician Objectives
- Objective 1.8

A+ Operating System Technologies Objectives
- Objectives 2.2 and 2.4

Required Materials

- Workstation with Windows 98, NT Workstation, and 2000 Professional installed and configured
- Updated video driver
- Internet access
- Windows 98, NT, and 2000 installation CD-ROMs

Part One: Downloading the Latest Video Driver

1. Using proper ESD precautions, remove the PC cover.
2. Identify the manufacturer and model number of your video adapter.
   - Enter this information below.

_____

3. From a workstation with Internet access, browse to your video adapter manufacturer's Web site.
4. Search the Web site and download the latest driver version for your video adapter.

Part Two: Updating a Video Adapter Driver in Windows 98

1. Start the workstation and ensure that Windows 98 loads properly.
2. From the **Start menu**, choose **Settings**, **Control Panel**, then double-click **System**.
3. Choose the **Device Manager** tab, then expand the **Display Adapters** category. (Figure 12.2.1)
4. Right-click your display adapter, and select **Properties**.
5. Select the **Driver** tab, and then click **Update Driver**.

232 Video

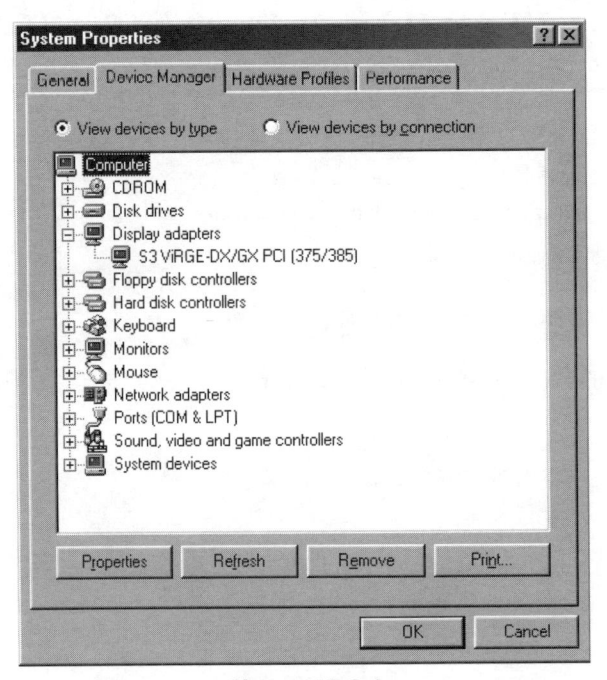

Figure 12.2.1

6. From the **Update Device Drive Wizard** screen, click **Next** twice, choose **Specify a Location**, enter a path to the downloaded driver file, and click **Next**. (Figure 12.2.2)

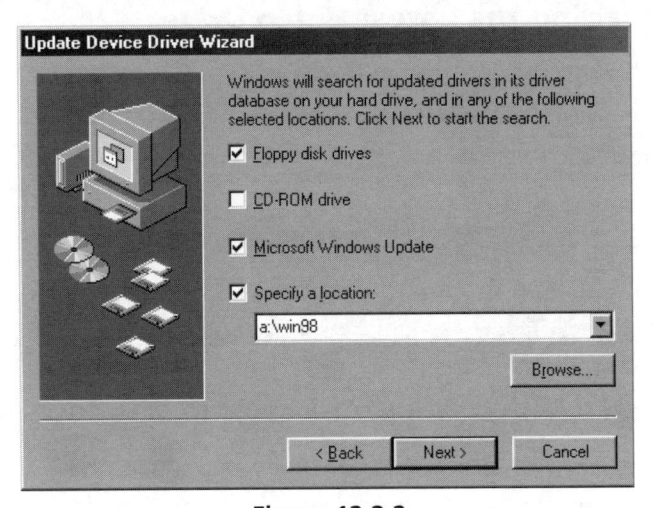

Figure 12.2.2

7. When the **Update Device Driver Wizard** finds the updated device driver, click **Next**, and then click **Finish**. The new driver will be installed.

Part Three: Updating a Video Driver in Windows NT

1. From the **Start Menu**, choose **Settings**, **Control Panel**, then double-click **Display**.
2. From the **Display Properties** screen, choose **Setting**, then click **Display Type**.
3. From the **Display Type** screen, click **Change**. (Figure 12.2.3)

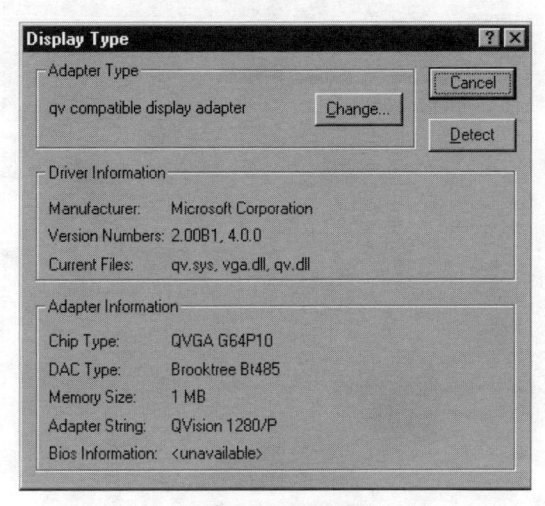

Figure 12.2.3

4. From the **Change Display** screen, choose **Have Disk**, enter a path to the downloaded driver files, and click **OK**.
5. When Windows NT finds the new driver files, click **Next** to start the update.

> **Note:** If prompted, insert the Windows NT installation CD-ROM or provide a path to the installation files.

6. When the driver files have been installed, restart your workstation.

Part Four: Updating a Video Driver in Windows 2000

1. Start the workstation and ensure that Windows 2000 loads properly.
2. Right-click the desktop and choose **Properties**.

3. From the **Display Properties** screen, choose **Settings**, then select **Advanced**. (Figure 12.2.4)

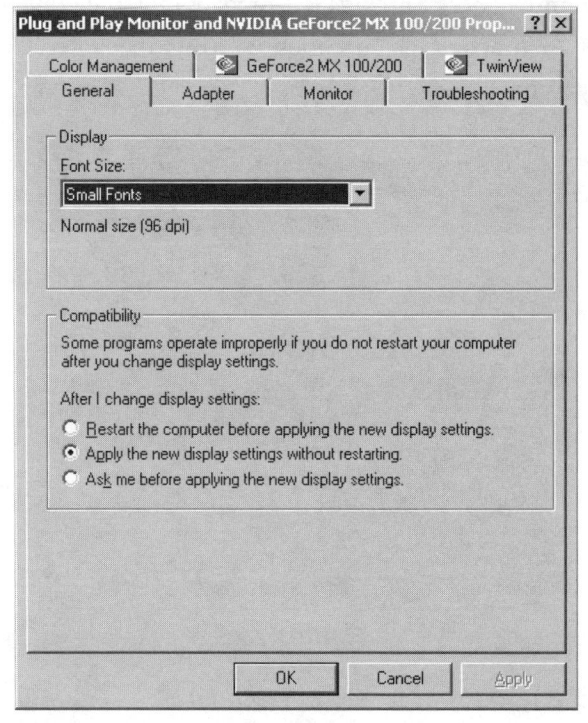

Figure 12.2.4

4. From the **Adapter** tab, choose **Properties**, select **Driver**, **Update Driver**, then click **Next**.
5. From the **Upgrade Device Driver** screen, choose **Next**, select **Specify a Location**, then click **Next**.
6. Enter a path to the downloaded driver file, then click OK. (Figure 12.2.5)

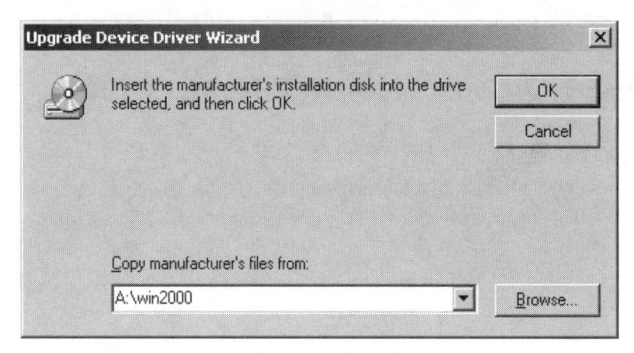

Figure 12.2.5

7. When Windows 2000 finds the driver file, click **Next** to allow the driver to be installed.

End of Exercise

✓ Instructor Check _____

Student Notes

Lab 12.3   Installing a Second Video Adapter and Monitor in Windows 2000

Introduction

Windows 98 and Windows 2000 allow you to install a second video adapter and monitor, and stretch your desktop across both monitors. In this lab you will install a second video adapter and monitor on a Windows 2000 Professional workstation.

Maps to the following CompTIA A+ Objectives

A+ Core Hardware Service Technician Objectives
- Objectives 1.2 and 1.8

A+ Operating System Technologies Objectives
- Objective 2.4

Required Materials
- Workstation with Windows 2000 Professional installed and configured
- Second PCI video adapter
- Second SVGA monitor and cable

Lab Procedure

1. Using proper ESD precautions, remove the workstation cover.
2. Install the second PCI video adapter in an available slot, and attach the monitor cable.
3. Start the workstation and ensure that Windows 2000 Professional loads properly. Windows 2000 will detect the new video adapter and install the drivers.
4. From the **Start Menu**, choose **Settings**, **Control Panel**, double-click **Display**, then select the **Settings** tab. (Figure 12.3.1)

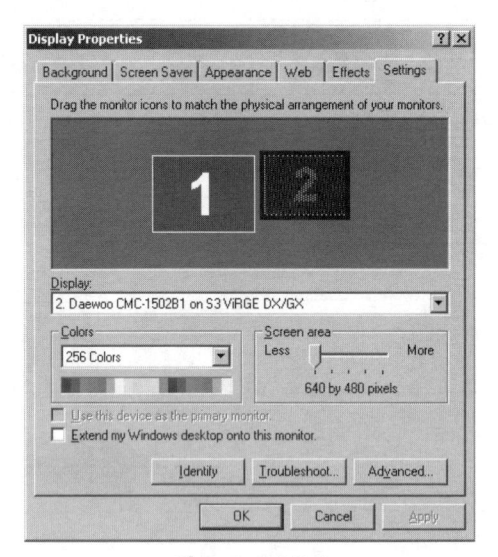

Figure 12.3.1

Lab 12.3 Installing a Second Video Adapter and Monitor in Windows 2000

❑ What other method can be used to access the Display properties screen?

___

___

___

___

5. Highlight the second monitor, select **Extend my Windows desktop onto this monitor**, then click **Apply**.
6. If prompted that Windows will try the new video settings for 15 seconds, click **OK**. If the new settings are working properly, click **Yes** to accept the new settings. Your desktop will now appear across both monitors and you can drag between the two. (Figure 12.3.2)

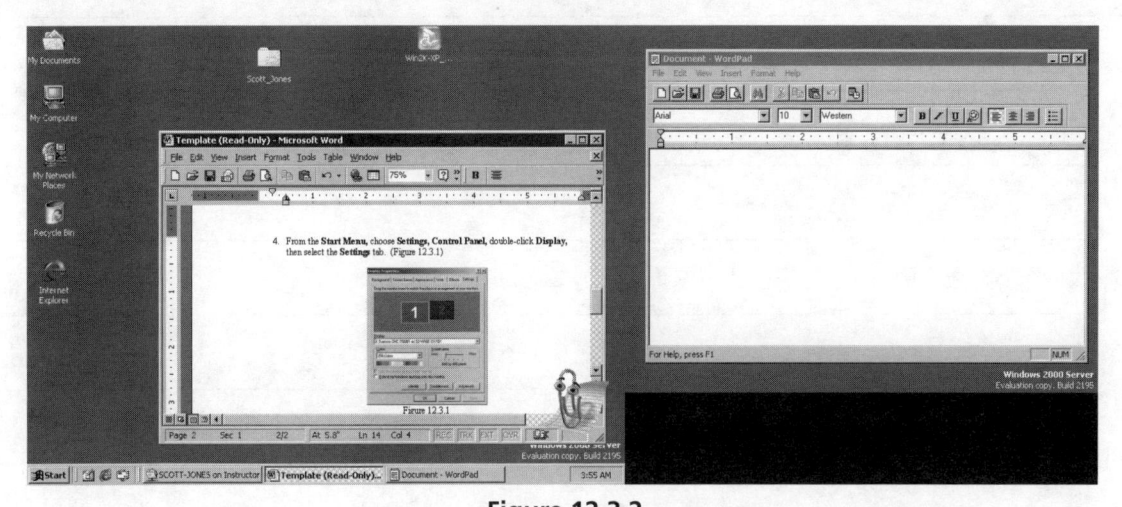

Figure 12.3.2

❑ What would be an advantage of using dual monitors?

___

___

___

___

___

End of Exercise

✓ Instructor Check _____

💡 Lab Notes

This lab will not work with every video adapter. At a minimum, the video adapters must be either AGP or PCI. Check the Microsoft Hardware Compatibility List (HCL) to verify that your adapters will work in a dual configuration.

Student Notes

CHAPTER 13

Printers

13.1 Installing a Printer in Windows 98   240

13.2 Installing a Printer in Windows NT Workstation   243

13.3 Installing a Printer in Windows 2000 Professional   246

13.4 Laser Printer Fundamentals   249

13.5 Ink Jet Printer Fundamentals   252

13.6 Troubleshooting Printers   255

Lab 13.1   Installing a Printer in Windows 98

Introduction

In this lab you will install and configure a printer in Windows 98.

Maps to the following CompTIA A+ Objectives

A+ Core Hardware Service Technician Objectives
- Objective 5.1

A+ Operating System Technologies Objectives
- Objective 2.4

Required Materials
- Workstation with Windows 98 installed and configured
- Printer and printer driver
- Bi-directional printer cable

Lab Procedure

1. Using the printer cable, attach the printer to the workstation and power on the printer.
2. Start your workstation and ensure that Windows 98 loads properly.
3. From **My Computer** double-click the **Printers** folder, then double-click **Add Printer**. The Add Printer Wizard will start. Click **Next**.
4. Choose **Local Printer**, then click **Next**. (Figure 13.1.1)

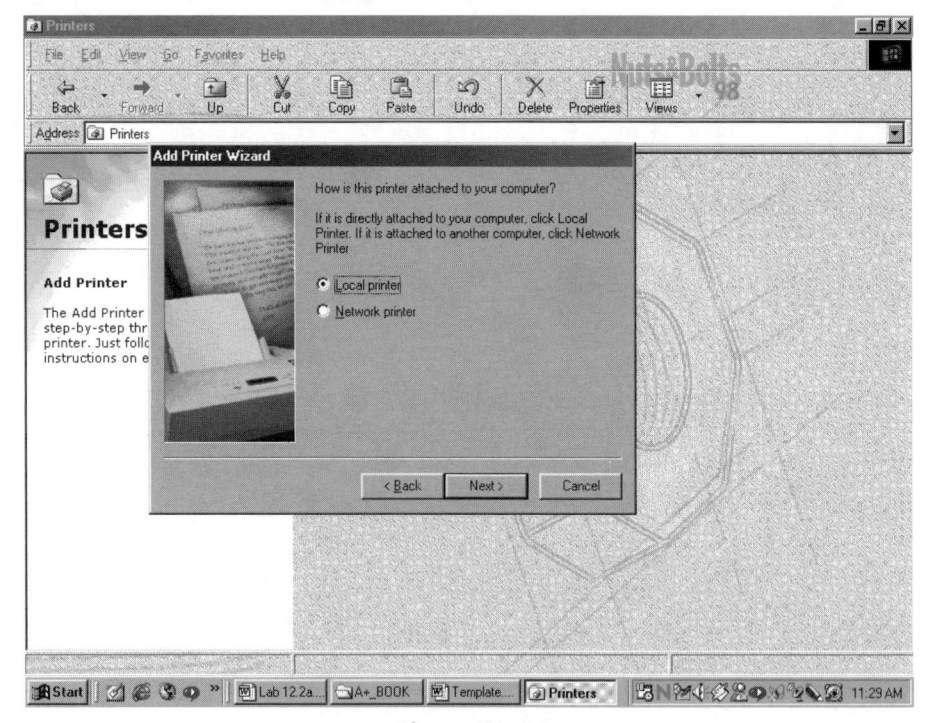

Figure 13.1.1

5. Choose your printer from the list, or if your printer is not listed, select **Have Disk**, enter a path to the printer driver files, and click **OK**. Click **Next** when your printer is selected. (Figure 13.1.2)

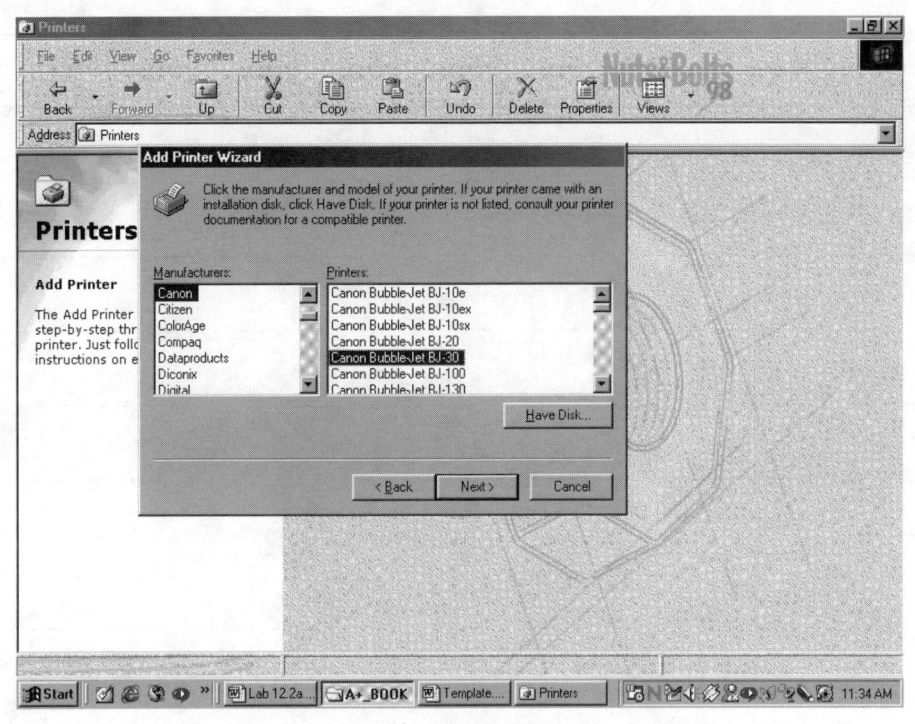

Figure 13.1.2

6. Select the proper printer port and click **Next**.
7. Enter a name for your printer, allow Windows 98 to use this printer as the default, then click **Next**.
8. Select **Yes** to allow Window 98 to print a test page, then click **Finish**. Windows 98 will install the driver for your printer. (Figure 13.1.3)

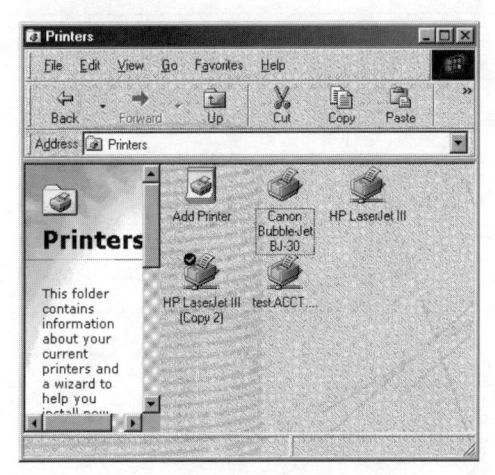

Figure 13.1.3

End of Exercise

✓ Instructor Check _____

Student Notes

Lab 13.2 Installing a Printer in Windows NT Workstation

Introduction

In this lab you will install and configure a printer in Windows NT.

Maps to the following CompTIA A+ Objectives

A+ Core Hardware Service Technician Objectives
- Objective 5.1

A+ Operating System Technologies Objectives
- Objective 2.4

Required Materials
- Workstation with Windows NT installed and configured
- Printer and printer driver
- Bi-directional printer cable

Lab Procedure

1. Using the printer cable, attach the printer to the workstation and power on the printer.
2. Start your workstation and ensure that Windows NT loads properly.
3. From the **Start Menu**, choose **Settings**, **Printers**, then click **Add Printer**.
    - What other method can be used to access the printers folder?

4. Choose **My Computer**, then click **Next**. (Figure 13.2.1)

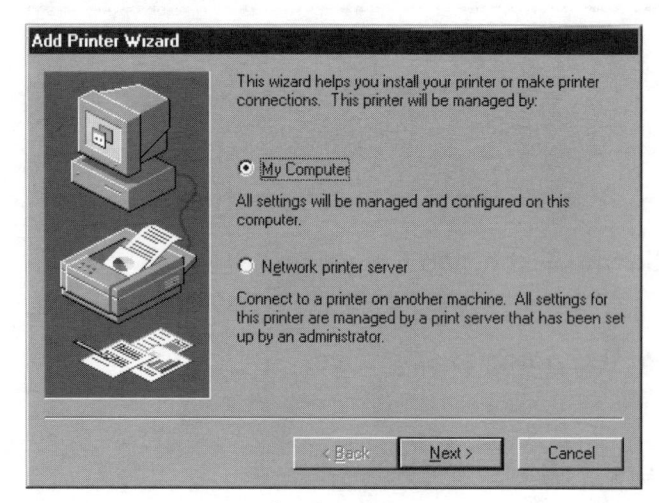

Figure 13.2.1

5. Select the proper printer port, then click **Next**.
6. Choose your printer from the list. If your printer does not appear, click **Have Disk**, enter a path to the driver files, then click **OK**. When the proper printer is selected, click **Next**. (Figure 13.2.2)

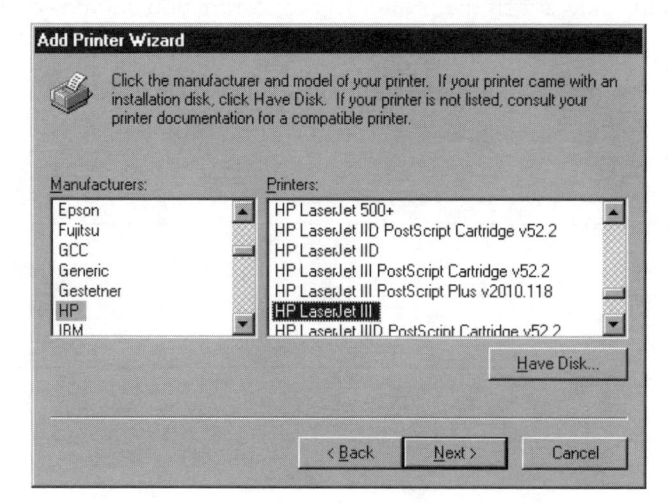

Figure 13.2.2

7. Enter a name for the printer, then click **Next**. Select **Not Shared**, then click **Next**.
8. Select **Yes** to print a test page, then click **Finish**.

> **Note:** If prompted, insert the Windows NT Installation CD-ROM or provide a path to the installation files.

9. Windows NT will install the drivers for your printer.

End of Exercise

✓ Instructor Check _____

Student Notes

246 Printers

Lab 13.3 Installing a Printer in Windows 2000 Professional

Introduction

In this lab you will install and configure a printer in Windows 2000.

Maps to the following CompTIA A+ Objectives

A+ Core Hardware Service Technician Objectives
- Objective 5.1

A+ Operating System Technologies Objectives
- Objective 2.4

Required Materials
- Workstation with Windows 2000 installed and configured
- Printer and printer driver
- Bi-directional printer cable

Lab Procedure

1. Using the printer cable, attach the printer to the workstation and power on the printer
2. Start your workstation and ensure that Windows 2000 loads properly.
3. From the **Start Menu**, choose **Settings**, **Control panel**, double-click **Printers**, then click **Add Printer**. The **Add Printer Wizard** will start. Click **Next**.
    - What other method can be used to access Control Panel?

    _____
    _____
    _____
    _____
    _____

4. Choose **Local Printer**, uncheck **Automatically Detect and Install my Plug and Play Printer**, then click **Next**.

5. Choose the proper printer port, then click **Next**. (Figure 13.3.1)

Figure 13.3.1

6. Choose your printer from the list, or if it is not listed, click **Have Disk** and enter a path to the driver files.
7. When the proper printer is selected, click **Next**. Enter a name for the printer and click **Next**.
8. Select **Do Not Share This Printer**, then click **Next**. Select **Yes** to print a test page, click **Next**, then **Finish**. Windows will install the driver files.
9. The new printer will now appear. (Figure 13.3.2)

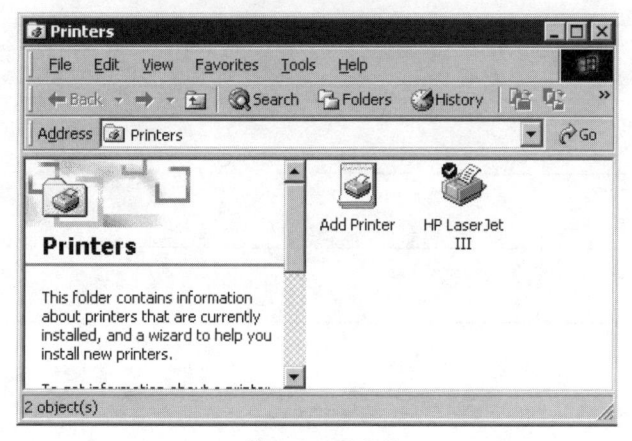

Figure 13.3.2

End of Exercise

✓ Instructor Check _____

Student Notes

Lab 13.4 Laser Printer Fundamentals

Introduction

In this lab you will review laser printer operation and troubleshooting fundamentals.

Maps to the following CompTIA A+ Objectives

A+ Core Hardware Service Technician Objectives
- Objectives 5.1 and 5.2

Required Materials
- Lab textbook
- Lab manual

Lab Procedure

1. There are six steps in the laser printing process:
   1. Cleaning
   2. Conditioning
   3. Writing
   4. Developing
   5. Transferring
   6. Fusing

   Study the following definitions and match them with the printing process step:

   _____ Toner is placed on the drum.

   _____ The surface of the drum is given a uniform electrical charge.

   _____ The electrical charge and any excess toner is removed from the drum.

   _____ Heat and pressure are applied to the paper and toner.

   _____ A laser beam draws an image on the drum.

   _____ Toner is drawn from the drum onto the paper.

1. Study the following laser printer problems and list possible causes and fixes for each problem:
   - Print jobs are becoming faded and hard to read

   _____

   _____

   _____

   _____

250 Printers

☐ Print jobs are totally black

☐ Print jobs are streaked or smeared

☐ Print jobs have repeating spots, streaks, or smears

☐ The laser printer prints unintelligible characters

End of Exercise

✓ Instructor Check _____

Student Notes

Lab 13.5 Ink Jet Printer Fundamentals

Introduction
In this lab you will review ink jet printer operations and troubleshooting fundamentals.

Maps to the following CompTIA A+ Objectives

A+ Core Hardware Service Technician Objectives
- Objectives 5.1 and 5.2

Required Materials
- Lab textbook
- Lab manual

Lab Procedure

1. Answer the following questions about how an ink jet printer operates:
    - Ink jet printers use a combination of three basic ink colors in addition to black. List those colors below:

        _____

        _____

        _____

    - What causes the ink to be sprayed onto the paper?

        _____

        _____

        _____

    - True or False: _____ Ink jet printers tend to print faster than laser jet printers.

2. Study the following ink jet printer problems and list possible causes and fixes for each problem:
    - Print jobs consistently have missing lines or parts of lines.

        _____

        _____

        _____

        _____

☐ Print jobs have ink streaks running lengthwise.

_____
_____
_____
_____
_____

☐ Color print jobs have faded color, or the colors are not the color they are supposed to be.

_____
_____
_____
_____
_____

☐ The ink jet printer prints unintelligible characters.

_____
_____
_____
_____
_____

End of Exercise

✓ Instructor Check _____

Student Notes

Lab 13.6 Troubleshooting Printers

Introduction
In this lab you will review printer troubleshooting techniques.

Maps to the following CompTIA A+ Objectives

A+ Core Hardware Service Technician Objectives
- Objective 5.2

Required Materials
- Workstation with Windows 2000 installed and configured
- Printer connected to a parallel or USB port, configured, and has power applied

Lab Procedure

> **Note:** There are four basic areas that can cause problems in the print process.
> - The workstation application
> - The operating system and/or printer driver
> - The connection between the printer and workstation
> - The printer itself
>
> In order to properly troubleshoot printer problems, the problem needs to be isolated to one of these four areas.

1. Disconnect the printer cable from the workstation.
2. Start your workstation and ensure that Windows 2000 loads properly.
3. Open the **Word Pad** application and type a simple sentence.
4. Attempt to print the **Word Pad** document.
   - What was the result of this action?

   _____
   _____
   _____
   _____

5. To see if the problem was with the application, attempt to print from a different application.

☐ Were you able to print from another application?

6. To see if the problem is with the operating system or driver files, from the **Start Menu**, choose **Settings**, then select **Printers**. Double-click the proper printer icon. From the **Printer** menu, choose **Properties**, then select **Print Test Page**. (Figure 13.6.1)

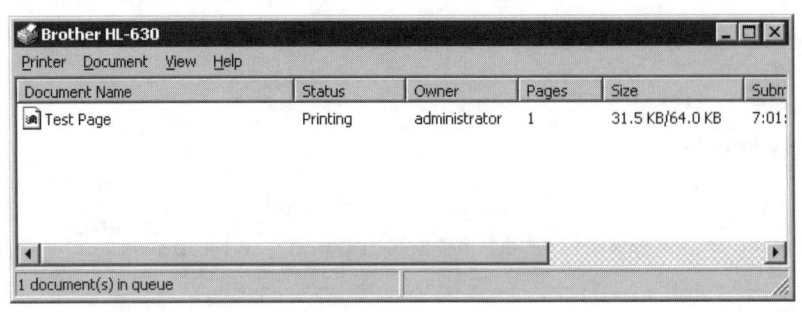

Figure 13.6.1

☐ Did the test page print job appear in the window?

7. If the print job appeared in the printer window, your operating system and driver files are functioning correctly.
8. To see if the problem is with the printer, use the onboard printer controls to print a test page. If your printer does not support this function, connect the printer to a different workstation and attempt to print.

   ☐ Was the printer test successful?

9. If the printer test was successful, the printer is working properly.
10. To test the printer and workstation connectivity, install a different printer cable and send a print job. (For the sake of this exercise, simply reconnect the printer cable to the workstation.)

    ☐ Were you able to successfully print?

End of Exercise

✓ Instructor Check _____

Student Notes

APPENDIX A

Using DOS in a Windows Environment

A.1 Opening a DOS Window in Windows 98, NT, and 2000   260

A.2 Finding Help for Using DOS Commands   264

A.3 Starting an Application from the DOS Command Line   267

A.4 Managing the File System from the DOS Command Line   268

Lab A.1   Opening a DOS Window in Windows 98, NT, and 2000

Introduction

Windows 98, NT, and 2000 allow some DOS applications to run. Windows 98 is best for this. Many times in the Windows NT/2000 environment, DOS applications must be upgraded to a newer Windows-based version.

Windows operating systems run DOS applications by creating a virtual DOS environment. In the Windows environment, the command prompt is accessed through a virtual DOS environment within a window.

In this exercise you will open a virtual DOS window in Windows 98, NT, and 2000.

Maps to the following CompTIA A+ Objectives:

A+ Operating System Technologies Objectives
- Objectives 1.1 and 1.2

Required Materials
- Workstation with Windows 98, NT, and 2000 installed and configured

Lab A.1 Opening a DOS Window in Windows 98, NT, and 2000   261

Part One: Opening a DOS Window in Windows 98

1. Start the workstation and ensure that Windows 98 loads properly.
2. From the **Start Menu**, choose **Run**, type **Command**, then click **OK**. A virtual DOS window will open on your desktop. (Figure A.1.1)

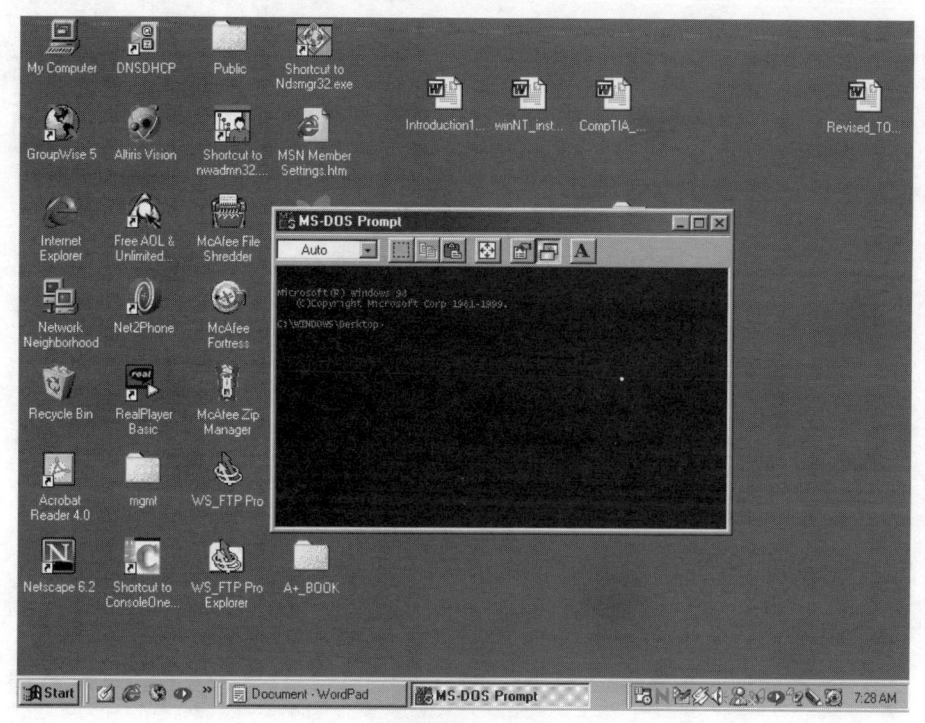

Figure A.1.1

□ What other method can be used to open a virtual DOS window in Windows 98?

_____

_____

_____

_____

_____

Using DOS in a Windows Environment

Part Two: Opening a DOS Window in Windows NT

1. Start the workstation and ensure that Windows NT loads properly.
2. From the **Start Menu**, choose **Programs**, then select **Command Prompt**. A virtual DOS window will open. (Figure A.1.2)

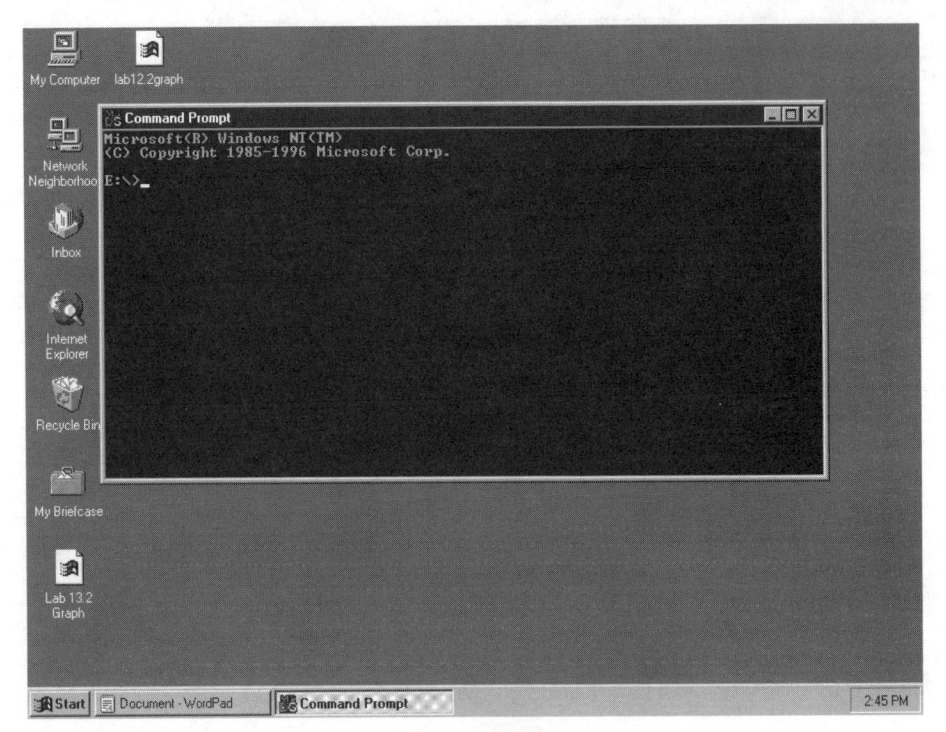

Figure A.1.2

□ What other method can be used to open a virtual DOS window in Windows NT?

___

Part Three: Opening a DOS Window in Windows 2000

1. Start the workstation and ensure that Windows 2000 loads properly.
2. From the **Start Menu**, choose **Run**, type **CMD**, and click **OK**. A virtual DOS window will open.

Lab A.1 Opening a DOS Window in Windows 98, NT, and 2000

☐ What other method can be used to open a virtual DOS window in Windows 2000

___

___

___

___

___

End of Exercise

✓ Instructor Check _____

> ### 💡 Lab Notes
> **Note:** From within a virtual DOS window, you can issue DOS commands, manipulate the file system, run utilities, and start applications.

Student Notes

Lab A.2 Finding Help for Using DOS Commands

Introduction

In this lab you will use the DOS Help to find DOS commands and their proper usage.

Maps to the following CompTIA A+ Objectives

A+ Operating System Technologies Objectives
- Objectives 1.1 and 1.2

Required Materials
- Workstation with Windows NT or 2000 installed and configured

Lab Procedure

> **Note:** This lab works in either Windows NT or 2000. To access help for DOS commands from within Windows 98, from a command prompt, type the command followed by a space then /? (e.g., FORMAT /?). Press enter. The help for the command will be displayed.

1. Start your workstation and allow Windows NT or 2000 to load.
2. Follow the steps in Lab A.1 and open a virtual DOS window.
3. From the command prompt, type **Help | more** and press **Enter**. A listing of the available DOS commands will appear. Press the space bar to scroll through the available commands. (Figure A.2.1)

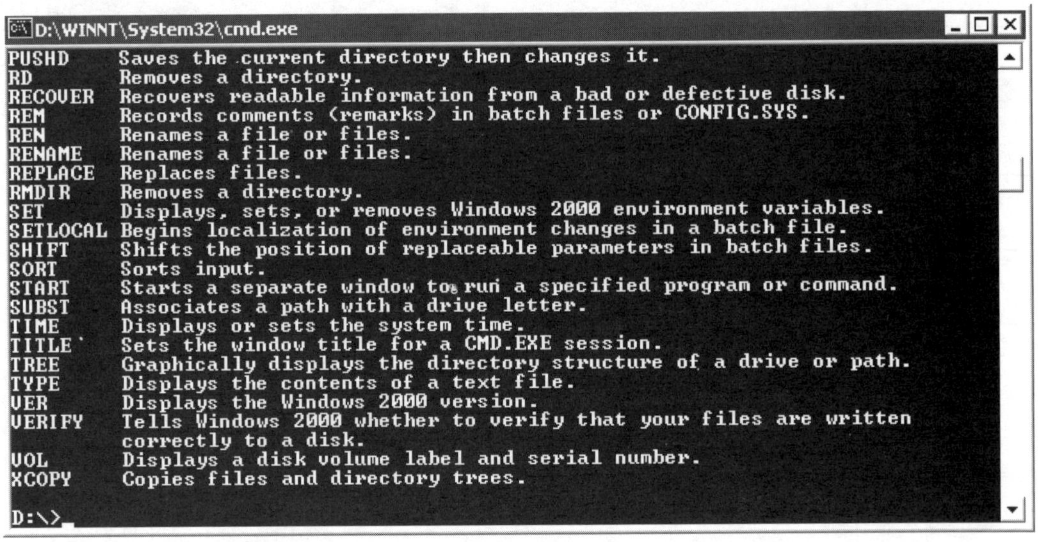

Figure A.2.1

Lab A.2 Finding Help for Using DOS Commands

4. To find help for a specific command, type *Command /?* (where *Command* is the specific command for which you need help) |, then press **Enter**. The usage and syntax for the specific command will be displayed. (Figure A.2.2)

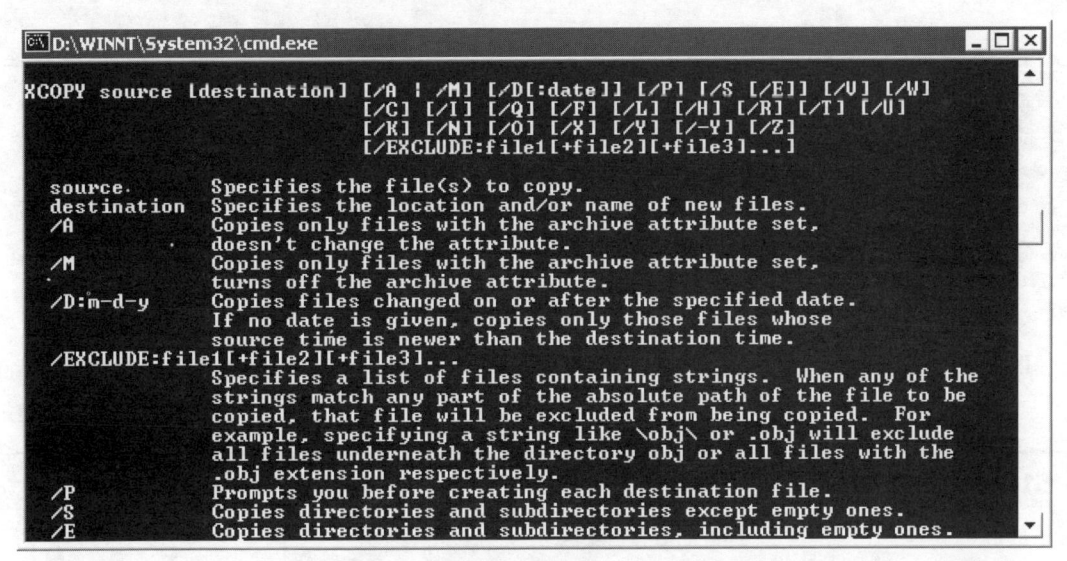

```
D:\WINNT\System32\cmd.exe

XCOPY source [destination] [/A | /M] [/D[:date]] [/P] [/S [/E]] [/V] [/W]
                           [/C] [/I] [/Q] [/F] [/L] [/H] [/R] [/T] [/U]
                           [/K] [/N] [/O] [/X] [/Y] [/-Y] [/Z]
                           [/EXCLUDE:file1[+file2][+file3]...]

  source       Specifies the file(s) to copy.
  destination  Specifies the location and/or name of new files.
  /A           Copies only files with the archive attribute set,
               doesn't change the attribute.
  /M           Copies only files with the archive attribute set,
               turns off the archive attribute.
  /D:m-d-y     Copies files changed on or after the specified date.
               If no date is given, copies only those files whose
               source time is newer than the destination time.
  /EXCLUDE:file1[+file2][+file3]...
               Specifies a list of files containing strings.  When any of the
               strings match any part of the absolute path of the file to be
               copied, that file will be excluded from being copied.  For
               example, specifying a string like \obj\ or .obj will exclude
               all files underneath the directory obj or all files with the
               .obj extension respectively.
  /P           Prompts you before creating each destination file.
  /S           Copies directories and subdirectories except empty ones.
  /E           Copies directories and subdirectories, including empty ones.
```

Figure A.2.2

5. Using DOS Help, answer the following questions:

    □ Which DOS command will give you a listing of all files in a directory?

    _____

    □ What does the XCOPY command do?

    _____

    _____

    □ Which DOS command would be used to change the name of a file?

    _____

    □ What command causes screen output to be displayed one screen at a time?

    _____

    □ Which command is used to make an exact copy of a disk?

    _____

266 Using DOS in a Windows Environment

- What would be the result of the following command: FORMAT C:

  _____

  _____

- What command graphically displays the directory structure of a path or drive?

  _____

End of Exercise

✓ Instructor Check _____

Student Notes

Lab A.3 Starting an Application from the DOS Command Line

Introduction

In this lab you will enter the proper DOS command to start an application.

Maps to the following CompTIA A+ Objectives

A+ Operating System Technologies Objectives
- Objectives 1.1 and 1.2

Required Materials
- Workstation with Windows 98, NT, or 2000 installed and configured

Lab Procedure

1. Start your workstation and ensure that Windows loads properly.
2. Open a virtual DOS window by following the steps in lab A.1.
3. From the DOS prompt, type **NOTEPAD.EXE** and press **Enter**. The Notepad utility should start.

End of Exercise

✓ Instructor Check _____

> ### 💡 Lab Notes
>
> **Note:** The Windows Graphical User Interface (GUI) uses icons to allow you to interface with the operating system (OS). The icon is nothing more then a shortcut to a command. Each icon has a command line associated with it as a property. By typing commands from a prompt, the computer is executing commands the same as when you click an icon.

Student Notes

Lab A.4 Managing the File System from the DOS Command Line

Introduction

In this lab you will use the DOS command line to create, browse, copy, and edit files and directories.

Maps to the following CompTIA A+ Objectives

A+ Operating System Technologies Objectives
- Objective 1.2

Required Materials
- Workstation with Windows 98, NT, and 2000 installed and configured

Part One: Creating Directories

1. Start the workstation and ensure Windows 2000 Professional loads properly
2. Open a virtual DOS window, following the steps in lab A.1.
3. At the command prompt, type **C:** and press **Enter**. This will ensure that you are working from the **C: drive**.
4. At the command prompt, type **CD ** and press **Enter**. This will ensure that you are at the **ROOT** of the **C: drive**. The command prompt should appear as **C:\>**.

   > **Note:** The Change Directory (CD or CHDIR) command allows you to navigate through the directory structure. **CD ..** will move you up one directory. **CD** *directory name* **(where** *directory name* **is the name of a directory or folder)** allows you to navigate up or down to adjacent directories.

5. At the command prompt, type **MD TESTDIR** and press **Enter**. This will create a directory named TESTDIR at the root of the C-Drive.
   - What other DOS command allows you to create a directory?

   _____

6. Use the **CD** command to change to the **TESTDIR** directory. Your command prompt should appear as **C:\TESTDIR>**.
   - What CD command did you use to change to the TESTDIR directory?

   _____

7. From the **TESTDIR** directory, create a directory called **MYDIR**.

Lab A.4 Managing the File System from the DOS Command Line

☐ What command did you use to create the **MYDIR** directory?

---

8. Navigate to the MYDIR directory and create the following directories:
   ☐ **DIR1**
   ☐ **DATADIR**
   ☐ **APPDIR**

Part Two: Creating Files

1. Navigate to the **C:\TESTDIR** directory.
2. At the command prompt, type **EDIT TESTFILE** and press **Enter**. The **DOS EDIT** utility will open. (Figure A.4.1)

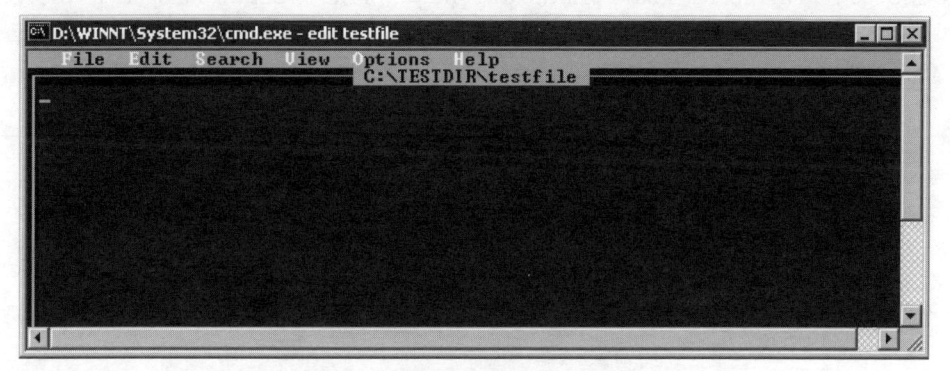

Figure A.4.1

3. From the **DOS EDIT** utility, type **This is a test file**.
4. Press the **Alt** key and then the **F** key. This will open the **File** menu. Using the arrow keys, select **Exit** and press **Enter**. When prompted to save the file, select **Yes**. The file will be saved.

> **Note:** The DOS EDIT utility can be used to create new files, or it can be used to open and edit existing files. DOS boot files such as CONFIG.SYS and AUTOEXEC.BAT can be created and edited with the EDIT utility.

5. Using the DOS EDIT utility, create the following files in your directory structure:
   ☐ In the **MYDIR** subdirectory, create **MYFILE** and **YOURFILE** files.
   ☐ In the **APPDIR** subdirectory, create **APPONE** and **APPTWO** files.
   ☐ In the **DATADIR** subdirectory, create **DATA1**, **DATATWO**, and **DATA-3** files.
   ☐ In the **DIR1** subdirectory, create **File1** and **File2** files.

Part Three: Browsing the Directory Structure

1. Navigate back to the **C:\TESTDIR** directory.
2. To see a listing of files and directories in the **TESTDIR** directory, type **DIR** and press **Enter**.

270 Using DOS in a Windows Environment

- What files and directories are listed in the **TESTDIR** directory?

3. Navigate to the **MYDIR**, **APPDIR**, **DATADIR**, and **DIR1** subdirectories and browse their contents using the **DIR** command.
4. To show a graphic representation of the directory and file structure, navigate to the **TESTDIR** directory. Type **TREE /F** and press **Enter**.
   - Draw the results of the **TREE** command below.

Part Four: Copying and Renaming Files and Directories

1. Navigate back to the **C:\TESTDIR** directory.
2. To rename the **TESTFILE** file, type **REN TESTFILE FILETEST** and press **Enter**.
3. Use the **DIR** command to ensure that the file name was changed.
   - Was the file name change successful?

___

4. To copy the **FILETEST** file, type **COPY FILETEST C:\TESTDIR\MYDIR\DIR1** and press **Enter**.
5. Navigate to the **C:\TESTDIR\MYDIR\DIR1** directory and ensure that the **FILETEST** file was copied.
   - Was the file copy successful?

___

End of Exercise

✓ Instructor Check _____

Lab Notes

Note: When using DOS commands to do directory searches, it is common to use wildcards to enable efficient searches. The asterisk character (*) can be used to replace an entire text string. (i.e., DIR *.TXT) A question mark can be used to replace a single character (i.e., DIR ?EAL.TXT).

Student Notes

___
___
___
___
___
___
___

Student Notes

APPENDIX B
Using Windows 98

B.1 Basic Windows 98 Operation 274

B.2 Managing the File System in Windows 98 279

B.3 Installing an Application in Windows 98 282

B.4 Starting an Application in Windows 98 284

Lab B.1   Basic Windows 98 Operation

Introduction

In this lab you will review basic Windows 98 operation.

Maps to the following CompTIA A+ Objectives

A+ Operating System Technologies Objectives
- Objectives 1.1 and 1.2

Required Materials
- Workstation with Windows 98 installed and configured

Part One: Navigating the Desktop

1. Start your workstation and ensure that Windows 98 loads properly.
2. To access the **Start Menu** programs, click the **Start** button, browse to the desired application, and click the applications icon to start the program. (Figure B.1.1)

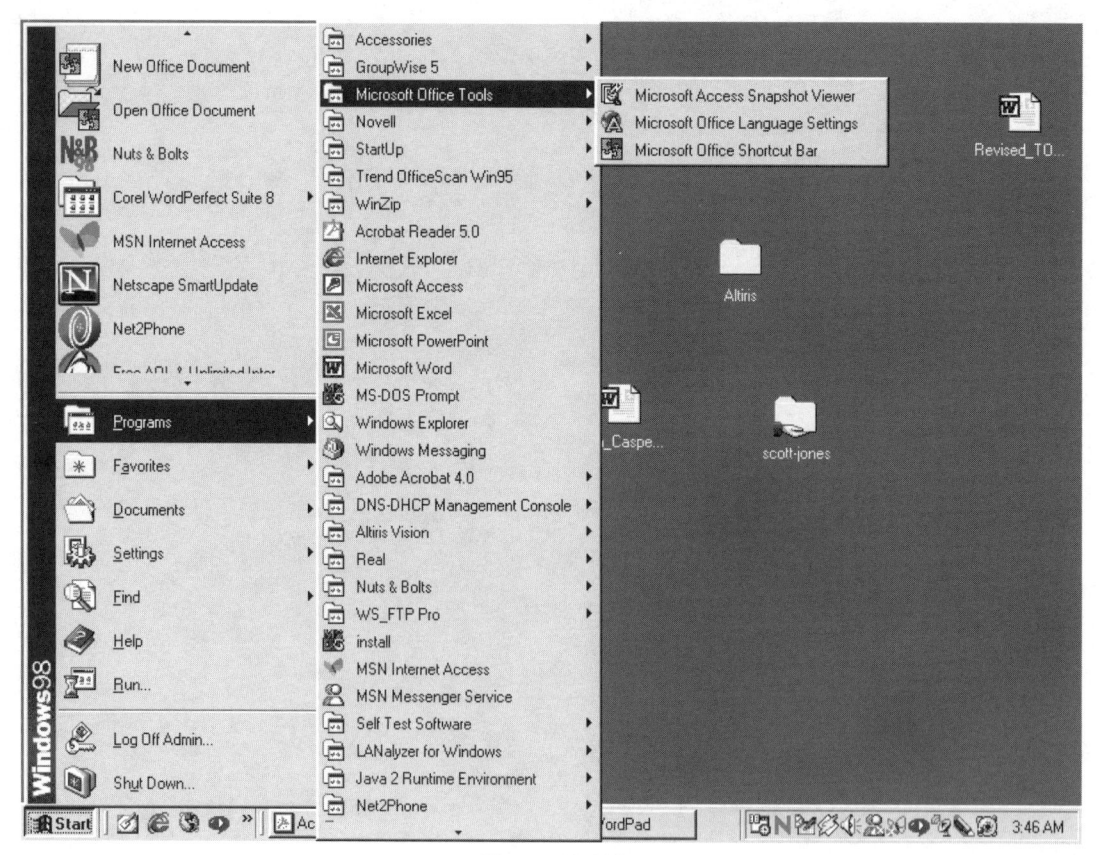

Figure B.1.1

Lab B.1   Basic Windows 98 Operation   275

3. To add a program to the **Start Menu**, right-click the **Start** button, then click **Open**. The **Start Menu** will open in a window. (Figure B.1.2)

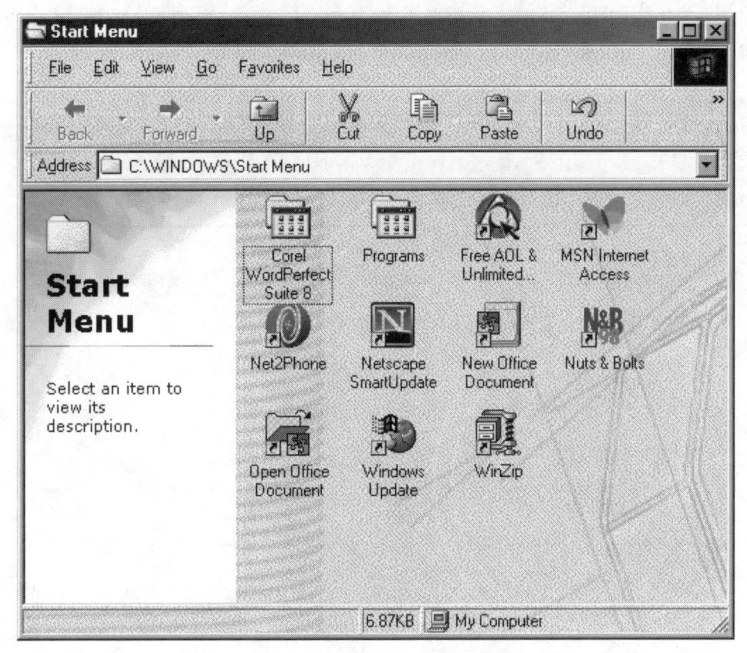

Figure B.1.2

4. Double-click the **Programs** folder. From the file menu, choose **New**, then select **Folder**.
5. Rename the new folder **Test Folder**, then open the folder.
6. From the **Start Menu**, choose **Find**, then select **Files and Folders**. Type **NOTEPAD.EXE**. Select your "C" drive to be searched, then click **Find Now**. (Figure B.1.3)

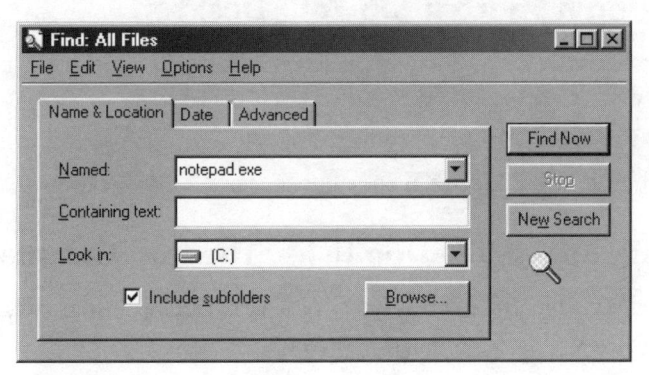

Figure B.1.3

7. When the **NOTEPAD.EXE** file is found, drag and drop the file into the **Test Folder** folder. Close all open windows on the desktop.
8. From the **Start Menu**, choose **Programs**, then select **Test Folder**. The **NOTEPAD.EXE** program should appear.

Part Two: Control Panel

1. From the **Start Menu**, choose **Settings**, then select **Control Panel**.
2. The **Control Panel** utility is used for adding and removing hardware, adding and removing software, and changing system configuration settings.

> **Note:** The utilities within the Control Panel are the safest way to manipulate your system configuration. These utilities directly access and edit the registry. It is much safer to allow the operating system to edit the registry than to do it yourself.

3. Browse the available Control Panel icons, then answer the following questions:
   - What icon would you access to remove a software program?

   _____

   - What icon would you access to change your networking protocols?

   _____

   - What icon allows access to device drivers and hardware profiles?

   _____

   - What icon allows you to configure a joystick?

   _____

Part Three: Creating a Shortcut on Your Desktop

1. From the **Start Menu**, choose **Find**, then select **Files and Folders**. Type **NOTEPAD.EXE**. Select your **C:** drive to be searched, then click **Find Now**.
2. When the **NOTEPAD.EXE** file is found, drag and drop the file onto the Desktop.
3. Double-click the **NOTEPAD.EXE** shortcut to start the application.

Part Four: Starting an Application Using the Run Command

1. From the **Start Menu**, choose **Run**, type **NOTEPAD.EXE**, then click **OK**.
2. The **NOTEPAD.EXE** application should run.

Part Five: Using Windows 98 Help

1. From the **Start Menu**, type **Help**. The **Windows Help** utility will open. (Figure B.1.4)

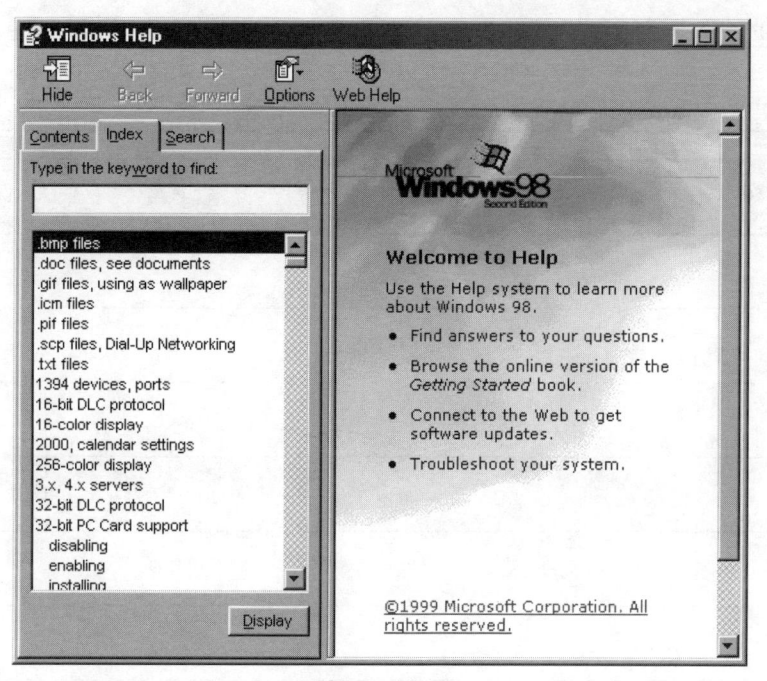

Figure B.1.4

2. Select the **Index** tab, type **TCP/IP**, then click the **Display** button.
3. From the **Topic Found** window, select **To assign a private IP address for a simple network**, then click the **Display** button. Read the displayed help file and answer the following questions:

   ▫ What is the name of the protocol that allows automatic IP addressing?

   _____

   ▫ What is the format of the Windows private automatic IP addresses?

   _____

   _____

End of Exercise

✓ Instructor Check _____

> ### 💡 Lab Notes
>
> **Note:** This lab has presented a very small portion of Windows 98 operation. Time and familiarity with the operating system will allow you to become proficient. Using the Windows Help utility will help to answer most questions you may have.

Student Notes

Lab B.2   Managing the File System in Windows 98

Introduction

In this lab you will use the Windows 98 My Computer and Windows Explorer utilities to create files and directories, rename files and directories, copy files and directories, and change the attributes of a file.

Maps to the following CompTIA A+ Objectives

A+ Operating System Technologies Objectives
- Objectives 1.1 and 1.2

Required Materials

- Workstation with Windows 98 installed and configured

Part One: Creating files and directories

1. Start the workstation and ensure that Windows 98 loads properly.
2. From **My Computer** browse to and open the **C:\TESTDIR** folder you created in Lab A.4.
3. From the **File** drop-down list, choose **New**, then select **Folder**. Name the folder **WIN98TEST**.
4. Open the **WIN98TEST** folder and create the following folders:
   - **WIN98-1**
   - **WIN98 ONE**
   - **WIN-98_1**
5. Open the **WIN98-1** folder. From the **File** drop-down list, choose **New**, then select **Text Document**. (Figure B.2.1)

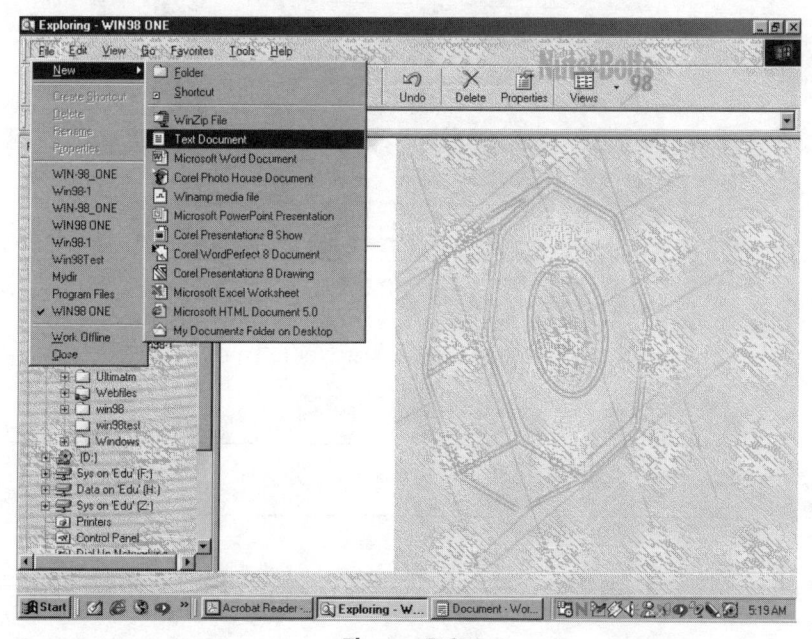

Figure B.2.1

6. Name the new text document **DOCUMENT ONE.TXT**, then create the following files:
   - In **WIN98 ONE** create **DOCUMENT TWO.TXT**
   - In **WIN-98_1** create **DOCUMENT THREE.TXT**

Part Two: Renaming and Copying Files

1. From the **Start Menu**, choose **Programs**, then select **Windows Explorer**.
2. Browse to the **C:\TESTDIR\WIN98TEST\WIN98-1\DOCUMENT ONE.TXT** file.
3. Right-click the **DOCUMENT ONE.TXT** file, then select **Rename**. Rename the file **DOC1.TXT** and press **Enter**.
4. To copy a file, right-click the **DOC1.TXT** file, and choose **Copy**. Browse to and open the **C:\TESTDIR\WIN98TEST** folder. Right-click in the folder window, and choose **Paste**. The **DOC1.TXT** file should be copied.

Part Three: Changing a File's Attributes

1. Right-click the **C:\TESTDIR\WIN98TEST\DOC1.TXT** file and select **Properties**. Select the **Read Only** attribute, and click **OK**. (Figure B.2.2)

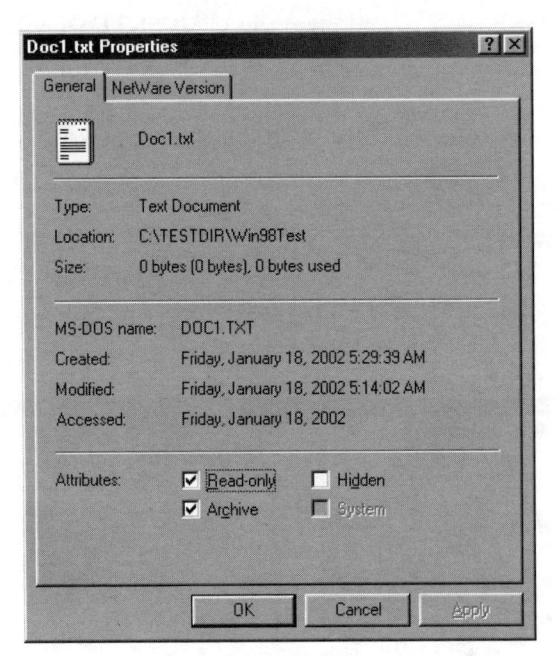

Figure B.2.2

- What will be the result of changing this file's attribute to read only?

Lab B.2 Managing the File System in Windows 98

☐ List the available attributes you can change:

_____
_____
_____
_____
_____

☐ What would be the result of changing this file's attribute to hidden?

_____
_____
_____
_____
_____

End of Exercise

✓ Instructor Check _____

💡 Lab Notes

A file's attributes are controlled by special "bits." These bits add special properties to a file when they are turned "on." You can also change a file's attributes by using the ATTRIB command from a command prompt.

Student Notes

_____
_____
_____
_____
_____

Lab B.3 Installing an Application in Windows 98

Introduction
In this lab you will download and install an application on Windows 98 workstation.

Maps to the following CompTIA A+ Objectives

A+ Operating System Technologies Objectives
- Objectives 1.1, 1.2, and 2.4

Required Materials
- Workstation with Windows 98 installed and configured
- Workstation with Internet access

Lab Procedure

1. From a workstation with Internet access, browse to the following URL: http://www.winzip.com/winzip/download.htm. Locate and download the latest version of the WinZip utility.

   > **Note:** WinZip is a file compression and unzipping utility. WinZip is distributed as shareware. You can install and evaluate this software for a period of 21 days. If you choose to use it beyond the 21-day limit, you must pay for and register the software. Be sure and follow the licensing and registration requirements for using this software.

2. From your Windows 98 workstation, execute the WinZip install executable. This can be done in one of several ways:
   - From the **Start Menu**, choose **Run**, type the path and file name of the installation executable, and click **OK**.
   - From **My Computer**, browse to and double-click the install executable.
   - If the workstation you are installing WinZip on is the same one you used to download the application, you will be given the option of starting the install process at the end of the download.
3. Follow all onscreen prompts to complete the install process.

End of Exercise

✓ Instructor Check _____

Lab Notes

In most cases, installing applications in Windows 98 will follow the above general steps. If your application is provided on a CD-ROM disk, it may be AUTORUN enabled. In this case, the installation process will start as soon as you insert the CD-ROM in the drive. Otherwise, you must browse the CD for the command that starts the installation process and double-click that command (which is normally SETUP.EXE).

Student Notes

Lab B.4 Starting an Application in Windows 98

Introduction

In this lab you will use various methods to start the application you installed in Lab B.3.

Maps to the following CompTIA A+ Objectives

A+ Operating System Technologies Objectives
- Objective 1.2

Required Materials

- Workstation with Windows 98 installed and configured
- Application from Lab B.3 installed

Part One: Starting an Application From the Start Menu

1. From the **Start Menu**, choose **Programs**, **WinZip**, then select the WinZip icon.
2. The WinZip application should run. (Figure B.4.1)

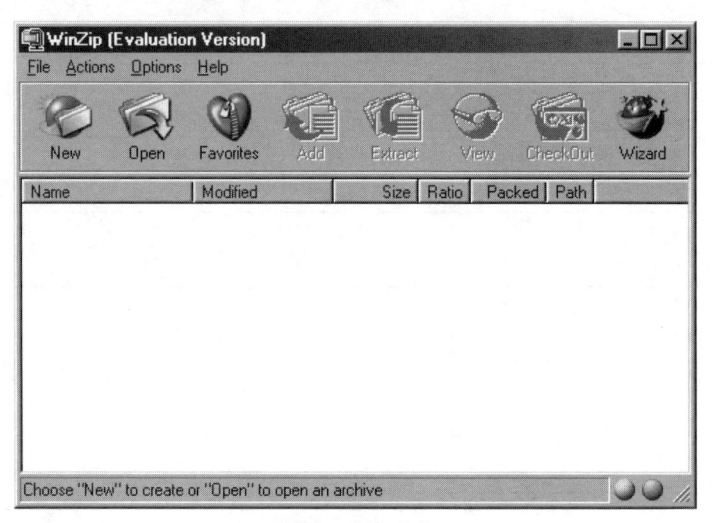

Figure B.4.1

Part Two: Starting an Application from the Run Command

1. From the **Start Menu**, choose **Run**, type **C:\PROGRAM FILES\WINZIP\WINZIP32.EXE**, then click **OK**.
2. The WinZip application should run.

Part Three: Starting an Application Using a File Extension

> **Note:** Windows 98 uses file extension associations to associate specific files with specific applications. When a file of this type is accessed, Windows 98 automatically starts the associated application and opens the file.

1. From **My Computer** browse to **C:\PROGRAM FILES\WINZIP**. Double-click the **EXAMPLE.ZIP** file. Using the file extension association, Windows 98 will automatically start the WinZip application, and the **EXAMPLE.ZIP** file will display in the window.

End of Exercise

✓ Instructor Check _____

Student Notes

APPENDIX C
Using Windows NT Workstation

C.1 Basic Windows NT Operation   288

C.2 Managing the File System in Windows NT   293

C.3 Installing an Application in Windows NT   296

C.4 Starting an Application in Windows NT   297

Lab C.1 Basic Windows NT Operation

Introduction

In this lab you will review basic Windows NT operation.

Maps to the following CompTIA A+ Objectives

A+ Operating System Technologies Objectives
- Objectives 1.1 and 1.2

Required Materials
- Workstation with Windows NT installed and configured

Part One: Navigating the Desktop

1. Start your workstation and ensure that Windows NT loads properly.
2. To access the programs that are on the **Start Menu**, click the **Start Menu** button, browse to the desired application, and click the applications icon to start the program.
3. To add a program to the **Start Menu**, choose **Settings**, **Task Bar**, then select **Start Menu Programs**. (Figure C.1.1)

Figure C.1.1

4. From the **Customize Start Menu** frame, choose **Add**.

5. Use the **Browse** button to browse to and select the **Notepad.exe** file (should be *X:*\WINNT\Notepad.exe where *X:* is the drive letter where NT is loaded). Click **Next**. (Figure C.1.2)

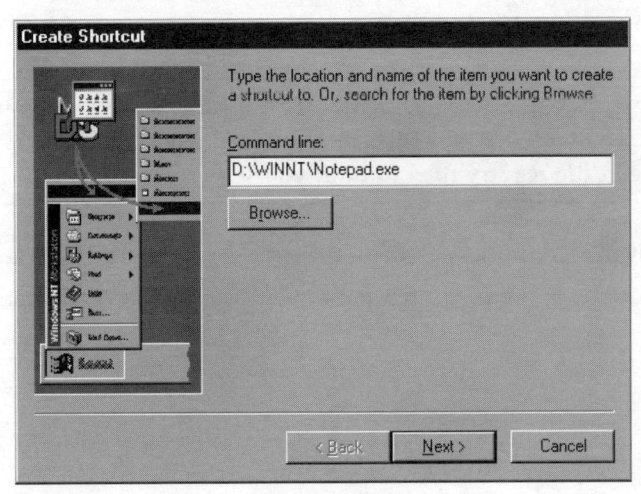

Figure C.1.2

6. From the **Select Program** folder, choose the **Programs** folder, and click **New Folder**.
7. Type **NOTEPAD** for the name of the new folder, and click **Next**.
8. Ensure that Notepad is listed for the name of the shortcut, and click **Finish**. The new Notepad Program should appear on the Start Menu. (Figure C.1.3)

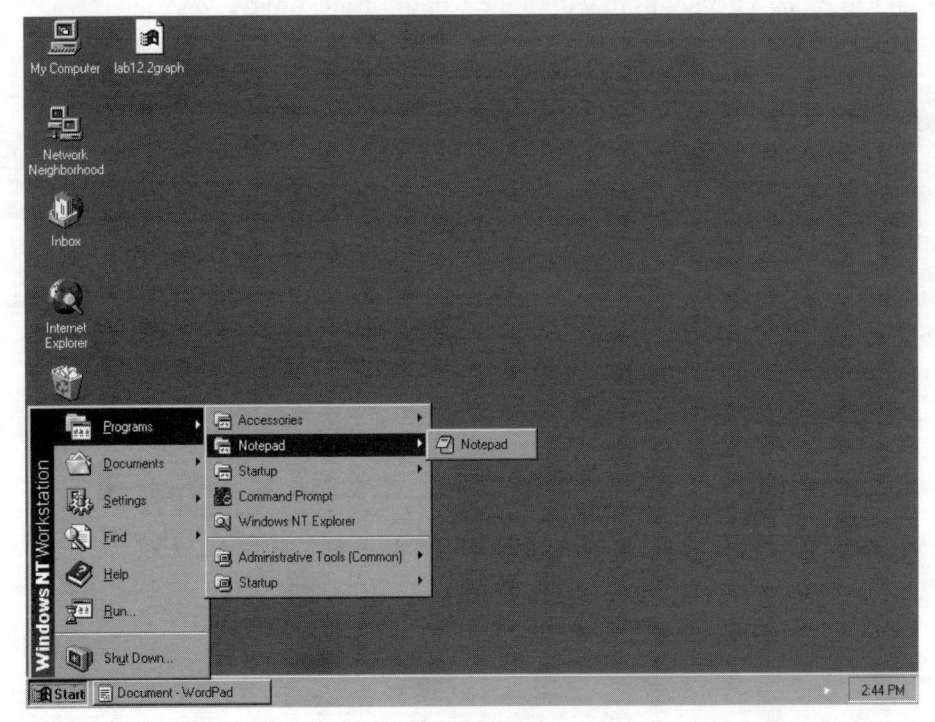

Figure C.1.3

290 Using Windows NT Workstation

Part Two: Control Panel

1. From the **Start Menu**, choose **Settings**, then select **Control Panel**.
2. The **Control Panel** utility is used for adding and removing hardware, adding and removing software, and changing system configuration settings.

> **Note:** The utilities within Control Panel are the safest way to manipulate your system configuration. These utilities directly access and edit the registry. It is much safer to allow the system to edit the registry then to do it yourself.

3. Browse the available Control Panel icons, then answer the following questions:
   - What icon would you use to configure the workstation shutdown options in case of a power failure?

   _____

   - What icon would you use to stop and start the Computer Browser Service?

   _____

   - What icon would you use to adjust the baud rate on a serial port?

   _____

   - Can you install a printer from within the Control Panel utility?

   _____
   _____

Part Three: Creating a Shortcut on Your Desktop

1. From the **Start Menu**, choose **Find**, then select **Files and Folders**. Type **Notepad.exe**. Select the drive where NT is loaded as the drive to be searched, then click **Find Now**.
2. When the **Notepad.exe** file is found, drag and drop the file onto the Desktop.
3. Double-click the **Notepad.exe** shortcut to start the application.

Part Four: Starting an Application Using the Run Command

1. From the **Start Menu**, choose **Run**, type **Notepad.exe**, then click **OK**.
2. **Notepad.exe** application should run.

Part Five: Using Windows NT Help

1. From the **Start Menu**, choose **Help**. The **Windows Help** utility will open. (Figure C.1.4)

Figure C.1.4

2. Select the **Index** tab, type **Emergency Repair Disk**, then click **Display**.
3. Read the displayed Help file and answer the following questions:
    - How often should you update your ERD?

    _____
    _____

    - What can you use an ERD for?

    _____
    _____
    _____
    _____
    _____

End of Exercise

✓ Instructor Check _____

> ### 💡 Lab Notes
>
> This lab has presented a very small portion of Windows NT operation. Time, use, and familiarity with the operating system will allow you to become proficient. Using the Windows Help utility will help to answer most questions you may have.

Student Notes

Lab C.2 Managing the File System in Windows NT

Introduction

In this lab you will use the Windows NT My Computer and Windows Explorer utilities to create files and directories, rename files and directories, copy files and directories, and change the attributes of a file.

Maps to the following CompTIA A+ Objectives

A+ Operating System Technologies Objectives
- Objectives 1.1 and 1.2

Required Materials
- Workstation with Windows NT installed and configured

Part One: Creating files and directories

1. Start the workstation and ensure that Windows NT loads properly.
2. From **My Computer** browse to and open the drive where NT is loaded.
3. From the **File** drop-down list, choose **New**, then select **Folder**. Name the folder **WINNTTEST**.
4. Open the **WINNTTEST** folder and create the following folders:
   - NT_TEST
   - NT-TEST
   - NT TEST
5. Open the **NT_TEST** folder. From the **File** drop-down list, choose **New** then select **Text Document**.
6. Name the new text document **NTDOC.TXT**, then create the following files:
   - In **NT-TEST** create **NTDOC TWO.TXT**
   - In **NT TEST** create **NTDOC THREE.TXT**

Part Two: Renaming and Copying Files

1. From the **Start Menu**, choose **Programs**, then select **Windows NT Explorer**.
2. Browse to the **X:\WINNTTEST\NT_TEST\NTDOC.TXT** file (where **X:** is the drive letter where NT is loaded).
3. Right-click the **NTDOC.TXT** file, then select **Rename**. Rename the file **NTRENAME.TXT** and press **Enter**.
4. To copy a file, right-click the **NTRENAME.TXT** file, and choose **Copy**. Browse to and open the **X:\WINNTTEST** folder (where **X:** is the drive letter where NT is loaded). Right-click in the folder window, and choose **Paste**. The **NTRENAME.TXT** file should be copied.

Part Three: Changing a File's Attributes

1. Right-click the **X:\WINNTTEST\NTRENAME.TXT** file (where **X:** is the drive letter where NT is loaded) and select **Properties**. Select the **Read Only** attribute and click **OK**. (Figure C.2.1)

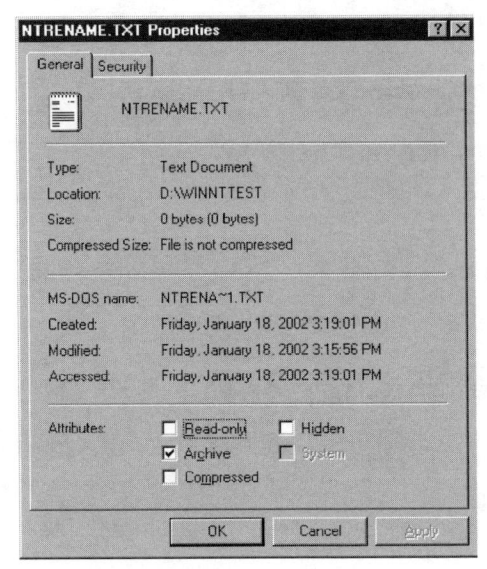

Figure C.2.1

- What will be the result of changing this file's attribute to read only?

- List the available attributes you can change:

☐ What would be the result of changing this file's attribute to compressed?

___

End of Exercise

✓ Instructor Check _____

> ### 💡 Lab Notes
> Windows NT (when using the NTFS file system) offers added file attributes that are specific to security and compression features.

Student Notes

___

Lab C.3 Installing an Application in Windows NT

Introduction
In this lab you will download and install an application on Windows NT workstation.

Maps to the following CompTIA A+ Objectives

A+ Operating System Technologies Objectives
- Objectives 1.1, 1.2, and 2.4

Required Materials
- Workstation with Windows NT installed and configured
- Workstation with Internet access.

Lab Procedure
1. From your Windows NT workstation, execute the WinZip install executable that was downloaded in Lab B.3. This can be done in one of several ways:
   - From the **Start Menu**, choose **Run**, type the path and file name of the installation executable, and click **OK**.
   - From **My Computer**, browse to and double-click the install executable.
2. Follow all onscreen prompts to complete the install process.

End of Exercise

✓ Instructor Check _____

> **Lab Notes**
>
> In most cases, installing applications in Windows NT will follow the previous general steps. Downloaded files may be zipped, and will require unzipping to uncompress the setup or other installation file. If your application is provided on a CD-ROM disk, it may be AUTORUN enabled. In this case, the installation process will start as soon as you insert the CD-ROM in the drive.

Student Notes

Lab C.4 Starting an Application in Windows NT

Introduction

In this lab you will use various methods to start the application you installed in Lab C.3.

Maps to the following CompTIA A+ Objectives

A+ Operating System Technologies Objectives
- Objective 1.2

Required Materials
- Workstation with Windows NT installed and configured
- WinZip application from Lab C.3 installed

Part One: Starting an Application from the Start Menu

1. From the **Start Menu**, choose **Programs**, **WinZip**, then select the WinZip icon.
2. The WinZip application should run. (Figure C.4.1)

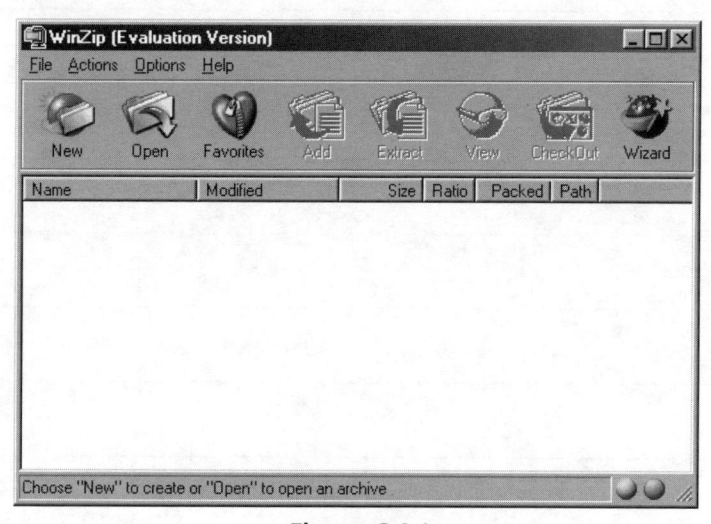

Figure C.4.1

Part Two: Starting an Application from the Run Command

1. From the **Start Menu**, choose **Run**, type **X:\PROGRAM FILES\WINZIP\WINZIP32.EXE** (where *X:* is the drive letter where NT is loaded), then click **OK**.
2. The WinZip application should run.

298   Using Windows NT Workstation

Part Three: Starting an Application Using a File Extension

> **Note:** Windows NT uses file extension associations to associate specific files with specific applications. When a file of this type is accessed, Windows NT automatically starts the associated application and opens the file.

1. From **My Computer** browse to **X:\PROGRAM FILES\WINZIP** (where **X:** is the drive letter where NT is loaded). Double-click the **EXAMPLE.ZIP** file. Using the file extension association, Windows NT will automatically start the WinZip application.

End of Exercise

✓ Instructor Check _____

Student Notes

APPENDIX D

Using Windows 2000 Professional

D.1 Basic Windows 2000 Operation 300

D.2 Right-click Managing the File System in Windows 2000 306

D.3 Installing an Application in Windows 2000 310

D.4 Starting an Application in Windows 2000 311

Lab D.1 Basic Windows 2000 Operation

Introduction

In this lab you will review basic Windows 2000 operation.

Maps to the following CompTIA A+ Objectives

A+ Operating System Technologies Objectives
- Objectives 1.1 and 1.2

Required Materials
- Workstation with Windows 2000 installed and configured

Part One: Navigating the Desktop

1. Start your workstation and ensure that Windows 2000 loads properly.
2. To access the programs that are on the **Start Menu**, click the **Start Menu** button, browse to the desired application, and click the applications icon to start the program.
3. To add a program to the **Start Menu**, choose **Settings**, **Task Bar and Start Menu**, then select **Advanced**. (Figure D.1.1)

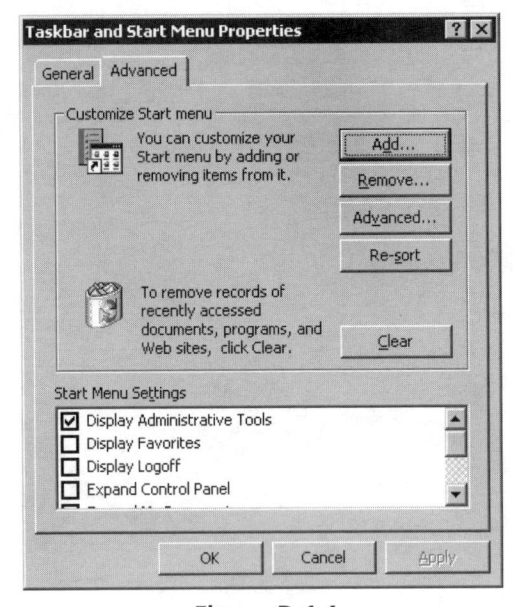

Figure D.1.1

4. From the **Customize Start Menu** frame, choose **Add**.

Lab D.1 Basic Windows 2000 Operation

5. Use the browse button to browse to and select the **NOTEPAD.EXE** file. (It should be *X:***WINNT\NOTEPAD.EXE**, where *X:* is the drive letter where Windows 2000 is loaded.) Click **Next**. (Figure D.1.2)

Figure D.1.2

6. From the **Select Program** folder, choose the **Programs** folder, and click **New Folder**.
7. Type **NOTEPAD** for the name of the new folder, and click **Next**.
8. Ensure that Notepad is listed for the name of the shortcut, and click **Finish**. The new Notepad Program should appear on the **Start Menu**.

Part Two: Control Panel

1. From the **Start Menu**, choose **Settings**, then select **Control Panel**.
2. The **Control Panel** utility is used for adding and removing hardware, adding and removing software, and changing system configuration settings.

> **Note:** The utilities within the Control Panel are the safest way to manipulate your system configuration. These utilities directly access and edit the registry. It is much safer to allow the system to edit the registry than to do it yourself.

3. Browse the available Control Panel icons, then answer the following questions:
   - What icon would you use to configure scanner and camera attachments on your workstation?

302 Using Windows 2000 Professional

☐ For what would you use the Administrative Tools folder?

___

___

___

___

___

☐ Which icon would you use to set options for people with handicaps?

___

Part Three: Using the MMC (Microsoft Management Console)

> **Note:** The MMC is a Windows 2000 system management and configuration utility. The MMC gives you the ability to create your own fully customizable management consoles and store them wherever you wish.

1. From the **Start Menu**, choose **Run**, type **CMD**, then click **OK**. The Windows command prompt window will appear.
2. From the Command prompt, type **MMC** and press **Enter**. The MMC Console1 utility will open. (Figure D.1.3)

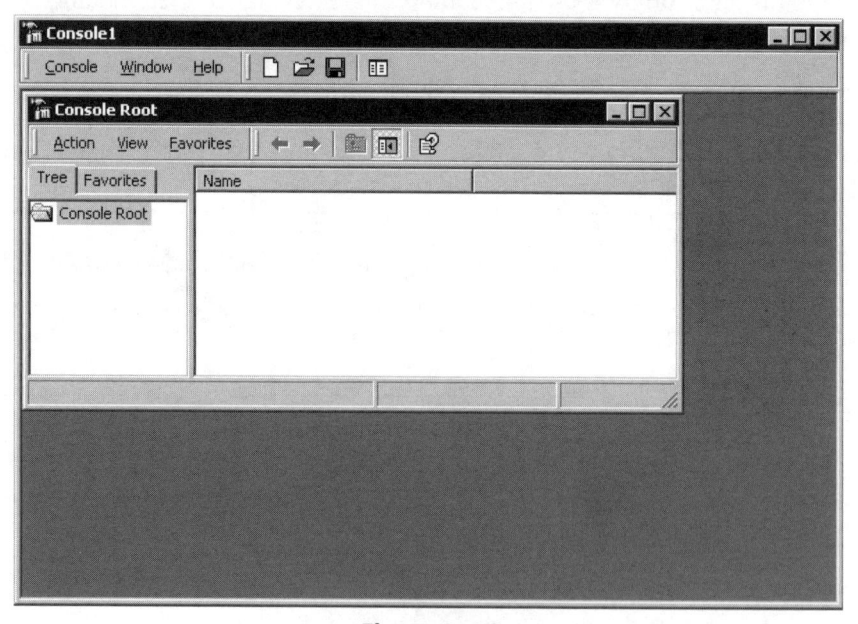

Figure D.1.3

3. From the **Console1** utility choose **Console**, then select **Add Remove Snapin**. (Figure D.1.4)

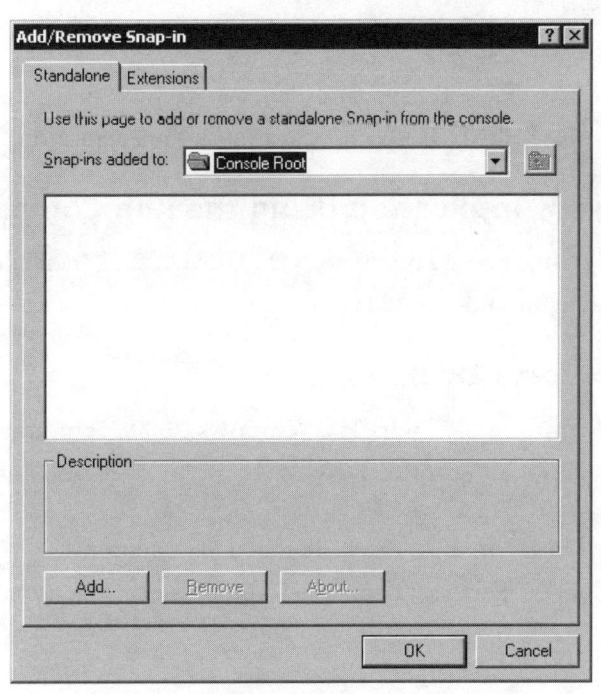

Figure D.1.4

4. From the **Standalone** tab, choose **Add**, select **Computer Management**, then click **Add**.
5. Select **Local Computer**, then click **Finish**. Close the **Add Standalone Snap-ins** Window and click **OK**. The **Computer Management** snap-in will appear in the **Console1** window. (Figure D.1.5)

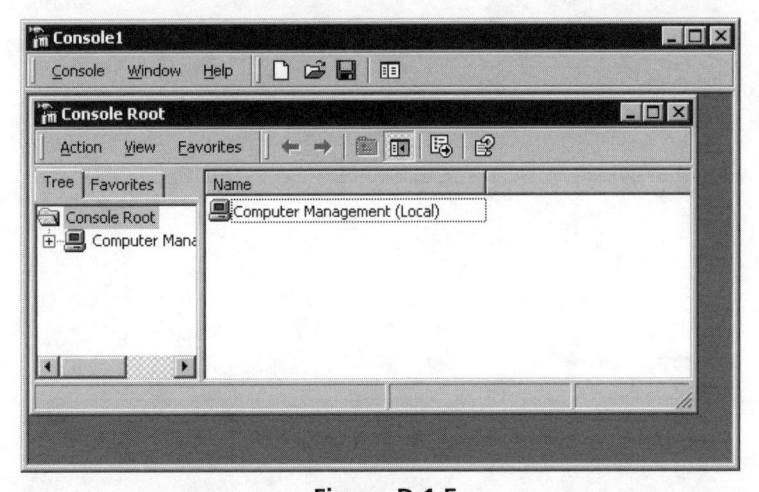

Figure D.1.5

6. From the **Console** drop-down menu, choose **Save As**. In the **Save in** window choose **Desktop**, for the **File name** type **Manager**, then click **Save**.
7. Close all open windows. The new **Manager** MMC should appear on your desktop.

Part Four: Creating a Shortcut on Your Desktop

1. From the **Start Menu**, choose **Find**, then select **For Files and Folders**. Type **NOTEPAD.EXE**. Select the drive where Windows 2000 is loaded as the search drive, then click **Search Now**.
2. When the **NOTEPAD.EXE** file is found, drag and drop the file onto the Desktop.
3. Double-click the **NOTEPAD.EXE** shortcut to start the application.

Part Five: Starting an Application Using the Run Command

1. From the **Start Menu**, choose **Run**, type **NOTEPAD.EXE**, then click **OK**.
2. **NOTEPAD.EXE** application should run.

Part Six: Using Windows 2000 Help

1. From the **Start Menu**, choose **Help**. The **Windows 2000 Help** utility will open.
2. Select the **Index** tab, type **Mapping Drives**, choose **to network computer or folder**, then click **Display**.
3. Read the displayed help file and answer the following questions:
   - Which utility does Windows 2000 Help tell you to use to map drives?

   _____

   - What would you do to ensure that the drive is mapped each time you log on to the network?

   _____

   _____

   _____

   _____

End of Exercise

✓ Instructor Check _____

> ### 💡 Lab Notes
>
> This lab has presented a very small portion of Windows 2000 operation. Time, use, and familiarity with the operating system will allow you to become proficient. Using the Windows Help utility will help to answer most questions you may have.

Student Notes

Lab D.2 Right-click Managing the File System in Windows 2000

Introduction

In this lab you will use the Windows 2000 My Computer and Windows Explorer utilities to create files and directories, rename files and directories, copy files and directories, and change the attributes of a file.

Maps to the following CompTIA A+ Objectives

A+ Operating System Technologies Objectives
- Objectives 1.1 and 1.2

Required Materials

- Workstation with Windows 2000 Professional installed and configured

Part One: Creating files and directories

1. Start the workstation and ensure that Windows 2000 loads properly.
2. From **My Computer**, browse to and open the drive where Windows 2000 is loaded.
3. From the **File** drop down list, choose **New**, then select **Folder**. Name the folder **2000TEST**.
4. Open the **WINNTTEST** folder and create the following folders:
   - **2000_TEST**
   - **2000-TEST**
   - **2000 TEST**
5. Open the **2000_TEST** folder. From the **File** drop-down list, choose **New**, then select **Text Document**.
6. Name the new text document **2000DOC.TXT**, then create the following files:
   - In the **2000-TEST** subdirectory, create **2000DOC TWO.TXT**.
   - In the **2000 TEST** subdirectory, create **2000DOC THREE.TXT**.

Part Two: Renaming and Copying Files

1. From the **Start Menu**, choose **Programs**, then select **Windows NT Explorer**.
2. Browse to the **X:\2000TEST\2000_TEST\2000DOC.TXT** file (where **X:** is the drive letter where Windows 2000 is loaded).
3. Right-click the **2000DOC.TXT** file, then select **Rename**. Rename the file **2000RENAME.TXT** and press **Enter**.
4. To copy a file, right-click the **2000RENAME.TXT** file, and choose **Copy**. Browse to and open the **X:\2000TEST** folder (where **X:** is the drive letter where Windows 2000 is loaded). Right-click in the folder window, and choose **Paste**. The **2000RENAME.TXT** file should be copied.

Lab D.2   Right-click Managing the File System in Windows 2000   307

Part Three: Changing a File's Attributes

1. Right-click the **X:\2000TEST\2000RENAME.TXT** file (where **X:** is the drive letter where Windows 2000 is loaded) and select **Properties**. Select the **Read Only** attribute, and click **OK**. (Figure D.2.1)

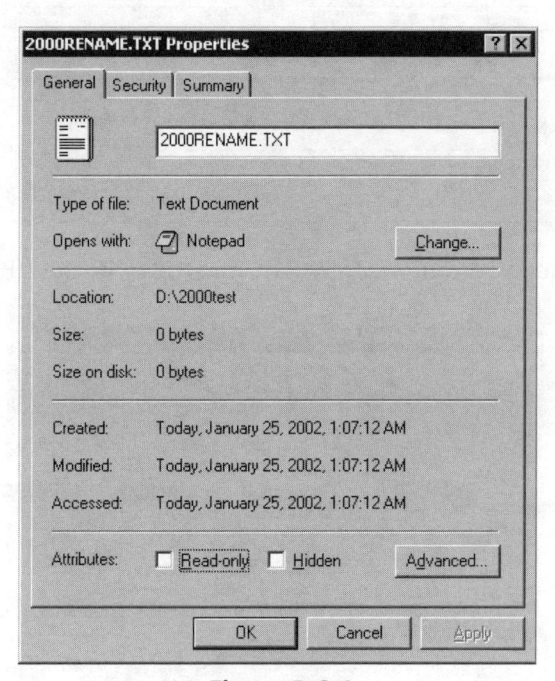

Figure D.2.1

- What will be the result of changing this file's attribute to read only?

_____

_____

_____

_____

_____

308 Using Windows 2000 Professional

- List the available attributes you can change:

_____

_____

_____

_____

_____

2. Choose the **Advanced** button to display **Advanced Attributes**. (Figure D.2.2)

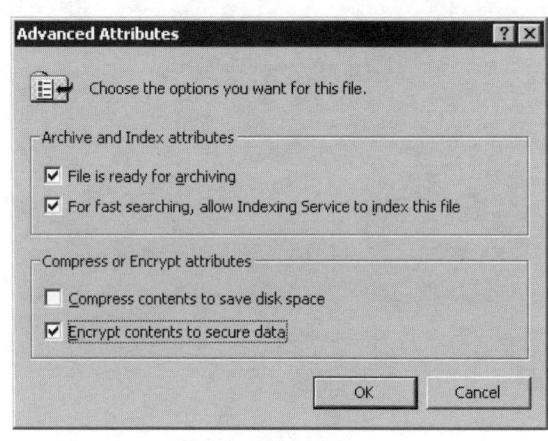

Figure D.2.2

- What would be the result of changing this file's attribute to compressed?

_____

_____

_____

_____

_____

- Can you select both **Compress contents to save disk space** and **Encrypt contents to secure data?**

_____

- Why or why not?

___

___

___

___

___

End of Exercise

✓ Instructor Check _____

> 💡 **Lab Notes**
>
> Windows 2000 (when using the NTFS file system) offers added file attributes that are specific to security, encryption, and compression features.

Student Notes

___

___

___

___

___

___

___

___

___

Lab D.3 Installing an Application in Windows 2000

Introduction

In this lab you will install an application on Windows 2000 Workstation.

Maps to the following CompTIA A+ Objectives

A+ Operating System Technologies Objectives
- Objectives 1.1, 1.2, and 2.4

Required Materials
- Workstation with Windows 2000 installed and configured

Lab Procedure

1. From your Windows 2000 Workstation, execute the WinZip install executable that was downloaded in Lab B.3. This can be done in one of several ways:
   - From the **Start Menu**, choose **Run**, type the path and file name of the installation executable, and click **OK**.
   - From **My Computer**, browse to and double-click the install executable.
2. Follow all onscreen prompts to complete the install process.

End of Exercise

✓ Instructor Check _____

💡 Lab Notes

In most cases, installing applications in Windows 2000 will follow the above general steps. Downloaded files may be zipped, and will require unzipping to uncompress the setup or other installation file. If your application is provided on a CD-ROM disk, it may be AUTORUN enabled. In this case, the installation process will start as soon as you insert the CD-ROM in the drive.

Student Notes

_____

_____

_____

_____

Lab D.4 Starting an Application in Windows 2000

Introduction
In this lab you will use various methods to start the application you installed in Lab D.3.

Maps to the following CompTIA A+ Objectives

A+ Operating System Technologies Objectives
- Objective 1.2

Required Materials
- Workstation with Windows 2000 installed and configured
- WinZip application from Lab D.3 installed

Part One: Starting an Application From the Start Menu
1. From the **Start Menu**, choose **Programs**, **WinZip**, then select the WinZip icon.
2. The WinZip application should run. (Figure D.4.1)

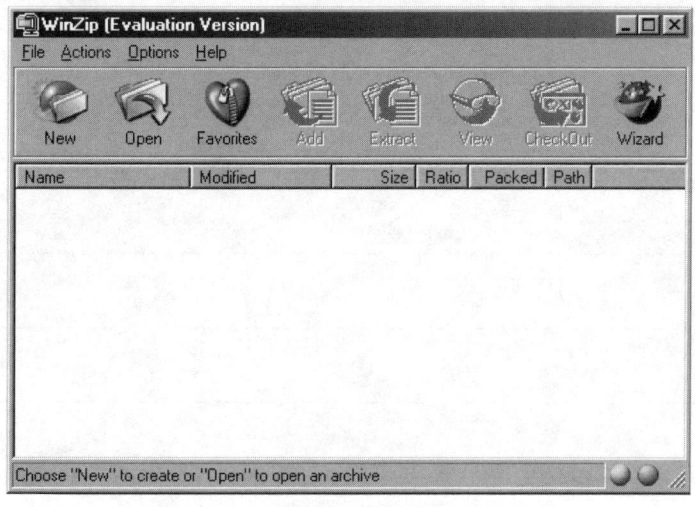

Figure D.4.1

Part Two: Starting an Application From the Run Command
1. From the **Start Menu**, choose **Run**, type **X:\PROGRAM FILES\WINZIP\WINZIP32.EXE** (where *X:* is the drive letter where Windows 2000 is loaded), then click **OK**.
2. The WinZip application should run.

Part Three: Starting an Application Using a File Extension

> **Note:** Windows 2000 uses file extension associations to associate specific files with specific applications. When a file of this type is accessed, Windows 2000 automatically starts the associated application and opens the file.

1. From **My Computer** browse to **X:\PROGRAM FILES\WINZIP** (where **X:** is the drive letter where Windows 2000 is loaded). Double-click the **EXAMPLE.ZIP** file. Using the file extension association, Windows 2000 will automatically start the WinZip application and display the **EXAMPLE.ZIP** file.

End of Exercise

✓ Instructor Check _____

Student Notes

_____

_____

_____

_____

_____

_____

_____

_____

_____

_____

_____

APPENDIX E
Using Windows XP

E.1 Installing Windows XP Professional 314
E.2 Basic Windows XP Operation 319
E.3 Managing the File System in Windows XP 325
E.4 Installing an Application in Windows XP 328
E.5 Starting an Application in Windows XP 329

Lab E.1 Installing Windows XP Professional

Introduction

In this lab you will install and configure Windows XP Professional on your workstation.

Maps to the following CompTIA A+ Objectives

A+ Operating System Technologies Objectives
- Objective 2.1

Required Materials

- Lab workstation that meets the following minimum requirements:
    - Intel Pentium (or compatible) 233 MHz (300 MHz recommended)
    - 64 MB RAM (128 MB RAM recommended)
    - 2 GB hard disk with 650 MB free space
    - VGA video adapter and monitor
    - Mouse or other pointing device
    - CD-ROM or DVD-ROM drive
    - Network Adapter (for network installations)
- Windows XP Professional Installation CD-ROM

Lab Procedure

> **Note:** Windows XP Professional setup can be started in one of four ways:
> 1. Boot disk with CD-ROM support
> 2. Bootable CD-ROM drive
> 3. Across the network
> 4. From within an existing Windows installation (autorun)
>
> For this exercise you will begin setup from a pre-existing Windows installation

1. Start your workstation and ensure that Windows 98, NT, or 2000 loads properly

   Note: If your workstation does not have a Windows operating already installed, enter the CMOS setup utility and ensure that your workstation is set to boot from the CD-ROM. After the workstation boots to the CD-ROM, it will enter the TEXT MODE phase of Windows XP setup. Continue the installation from step 10 below.

2. Insert the **Windows XP Professional** installation disk into the CD-ROM drive. The disk will auto run. (Figure E.1.1)

   Note: If the autorun feature is turned off, open My Computer and double-click the CD-ROM.

Lab E.1   Installing Windows XP Professional   315

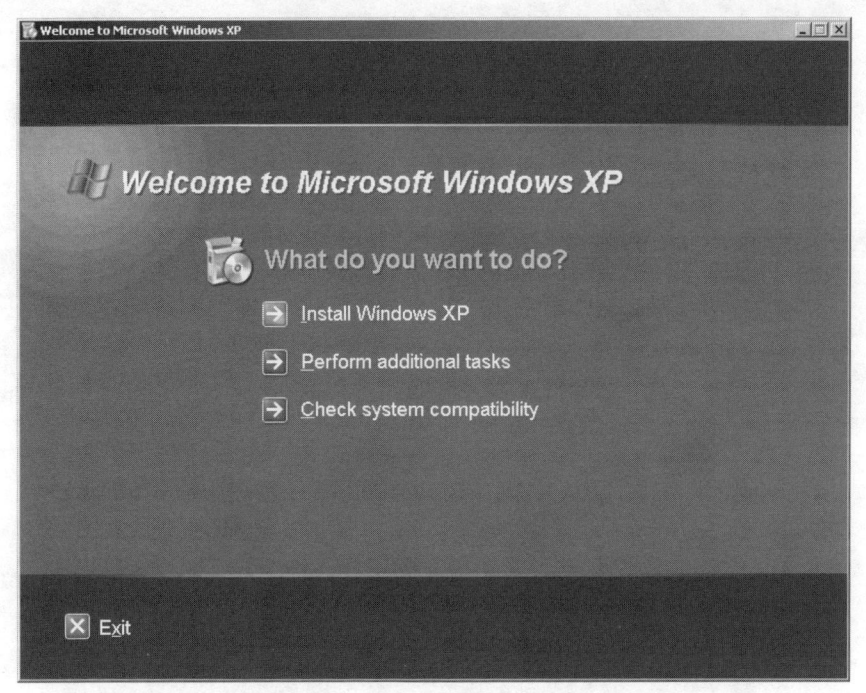

Figure E.1.1

3. Choose **Install Windows XP**. The **Welcome to Windows XP Setup** screen will open. (Figure E.1.2)

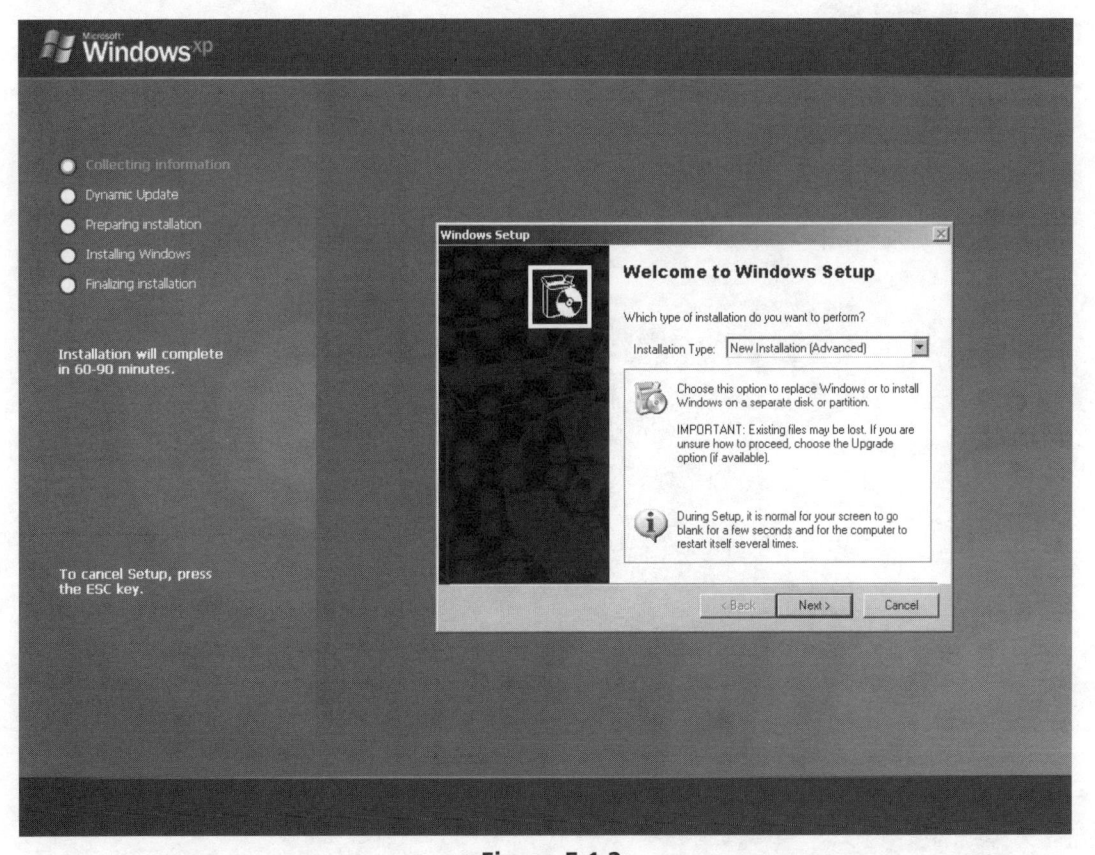

Figure E.1.2

4. Choose **New Installation** from the drop-down menu, then click **Next**.
5. At the **License Agreement** screen, select **I Accept the Agreement**, then click **Next**. (Figure E.1.3)

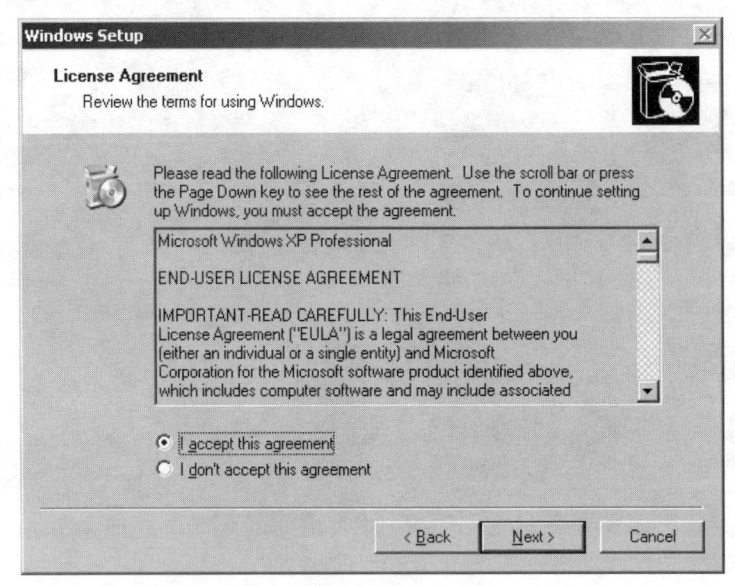

Figure E.1.3

6. At the **Product Key** screen, type in your product key number (provided with installation CD), then select **Next**.
7. At the **Setup Options** screen, click **Next**.
8. At the **Get Updated Setup Files** screen, select **No, skip this step and continue installing Windows**, then click **Next**. (Figure E.1.4)

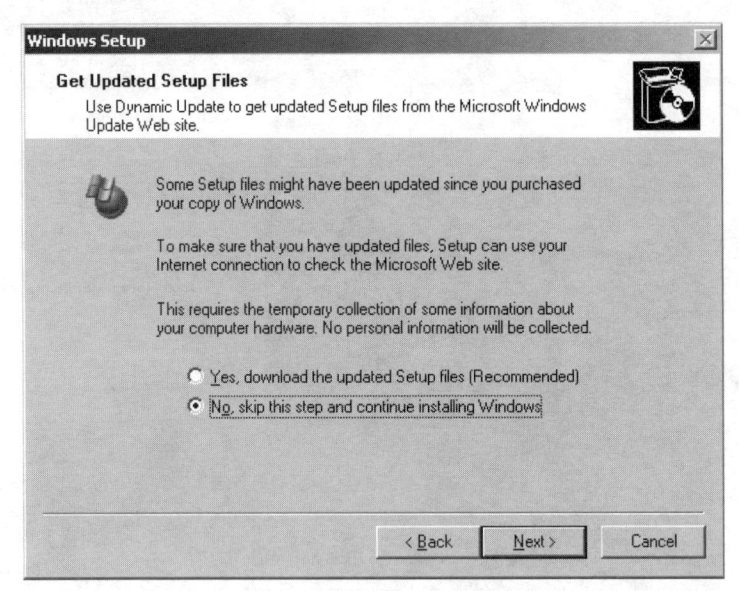

Figure E.1.4

9. Setup will copy files needed for setup, then restart your computer.

Lab E.1 Installing Windows XP Professional

10. When your computer restarts, setup will begin the **Text Phase** of setup. When prompted, press **Enter** to continue setting up Windows XP Professional.
11. At the disk partitions screen, use the up and down arrow keys, highlight **Unpartitioned Space** on your hard drive, and press the "**C**" key to create a partition.
12. Windows XP requires a partition size of at least 2000 MB. Type in **2000 MB** (or greater) as the size for the new partition, then press **Enter**.
13. Using the up and down arrow keys, select the new partition, then press **Enter**.
14. Choose **Format the Partition using the NTFS file system**, then press **Enter**. Setup will begin formatting the drive.
15. When the format is finished, setup will enter the **File Copy Phase** of setup and begin copying files to the Windows installation folders.
16. When the file copy completes, setup will reboot your computer. When the computer reboots, setup will enter the **GUI phase** of setup.
17. At the **Regional and Language Options** screen, accept the default settings and click **Next**.
18. At the **Personalize your Software** screen, type your name and the name of your organization, then click **Next**.
19. At the **Computer Name** and **Administrator Password** screen, type **WINXPXX** (where *XX* is the number assigned by your instructor). For the computer name, enter and confirm a password for the Administrator Account, then click **Next**.

> **Note:** For convenience, use password (all lower-case) for your password.

20. If the **Modem Dialing Information** screen is displayed, enter your country, area code, and dialing information, then click **Next**.
21. At the **Date and Time Settings** screen, enter the correct date, time, and time zone. Then click **Next**.
22. At the **Networking Settings** screen, choose **Custom Settings**, then click **Next**.
23. At the **Networking Components** screen, highlight the **Internet Protocol (TCP/IP)**, then select **Properties**. Choose **Use the Following IP Address**, enter **10.0.0.X** (*X* being a number supplied by your Instructor) in the IP address field, **255.0.0.0** in the Subnet Mask field, click **OK**, and then click **Next**.
24. At the **Workgroup or Computer Domain** screen, choose **No, this computer is not on a network, or is on a network without a domain**, ensure that **Workgroup** appears in the **Workgroup or Computer Domain** field, then click **Next**. Setup will begin installing Windows 2000 components and performing final configuration tasks.
25. When the Windows 2000 Professional setup completes, your workstation will reboot.
26. When the computer restarts, Windows setup will lead you through a step-by-step process to finalize the workstation's settings. Follow the prompts to setup your Internet access, register with Microsoft, and create users.

318 Using Windows XP

27. To begin using Windows XP, click your user icon. (Figure E.1.5)

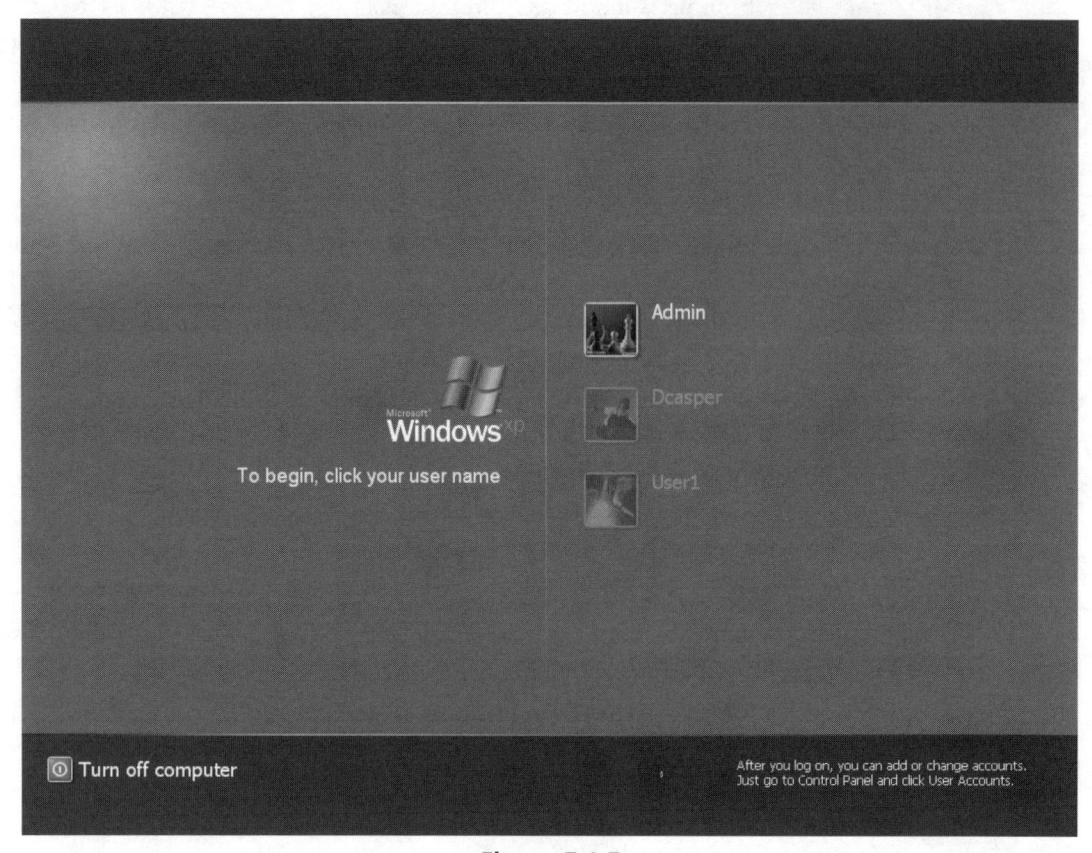

Figure E.1.5

End of Exercise

✓ Instructor Check _____

Student Notes

_____
_____
_____
_____
_____

Lab E.2 Basic Windows XP Operation

Introduction

In this lab you will review basic Windows XP operation.

Maps to the following CompTIA A+ Objectives

A+ Operating System Technologies Objectives
- Objectives 1.1 and 1.2

Required Materials
- Workstation with Windows XP installed and configured

Part One: Navigating the Desktop

1. Start your workstation and ensure that Windows XP loads properly.
2. To access the programs that are on the **Start Menu**, click the **Start Menu** button, choose **All Programs**, browse to the desired application, and click the applications icon to start the program.
3. To add an application to the **Start Menu**, from **My Computer**, browse to the *X:***Windows****NOTEPAD.EXE** file (where *X:* is the drive letter where Windows XP is loaded). Click and drag the NOTEPAD.EXE file to the **Start Menu**, and then to the folder you want it to appear in. (Figure E.2.1).

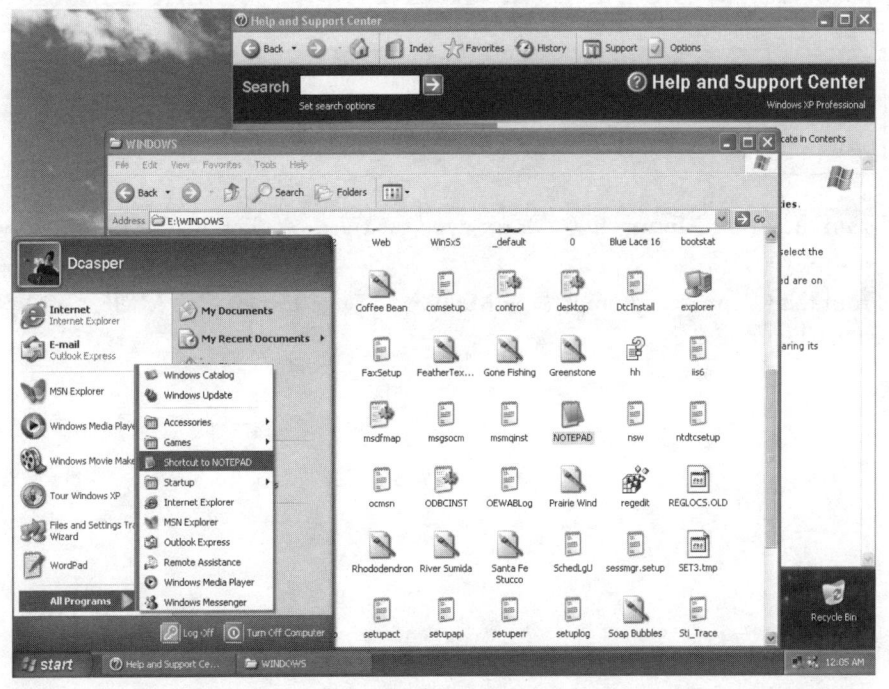

Figure E.2.1

4. The new Notepad Program should appear on the **Start Menu**.

320 Using Windows XP

Part Two: Control Panel

1. From the **Start Menu**, choose **Control Panel**.
2. The **Control Panel** utility is used for adding and removing hardware, adding and removing software, and changing system configuration settings.

> **Note:** The utilities within Control Panel are the safest way to manipulate your system configuration. These utilities directly access and edit the registry. It is much safer to allow the system to edit the registry then to do it yourself.

3. Browse the available Control Panel icons, then answer the following questions:
   - What icon would you use to configure scanner and camera attachments on your workstation?

   _____

   - Which icon would you use to set up networking on your workstation?

   _____

   - Which icon would you use to set options for people with handicaps?

   _____

Part Three: Using the MMC (Microsoft Management Console)

> **Note:** The MMC is a Windows XP system management and configuration utility. The MMC gives you the ability to create your own fully customizable management consoles, and store them wherever you wish.

1. From the **Start Menu**, choose **Run**, type **CMD**, then click **OK**. The Windows command prompt window will appear.
2. From the Command prompt, type **MMC** and press **Enter**. The MMC Console1 utility will open. (Figure E.2.2)

Lab E.2 Basic Windows XP Operation 321

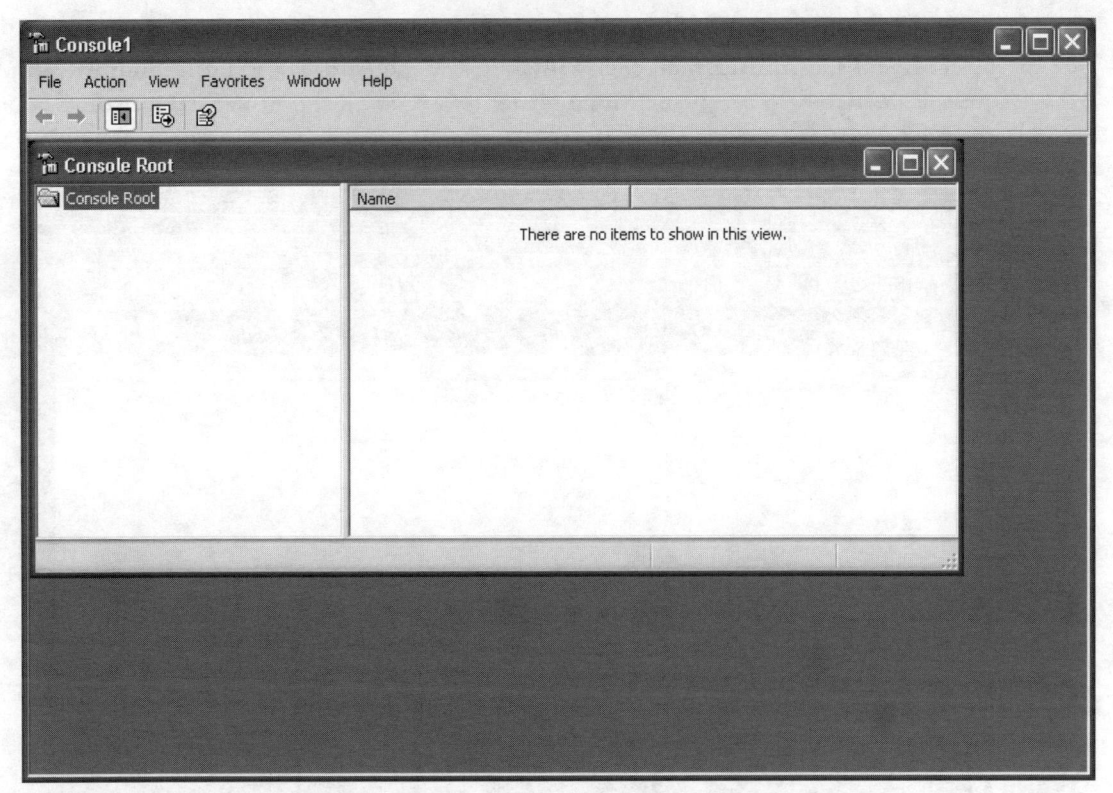

Figure E.2.2

3. From the **Console1** utility, choose **File**, then select **Add Remove Snapin**. (Figure E.2.3)

Figure E.2.3

4. From the **Standalone** tab, choose **Add**, select **Computer Management**, then click **Add**.
5. Select **Local Computer**, then click **Finish**. Close the **Add Standalone Snapins** Window and click **OK**. The **Computer Management** snapin will appear in the **Console1** window. (Figure E.2.4)

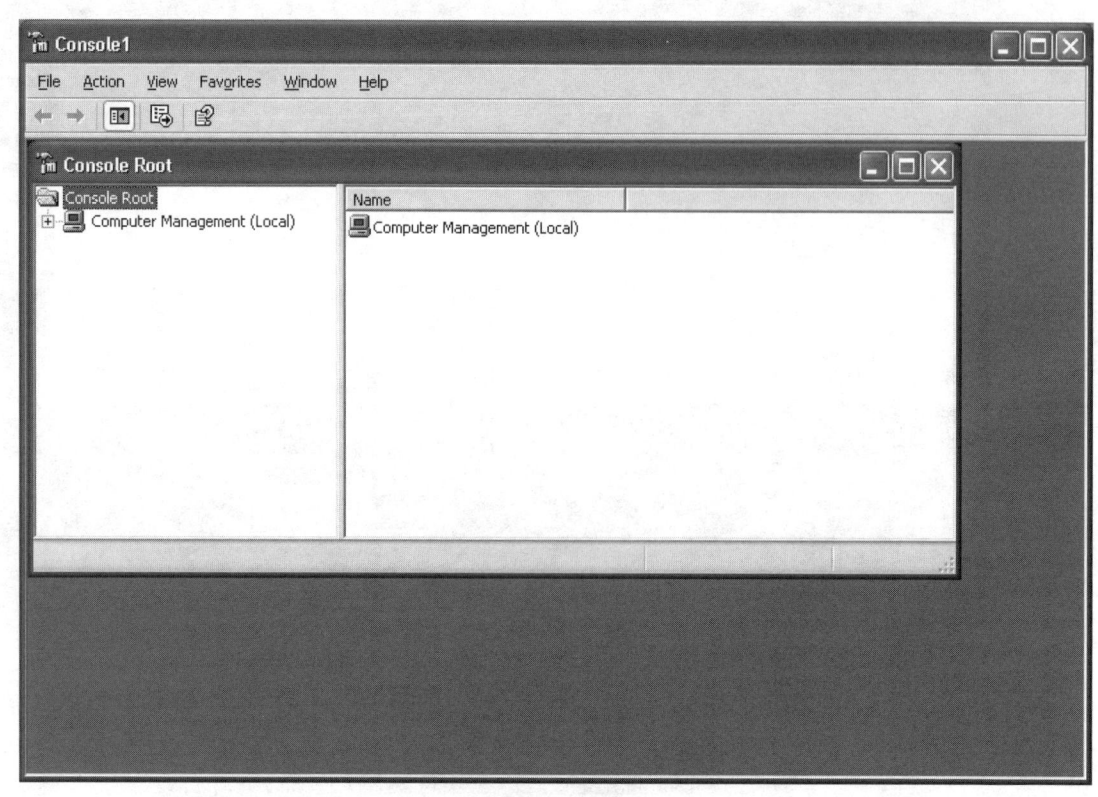

Figure E.2.4

6. From the **Console** drop-down menu, choose **Save As**. In the **Save in** window, choose **Desktop**, for the **File name**, type **Manager**, then click **Save**.
7. Close all open windows. The new **Manager** MMC should appear on your desktop.

Part Four: Creating a Shortcut on Your Desktop

1. From the **Start Menu**, choose **Search**, then select **All Files and Folders**. Type **NOTEPAD.EXE**. Select the drive where Windows XP is loaded as the **Look in** drive, then click **Search**.
2. When the **NOTEPAD.EXE** file is found, drag and drop the file onto the Desktop.
3. Double-click the **NOTEPAD.EXE** shortcut to start the application.

Part Five: Starting an Application Using the Run Command

1. From the **Start Menu**, choose **Run**, type **NOTEPAD.EXE**, then click **OK**.
2. **NOTEPAD.EXE** application should run.

Part Six: Using Windows XP Help

1. From the **Start Menu**, choose **Help and Support**. The **Windows XP Help** utility will open.
2. Select the **Index** button, type **Mapping Drives**, choose **How to**, then click **Display**.
3. Read the displayed help file and answer the following questions:
   - Which utility does Windows XP Help tell you to use to map drives?

   _____

   - What would you do to ensure that the drive is mapped each time you log onto the network?

   _____

   _____

   _____

   _____

End of Exercise

✓ Instructor Check _____

Lab Notes

This lab has presented a very small portion of Windows XP operation. Time, use, and familiarity with the operating system will allow you to become proficient. Using the Windows Help utility will help to answer most questions you may have.

Student Notes

_____

_____

_____

_____

Student Notes

Lab E.3 Managing the File System in Windows XP

Introduction

In this lab, you will use the Windows XP **My Computer** and **Windows Explorer** utilities to create files and directories, rename files and directories, copy files and directories, and change the attributes of a file.

Maps to the following CompTIA A+ Objectives

A+ Operating System Technologies Objectives
- Objectives 1.1 and 1.2

Required Materials
- Workstation with Windows 2000 Professional installed and configured

Part One: Creating Files and Directories

1. Start the workstation and ensure that Windows XP loads properly.
2. From the **Start Menu**, click **My Computer**. Browse to and open the drive where Windows XP is loaded.
3. From the **File** drop-down list, choose **New**, then select **Folder**. Name the folder **XPTEST**.
4. Open the **WINNTTEST** folder and create the following folders:
   - **XP_TEST**
   - **XP-TEST**
   - **XP TEST**
5. Open the **XP_TEST** folder. From the **File** drop-down list, choose **New** then select **Text Document**.
6. Name the new text document **XPDOC.TXT**, then create the following files:
   - In the **XP-TEST** subdirectory, create **XPDOC TWO.TXT**.
   - In the **XP TEST** subdirectory, create **XPDOC THREE.TXT**.

Part Two: Renaming and Copying Files

1. From the **Start Menu**, choose **All Programs**, select **Accessories**, then select **Windows Explorer**.
2. Browse to the **X:\XPTEST\XP_TEST\XPDOC.TXT** file (where *X:* is the drive letter where Windows XP is loaded).
3. Right-click the **XPDOC.TXT** file, then select **Rename**. Rename the file **XPRENAME.TXT** and press **Enter**.
4. To copy a file, right-click the **XPRENAME.TXT** file and choose **Copy**. Browse to and open the **X:\XPTEST** folder (where *X:* is the drive letter where Windows XP is loaded). Right-click in the folder window, and choose **Paste**. The **XPRENAME.TXT** file should be copied.

Part Three: Changing a File's Attributes

1. Right-click the **X:\XPTEST\XPRENAME.TXT** file (where **X:** is the drive letter where Windows XP is loaded) and select **Properties**. Select the **Read Only** attribute, and click **OK**.
   - What will be the result of changing this file's attribute to read only?

   _____

   - List the available attributes you can change:

   _____

2. Choose the **Advanced** button to display **Advanced Attributes**.
   - What would be the result of changing this file's attribute to compressed?

   _____

   - Can you select both **Compress contents to save disk space** and **Encrypt contents to secure data**?

   _____

- Why or why not?

End of Exercise

✓ Instructor Check _____

> 💡 **Lab Notes**
>
> Windows XP (when using the NTFS file system) offers added file attributes that are specific to security, encryption, and compression features.

Student Notes

Lab E.4 Installing an Application in Windows XP

Introduction
In this lab you will install an application on Windows XP Professional.

Maps to the following CompTIA A+ Objectives

A+ Operating System Technologies Objectives
- Objectives 1.1, 1.2, and 2.4

Required Materials
- Workstation with Windows XP installed and configured

Lab Procedure
1. From your Windows XP workstation, execute the WinZip install executable that was downloaded in Lab B.3. This can be done in one of several ways:
   - From the **Start Menu**, choose **Run**, type the path and file name of the installation executable, and click **OK**.
   - From **My Computer**, browse to and double-click the install executable.
2. Follow all onscreen prompts to complete the install process.

End of Exercise

✓ Instructor Check _____

💡 Lab Notes
In most cases installing applications in Windows XP will follow the above general steps. Downloaded files may be zipped, and will require unzipping to uncompress the setup or other installation file. If your application is provided on a CD-ROM disk, it may be AUTORUN enabled. In this case, the installation process will start as soon as you insert the CD-ROM in the drive.

Student Notes

_____

_____

_____

_____

Lab E.5 Starting an Application in Windows XP

Introduction

In this lab you will use various methods to start the application you installed in Lab E.4.

Maps to the following CompTIA A+ Objectives

A+ Operating System Technologies Objectives
- Objective 1.2

Required Materials
- Workstation with Windows XP installed and configured
- WinZip application from Lab E.4 installed

Part One: Starting an Application from the Start Menu

1. From the **Start Menu**, choose **All Programs**, **WinZip**, then select the WinZip icon.
2. The WinZip application should run. (Figure E.5.1)

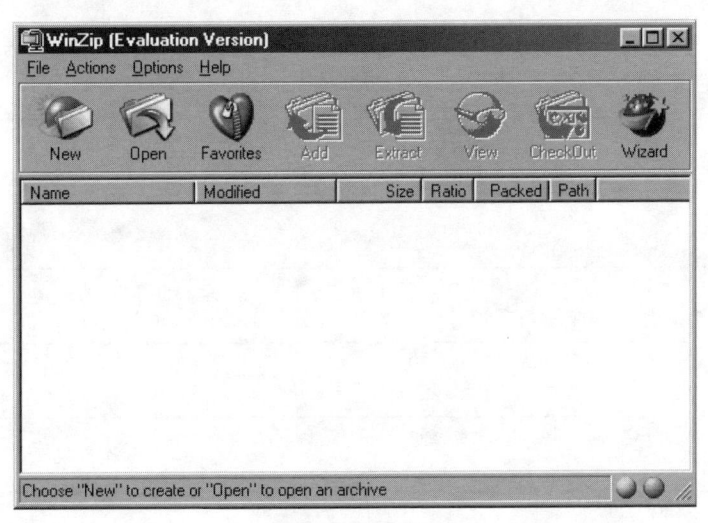

Figure E.5.1

Part Two: Starting an Application from the Run Command

1. From the **Start Menu**, choose **Run**, type **X:\PROGRAM FILES\ WINZIP\ WINZIP32.EXE** (where *X:* is the drive letter where Windows XP is loaded), then click **OK**.
2. The WinZip application should run.

Part Three: Starting an Application Using a File Extension

> **Note:** Windows XP uses file extension associations to associate specific files with specific applications. When a file of this type is accessed, Windows XP automatically starts the associated application and opens the file.

1. From **My Computer**, browse to **X:\PROGRAM FILES\WINZIP** (where **X:** is the drive letter where Windows XP is loaded). Double-click the **EXAMPLE.ZIP** file. Using the file extension association, Windows XP will automatically start the WinZip application and display the **EXAMPLE.ZIP** file.

End of Exercise

✓ Instructor Check _____

Student Notes

_____

_____

_____

_____

_____

_____

_____

_____

_____

_____

APPENDIX F
CMOS Beep and Error Codes

Standard IBM POST Error Beep Codes

1 short beep	Normal POST
2 short beeps	POST error, error code will appear on screen
No beep	System problem, check power supply and system board
1 long and 1 short beep	Bad system board
1 long and 2 short beeps	MDA or CGA video adapter problem
1 long and 3 short beeps	EGA video adapter problem
3 long beeps	Keyboard error
Repeating short beeps	System problem, check power supply and system board
Continuous beep	Check system board, power supply, or keyboard

Standard IBM POST Diagnostic Codes

100–199	System board errors
200–299	Memory errors
300–399	Keyboard errors
400–499	Monochrome display errors
500–599	Color graphics display errors
600–699	Floppy disk errors
700–799	Math coprocessor errors
900–999	Parallel port errors
1100–1299	Asynchronous communication port errors
1300–1399	Game port errors
1500–1599	Synchronous communication port errors
1700–1799	Hard drive/hard drive controller errors

332 CMOS Beep and Error Codes

Standard IBM POST Diagnostic Codes (continued)

2000–2199	Binary synchronous communication port errors
2400–2599	EGA video display errors
3000–3199	Network Interface Card errors
4800–4999	Internal modem errors
11200–11299	SCSI adapter errors
21000–21099	SCSI fixed disk errors
21500–21599	SCSI CD-ROM errors

AMI BIOS Beep Codes

1 short beep	Normal POST
2 short beeps	Memory errors
3 short beeps	Memory errors
4 short beeps	Memory errors, possible bad timer
5 short beeps	System board errors
6 short beeps	Keyboard controller errors
7 short beeps	CPU errors
8 short beeps	Video adapter errors
9 short beeps	BIOS errors
10 short beeps	CMOS errors
11 short beeps	Cache memory errors
1 long and 3 short beeps	Conventional or extended memory errors
1 long and 8 short beeps	Display/video errors

Award BIOS Beep Codes

1 long and 2 short beeps	Video display errors
Any other beep codes	Probably caused by system RAM errors

Phoenix BIOS Beep Codes
Phoenix beep codes are always a series of three sets of beeps

1-1-3	CMOS configuration read errors
1-1-4	BIOS errors
1-2-1	Timer chip errors
1-2-2	System board errors
1-2-3	System board errors

Phoenix BIOS Beep Codes (continued)
Phoenix beep codes are always a series of three sets of beeps

1-3-1	System board errors
1-3-3	System board errors
1-3-4	System board errors
1-4-1	System board errors
1-4-2	Memory errors
2-x-x	Memory errors (any combination of beeps after 2)
3-1-x	Chipset errors
3-2-4	Keyboard controller errors
3-3-4	Video adapter errors
3-4-x	Video errors
4-2-1	Chipset errors
4-2-2	Keyboard or system board errors
4-2-3	Keyboard or system board errors
4-2-4	Expansion card or bus slot errors
4-3-1	System board errors
4-3-2	System board errors
4-3-3	System board errors
4-3-4	Clock errors, possible bad CMOS battery
4-4-1	Serial port errors
4-4-2	Parallel port errors
4-4-3	Math co-processor errors
Low 1-1-2	System board errors
Low 1-1-3	CMOS RAM problem

> **Note:** The CMOS beep and error codes listed above are given as general information. For detailed information about specific beep and error codes, visit the Web site of your BIOS manufacturer or your computer manufacturer.

APPENDIX G

Standard IRQ, I/O, and DMA Assignments

Standard IRQ Assignments

IRQ 0	System timer
IRQ 1	Keyboard controller
IRQ 2	Bridge to IRQs 8–15
IRQ 3	COM 2 and COM 4
IRQ 4	COM 1 and COM 3
IRQ 5	Available, or used for sound card
IRQ 6	Floppy Disk controller
IRQ 7	LPT1
IRQ 8	Real-time clock
IRQ 9	Available
IRQ 10	Available
IRQ 11	Available
IRQ 12	PS2 mouse
IRQ 13	Math coprocessor
IRQ 14	Primary IDE controller
IRQ 15	Secondary IDE controller

Standard IRQ, I/O, and DMA Assignments

Standard I/O Assignments

060h–061h	Keyboard
0F0h–0FFh	Math coprocessor
1F0h–1F7h	Primary hard disk controller
170h–177h	Secondary hard disk controller
3F8h–3FFh	COM 1
2F8h–2FFh	COM 2
3E8h–3EFh	COM 3
2E8h–2EFh	COM 4
200h–207h	Game port
378h–37Fh	LPT1
278h–27Fh	LPT2
220h–22Fh	Sound cards
2F8h–30Fh	Network cards

Standard DMA Channel Assignments

DMA 0	DRAM refresh
DMA 1	Available
DMA 2	Floppy disk controller
DMA 3	Available
DMA 4	Link to second DMA controller
DMA 5	Available
DMA 6	Available
DMA 7	Available

APPENDIX H

PC Power Connector Diagrams

AT-Style System Board power Connectors

Pin	Wire Color	Standard Voltage
P8-1	Orange	+5V
P8-2	Red	+5V
P8-3	Yellow	+12V
P8-4	Blue	−12V
P8-5	Black	Ground
P8-6	Black	Ground
P9-1	Black	Ground
P9-2	Black	Ground
P9-3	White	−5V
P9-4	Red	+5V
P9-5	Red	+5V
P9-6	Red	+5V

ATX-Style System Board Power Connectors

Pin	Wire Color	Standard Voltage
1	Orange	+3.3V
2	Orange	+3.3V
3	Black	Ground
4	Red	+5V
5	Black	Ground
6	Red	+5V
7	Black	Ground
8	Gray	+5V
9	Purple	+5V
10	Yellow	+12V
11	Orange	+3.3V
12	Blue	-12V
13	Black	Ground
14	Green	Power Signal
15	Black	Ground
16	Black	Ground
17	Black	Ground
18	White	–5V
19	Red	+5V
20	Red	+5V

Note: These are standard color codings. Some power supply manufacturers may change the wire colors. If this is the case with your workstation, refer to the PINs for the voltage assignments.

MOLEX Power Connectors

Pin	Wire Color	Standard Voltage
1	Yellow	+12V
2	Black	Ground
3	Black	Ground
4	Red	+5V